WORK AND PEOPLE

WORK AND PEOPLE

An Economic Evaluation
of Job-Enrichment

by

HENRI SAVALL

*Director, ISEOR (Institut de Socio-économie des
Entreprises et des Organisations) Research Centre,
in Association with the University of Lyon II
and the École Supérieure de Commerce de Lyon*

Translated from the French by

M. A. Woodhall

*Professeur à l'École Supérieure de Commerce de Lyon
Director, Manchester Business School Language Learning Centre*

CLARENDON PRESS · OXFORD

1981

Oxford University Press, Walton Street, Oxford OX2 6DP
London Glasgow New York Toronto
Delhi Bombay Calcutta Madras Karachi
Kuala Lumpur Singapore Hong Kong Tokyo
Nairobi Dar Es Salaam Cape Town
Melbourne Wellington
and associate companies in
Beirut Berlin Ibadan Mexico City

Published in the United States
by Oxford University Press, New York

First published as Enrichir le travail humain dans les
entreprises et les organisations
© Bordas 1975, 1978
English translation © Oxford University Press, 1981

British Library Cataloguing in Publication Data

Savall, Henri
    Work and people.
    1. Work design
    I. Title
    658.3'06   T60.8   80-41354
    ISBN 0-19-874093-X

Typeset by Anne Joshua Associates, Oxford
and printed in Great Britain by
Richard Clay (The Chaucer Press) Ltd., Bungav, Suffolk

FOREWORD TO THE SECOND EDITION

The early steps toward job-enlargment and job-enrichment were focused on reversing the dehumanizing effects of Taylorism. Important as it was for the individuals involved, the work-structure issue was a local one, unconnected with the global strategic problems of the enterprise.

Today, some half-century after the seminal Hawthorne experiments, the purpose and design of work have become one of the central issues in society's transition into the post-Industrial Era. From a functional concern of the personnel manager, it has become one of the key issues in the design and the strategy of the firm.

The issue is conflict-laden as a result of several conflicting tendencies:

(1) the disappearance of the Protestant ethic of hard work and its replacement by as yet poorly articulated expectations for self-fulfilment and positive non-economic rewards through work;

(2) the inexorable march of technology which continues to make attractive automation, routinization, and standardization of work;

(3) the emergence of the right to a job as a societal norm at a time when job formation is not keeping up with the growth of the labour pool;

(4) the (frequently implicit) assumption that the economic standard of living in the Western world can continue to improve at the same time that the work-week is made shorter, work easier, and while full employment is maintained.

It is clear from these tendencies that the purpose and meaning of work in the post-Industrial society will be determined through a complex and subtle interplay of human, technological, and economic factors. But the historical progress in definition of work has been one-sided. Taylorism treated work as an economic–technological phenomenon. The post-Taylor development swung the pendulum to the other extreme and focused on the human variables. In industry this focus was frequently justified on an implicit assumption 'that the happy worker is a productive worker', and that new work participation and enrichment schemes will continue to bring about increased productivity. Outside industry, psychologists and sociologists, unfamiliar and unconcerned with problems of economic productivity and profitability, frequently neglected altogether the economic consequences of work redesign. They tended to treat work enrichment almost as 'wages of sin' which the firm must pay in order to atone for the excesses of Taylorism.

In this book Savall advocates a multi-disciplinary integration of the humanist and techno-economic perspectives. His focus is on an economist's contribution to this restructuring through two major aspects:

measuring the economic consequences, including all hidden social costs, of changes in the work structure developing a measuring apparatus 'which spotlights the "real and complete" comparative costs of the different forms of the job-design'.

In the latter aspect he includes proxy criteria which assure 'proper and decent working conditions' (see page 00).

Thus his viewpoint is that of an economist who treats social aspects of work-satisfaction as constraints. When and if Savall's contribution is married to those of humanist job designers, the pendulum of the perspective on job design will move towards the centre position at which the trade-offs between the positive humanist and the economic criteria, which Savall advocates, can be made in an explicit and measured manner.

H. Igor Ansoff

AUTHOR'S PREFACE TO THE SECOND EDITION

The major part of the present work was published in 1975 under the title *Enrichir le travail humain dans les entreprises et les organisations.* The book was written in the summer of 1974 at which time the socio-economic approach to working conditions was very much an innovation, in an area where psychosociology and ergonomics reigned supreme.

When, in 1976, the Délégation Générale à la Recherche Scientifique et Technique (DGRST) asked for projects dealing with the improvement of working conditions to be submitted, it made no specific mention of the economic aspect. Of the 120 research projects consequently submitted only very few mentioned an economic approach. Only one of a dozen or so research projects that were awarded DGRST grants was specifically concerned with a socio-economic analysis.[1]

Not until late 1976 did people become aware of the interest that a socio-economic approach to working conditions might have. One year later it was very satisfying to observe that my ideas had made headway and had gained a foothold in numerous sectors of the economy where decisions about encouragement and analysis of working conditions were taken.

In 1976 L. Stoleru, Secretary of State for manual workers, asked the French Foundation for Management Education (FNEGE) to set up a working party to examine the contribution made by compulsory schooling to the improvement of working conditions. The working party was led by the head of training, communication, and management of the Pechiny Ugine Kuhlmann group, M. Jacques Morin. It comprised industrialists, civil servants, and educationalists. It published its findings[2] in February 1977 and recommended that all the disciplines currently on the syllabus should be taught from an all-embracing *socio-economic* point of view. A working party of FNEGE teachers is currently continuing its investigations along these lines with the aim of producing concise details for the content of such a syllabus, and bringing them to the notice of the heads of institutes of higher education.

The Ministry of Employment has now inserted a clause into agreements made with companies which benefit from FACT grants (Fondation d'Amélioration des Conditions de Travail) to the effect that there should be an *economic* evaluation of the experiments carried out.

In 1977 ANACT (l'Agence Nationale pour l'Amélioration des Conditions de Travail) set up two study groups, one into the methodology of multi-disciplinary evaluation (*economic*, sociological, ergonomic) of job-restructuring in industry, the other into the *economic evaluation* of attempts to improve working conditions. Under the auspices of ANACT, methodologies are being worked out and applied in various companies. On the one hand are the companies which belong to the Institut Entreprise et Personnel, on the other hand are the companies which are in receipt of FACT grants. In addition the Secretary of State has given ANACT and FNEGE the task of organizing a pilot course for training people in charge of training. A large part of this course is devoted to the *socio-economic* approach.

Since 1977 several large French firms and a number of training centres have been offering training courses which include a *socio-economic* approach (investment models, evaluation of working conditions, decision-making for projects dealing with the improvement of working conditions).

Trade-union journals and others gave a very favourable reception to the first edition of this book. It shows the extent to which all sides of industry are beginning to realize how important is the *economic aspect* of working conditions. Industrial negotiation is now, in fact, allocating a much more important role to the improvement of working conditions.

All the above results have led to the idea of a new edition of *Enrichir le travail humain* . . . with a new, more appropriate title. This new edition contains a new chapter devoted to the methodology which I have worked out and which is at present being tested. There is also a complementary bibliography. In the near future it is hoped to bring out a second volume containing a complete and operational methodology of socio-economic evaluation and giving the results obtained by a number of French companies which have agreed to apply the system of evaluation.

We should like to thank first of all Henri Bartoli, Alain Bienaymé, Jacques Delors, Jean-Daniel Reynaud, and Henri Tezenas du Montcel for all the advice given during the preapration of this book.

We are indebted to Yves Delamotte, Pierre-Louis Remy, and Oscar Ortsman for their invitation to attend the March 1974 Royaumont conference on new forms of job design. This important conference was organized by the French Foundation for Management Education (FNEGE) under the auspices of the Minister of Employment. Participants included experts from the Tavistock Institute, London, and a number of their Dutch and Norwegian colleagues.

Finally our thanks are due to those industrialists, consultants, and researchers who supplied us with valuable documents and gave us the benefit of their practical experience.

NOTES

(1) Cf. the research programme run by H. Savall, 'Conditions de Travail' (University of Lyon II and École Supérieure de Commerce de Lyon), with the support of the DGRST and the FNEGE.
(2) H. Savall was the general secretary of this working party. The report was compiled by H. Savall and Messrs Agid and Bernard of the FNEGE, and Mlle Théophile of the CFSM. Cf. also H. Savall, 'Formation et conditions de vie au travail', *Revue française de gestion*, May 1977, and 'Propositions en vue de développer la contribution de la formation initiale à l'amélioration des conditions de vie au travail', in *Enseignement et gestion*, no. 3, 1977.

FOREWORD TO THE FIRST EDITION

In this book Henri Savall deals with a subject which has been at the fore-front of discussion for several years. In spite of the vast quantity of documentation which the author so carefully refers to, this is an area which has not been the object of a great deal of close investigation. This is especially so in France.

Job-enrichment requires a multi-disciplinary scientific approach. Henri Savall is an economist by training and is well versed in the history of economic thought, as shown in his work on Bernacer, one of Keynes's forerunners. He has been able to put right a number of mistaken ideas about traditional doctrines, especially where F. W. Taylor is concerned.

If one were to keep to traditional presentations of the theory of labour supply and demand, the price of labour would be a mere caricature of the working conditions which workers are in reality faced with on the job. Seen from this angle, the sizeable and relatively continual increase in the purchasing power of the average wage hides the extent to which workers in their workshops, factories, and offices really perceive a deterioration in their condition.

The author examines a number of experiments that are being carried out and tries to determine the results which we can expect. He then endeavours to demonstrate how the economic approach to problems concerning work could be revised so as to enlighten management about the possibilities and advantages of modifying organization methods. Although the accounting techniques which the author suggests are open to discussion, his hypothesis is a most fruitful one. We have to analyse the performance of any organization from two points of view: the external performance which is expected by society at large based on the specific vocation of the particular enterprise (car-production, services, etc.) and the internal performance based on the aspirations of the workers. No enterprise can remain competitive unless it can offer attractive working conditions.

Henri Savall's study raises new questions. On the level of scientific knowledge we have to ask ourselves whether a strategy of organizational change which implies long-term expenditure on fixed assets can be based on such a fleeting reality as the workers' psychological satisfaction. At the risk of drifting into an exclusively 'functionalist' view of things, any in-depth research has to cover both the complex trade union attitude and the demands made by the reorganization of the enterprise.

At a time when government bodies are dealing with the conclusions drawn by the Sudreau Report, the publication of this book is most opportune. It will break new ground. It is our hope and belief that the author will carry on with the research he has begun, an undertaking which will rightly throw out the artificial and 'disappointing' opposing of economic and social elements.

ALAIN BIENAYMÉ
Paris IX – Dauphine
Member of the Economic and
Social Council

PREFACE TO THE FIRST EDITION

When Henri Savall decided to devote his complementary thesis to the enrichment of human work, he wanted, above all, to reintroduce the economic dimension to an area in which it appeared that psychology and sociology reigned supreme. He knew how difficult his task would be and that he could only hope to make a small contribution to a non-finite discourse. Although experiments in the improvement of working conditions are making rapid headway in certain countries, they are still rare in the world of the production of goods and services, a world which is dominated by Taylorism, automation, and constraints imposed by the computer.

This explains the author's chosen angle of attack. His aim has been to give a historical summary and explanation of the problems involved in job-design so as to give both researchers and practitioners the essential ideas and necessary bibliography. The former can thereby extend their research; the latter can deepen their knowledge with a view to taking action.

Three current experiments, each with its own specificity, have been used to focus the problem and to provide a useful basis for reflection: factories which are attempting to transcend the technological constraints imposed by job-fragmentation and production-line work; areas of the banking world which suffer from the demands made by computerization and which are consequently faced with the problems of an over-qualified, psychologically ill-at-ease workforce; a company which is looking for and experimenting with a method by which to involve its workers in a discussion about their own working conditions and enable them to participate in the actual improvement of those conditions. The sum total of these three cases is, of course, not representative of all the problems raised by the enrichment of human work. By examining them, however, we are able to understand in a more lively and precise way the major difficulties encountered by the people conducting the experiments.

From this basis, Henri Savall has attempted to draw up an inventory of the factors which have to be taken into account in organizational innovation. No doubt his analyses will lead to both reflection and controversy. In an area as new as this, where the ground is still virtually unbroken, there is not enough factual information to enable one to make a neat division between the different theses available. There are, at least to my mind, a number of questions to be answered: how will the various attitudes and behaviour patterns develop? What will be the function of work in society tomorrow? How strong will the rejection of fragmented, monotonous work be? Will those involved — Government, management, workers and their unions — have converging or radically opposing strategies?

It is a question of social change in the full sense of the term. It is easy to understand that the author did not want to introduce his practical proposals for an economic and financial evaluation of the enrichment of human work without first having considered the central problem of the path to be taken and the strategy to be adopted.

For the same reasons he could do nothing more than erect a few signposts. By working in this way the author remained true to his initial motivation not to be afraid of taking paths which were still unclear, full of obstacles, and largely unexplored. This demanded a great deal of intellectual courage and a mind bent on action. As a result the author has been able to put forward an accounting system which is both simple and rigorous, and which will tempt a large number of potential users by its practical nature.

I find that Henri Savall's suggested procedure is all the more useful in that he has attempted to extend traditional limits and examine social indicators. I know well that very fruitful research has been carried out with a view to measuring working conditions by means of a battery of social indicators.[1] This has led to extensive progress in measuring large-scale social phenomena. It still remains, however, to integrate these findings into an accounting system which enables one to link means and objectives, to evaluate the results of policies where the cost of carrying them out is known.

The method suggested in this book is not a substitute for what has just been mentioned. It is at one and the same time simpler and more immediately operational. There are four elements which have been selected: absenteeism, turnover, rejects, physical productivity. It is relatively easy to evaluate their cost or monetary yield. Thereafter it is easy to integrate the quantified findings into a table which will allow one to measure the financial advantage accruing from new ways of working. Although such accounts may not reflect every aspect of economic, social, and psychological reality, they do provide a practical basis both for the problems involved in the decision and for the emergence of a social dialogue. In this way workers' and managements representatives can use these findings in discussing the experiments being undertaken and the sharing-out of the benefits arising from the new working conditions. Workers and unions are reticent about projects for improving working conditions where they are unable to measure the underlying aims, the means of implementation by the workers themselves, and the calculated advantages. Knowing this, it is important to underline the tangible contribution made by Henri Savall's suggested accounting system.

For this reason I hope that management and unions will take up and experiment with the tool which Henri Savall is offering them. Without any doubt this would be the best test possible.

Later on it will be possible to improve and then extend our measuring instruments to cover all the findings, not merely economic, but also psychological and social. The test and the sanction will then be the operational value of the social indicators, something which has still to be demonstrated.

---

[1] Cf. G. Roustang *et al., Pour une analyse des conditions de travail ouvrier dans L'entreprise*, Armand Colin, Paris, 1975. This publication is based on research carried out by the Laboratoire d'Économie et de Sociologie du Travail in Aix-en-Provence.

The present work is one which forces us, with good reason, to stop and think for a moment about the effort involved in reconciling the economic and the social aspect of man at work.

It is one of the author's merits that he attacks the unhealthy division which is to be found everywhere in numerous economic and social comments. It is not that harmony between the economic and the social aspect is a matter of course, or that harmony can come about without having to encounter and overcome certain conditions, but it is because the opposition between the two has given rise to forms of deviation which we have to condemn over and over again. The social aspect must never be thought of as the 'salvation army' of the economic aspect, as a sort of latter-day correction of certain excesses induced by a kind of purely rational economic reasoning. For my part I have always advocated integrating both dimensions, be it a question of planning development, or be it a question of dealing in a specific way with a social question. If the economic aspect produces social consequences, the social aspect in itself is both the condition of and reason for economic activity.

The present study of the enterprise brings us a new illustration of this debate.

Henri Savall is right to challenge the traditional concept of economic man. Of Taylor's 'vision of the world' he declares: 'There are three grounds for complaint against Taylor. He believes that work can be rationalized by reducing or suppressing initiative and stimulants (except wages), thereby ending up with another variety of a familiar monster: homo economicus at work, and thereby plagiarizing one of the most sterile creations of political economy of the last two centuries.'

Still speaking of Taylor, he adds: 'He believes that the impersonalization of the finality of work — productivity equally shared — should resolve *sui generis* the difficulty of social co-operation.'

This reductionist vision of man was bound to stir up political, social, and ideological disagreement. Marx criticized both the classical economists and Taylor when he contested the equity of the sharing between capital and labour. He also criticized the capitalist division of labour as something which 'cripples the worker and turns him into a sort of monster'. Writing about the working classes in England, Engels had already condemned the pitiable routine of endless toil, where the same mechanical process is repeated endlessly. He equated work with the labour of Sisyphus; like the rock, the weight of work falls back down on to the exhausted worker. Of the effects of capitalist production Marx said that the worker does not dominate his working conditions, but is dominated by them.

Such references are used to indicate the roots of a dispute which was to be taken up by the trade-union struggles of the late nineteenth century. By referring to man in his entirety, this movement was to take up arms in a never-ending battle for the defence of the worker's integrity, for the recognition of his whole personality. Even if, at certain moments in the history of labour or in certain countries, it has seemed as though a purely instrumentalist concept of trade-union objectives has triumphed, i.e. the emphasis placed on the external advantages to be gained from paid employment (direct wage, social advantages, working hours, . . .), the defence of man's integrity has never been forgotten. This defence was based on, amongst other things, a non-reductionist concept and therefore on a rejection of *homo economicus*.

For a long time work-theoreticians were to reply to this action by workers with proposals based, albeit unconsciously, on the maintenance of the division between the economic and the social aspects.

Since it was not enough to satisfy workers' demands by raising the standard of living and cutting working hours, the idea of attacking the economic environment and not the content of work itself was introduced. In this way the division was accepted. Job-design could not be altered without leading to a decrease in economic effectiveness. So it was a question of looking for new objectives 'for a new salvation army'. In particular this is the origin of the human relations school and, more recently, the social systems school. Henri Savall is right to emphasize that neither really questions the command unit, the degree of sub-ordination, or the extent of centralization.

It is really only a question of making certain amendments to Taylor's system by using external advantages. This is not negligible, but it does not call into question *homo economicus*, i.e. the man whose potential has been mutilated, a being stripped of autonomy, prevented from having any control whatsoever over his work.

Since the late fifties there has been a movement afoot to reconcile the economic and social aspects of work. It is one of Henry Savall's merits that he has given us an illustration of this idea through an analysis of the various problems of job-design.

The motor has been wound up. How far will it run? If it is possible to integrate economic and social aspects in new concepts of job-design, will it also be easy by the same token to reconcile political projects and ideologies?

This is an area which I for one would like to discuss with the author in greater depth.

This is the way he describes the universality of the present situation: 'The economies of the Western industrialized countries, of the countries of Eastern Europe, and of Yugoslavia are all organized on the Taylor model . . . The logical conclusion is that the form of job-design appears to be independent of *existing* political, social, and economic systems and that the management of human resources towards economic ends poses universal problems, in the same way that reputedly more "objective" arts and science subjects do.'

This assertion is doubtless acceptable. The proof can be seen in the degree of interest shown by delegations from all nations of whatever political colour in the report presented by the Director General of the ILO at the 1974 Geneva Conference.

We must not, however, underestimate what one might call the socio-political working environment or the social motivators. Although I have no wish to enter into a comparison of the various systems, I would like to stress the importance of the political and ideological dimension, be it only for the sake of a better understanding of the phenomena observed.

In other words, and to return to France, it is not possible to analyse the findings of our situation without bearing in mind the reality of our system of industrial relations: the impact of the class struggle both on the facts and on people's minds, opposition to projects from both employers and unions, the diversity of employers' concepts, the plurality of trade-union organization, the effective role of the Government . . .

For this reason I cannot agree with Henri Savall's analysis of French trade-union behaviour. He deals too summarily with the social aspect. Although he is right in saying that union attitudes are not yet fixed, he does not lay enough stress on the strategic difficulties which face trade unions at the present time.

It is, for example, not enough to illustrate his statement with the fact that neither the CGT nor the CFDT wanted to sign the national employer–union agreement on working conditions. Just before this point Henri Savall mentions the ideological reticence of the CGT. But did he ask himself about the effective value of this agreement, as did the two unions in question? It is only a matter of an outline agreement, interspersed with declarations of intent. There are, though, no concise agreements on the burning questions of shift work or piece-work. This makes it easier to understand why the two groups are opposed to the agreement. They are well acquainted with the political context they have to operate in. They know very well how their signature to the agreement would have been exploited and that their members would have been given no tangible counterpart.

It seems to me that it is impossible to appreciate the trade-union context as regards the problem of working conditions unless one bears in mind the two principal dilemmas faced by workers' representatives.

The first arises from the technique of industrial relations: which is the right level for dealing with the problem? National level, sector level, company level? A national agreement is not useful and effective unless it contains concrete undertakings which can be applied in all companies. This was the case for the July 1970 agreement on Continuing Education, which all the unions signed. The details of the study-leave system were sufficiently simple to enable them to be applied in all companies. This was not the case for the 1975 agreement on working conditions. It was vague on topics which required homogeneity; it was by its very nature incapable of touching on the other subjects, the diversity of which prevented their being dealt with at national level. It would have been more sensible to have envisaged another strategy based on experimentation at company level and to have allocated the necessary means to help and encourage any action which aimed at job-enrichment. Lessons could then have been learnt from facts and results.

As for the second dilemma, it is the trade unions themselves who will have to solve it. It is too easy to criticize the ideological opposition of certain unions. In reality such unions have to take account of the workers' state of mind, their awareness of the problems, the risks of mystification which threaten them. The French trade-union movement has always been faced by the following alternatives: it can either bolster up its ideological critique of society by stressing the shortcomings of capitalist society, at the risk of seeing the workers criticize the ineffectiveness of its action; or it can risk weakening its own role by obtaining, through struggle and negotiation, substantial improvements in workers' moral and material well-being. Depending on the time, depending on the problems, the trade-union movement has taken one or other of these risks. It has certainly been guilty of errors of judgement. It has sometimes underestimated the importance of a problem raised by the Government or by employers. But it has, on the other hand, often been right, either because the facts have justified *a posteriori* its refusal to enter into a particular kind of co-operation, or because it knew the way things would turn out.

Be that as it may, the important thing is that the person engaged on research in economics and social sciences in our country does not forget, whatever his personal preferences are, the trade-union and industrial-relations dimension. I make so bold as to add that this remark is equally applicable to those politicians and industrialists who are genuinely interested in undertaking some form of realistic and effective action and at the same time respecting the political and ideological pluralism on which our society is founded.

JACQUES DELORS

CONTENTS

Foreword to the second edition   v

Preface to the second edition   vii

Foreword to the first edition   ix

Preface to the first edition   xi

INTRODUCTION   1

A.   Factual Observation: a troubled present   1
    i.   *The recent disputes*   1
    ii.   *The conditions of life at work*   2
    iii.   *The universality of the situation*   4

B.   The economic approach to new forms of job-design   6
    i.   *The historical precedence of the contribution from*
       psychologists and sociologists   6
    ii.   *The theoretical insufficiency of the socio-psychological view*   6
    iii.   *The pragmatic insufficiency of the socio-psychological method*   8
    iv.   *The area of our study*   9

CHAPTER 1 – THE PROBLEM OF JOB DESIGN   13

1.   **The heritage of the past**   13

A.   The dominant theory questioned   13
    i.   *Taylorism and its substitutes*   13
       (*a*)   *F. W. Taylor's theory*   13
       (*b*)   *Scientific management or the classical school of*
          organization   16
    ii.   *The criticisms*   18
       (*a*)   *Taylorism and its deviations or caricatures*   18
       (*b*)   *The effects of Taylorism*   19
          The instrumental concept of man at work   19
          Technological hegemony   19
          The reasons for progressive deviationism   20
       (*c*)   *The Taylor paradox and the internal contradictions of*
          Taylorism   21
          The development of the perverse effects of Taylorism   22
          Unavoided wastage   22
          The entropy of the work system   23
    iii.   *The palliatives*   24
       (*a*)   *Compensations-deviations*   24
          Time spent at work and productivity   25
          Reduction in the number of hours worked – a necessary
          and insufficient condition   28
       (*b*)   *The incorporation of categories of less-qualified and/or*
          more docile workers   29

B. The theories inspired by human and social sciences   32
   i. *The amendments to Taylorism*   32
     (a) *The need to understand the enterprise in its entirety, as a really living being*   32
     (b) *The school of human relations*   33
     (c) *The social systems school*   35
   ii. *Taylorism overtaken*   36
     (a) *The French forerunners*   36
     (b) *The dichotomy of motivation to work: F. Herzberg*   39
     (c) *A synthetic vocation theory: the socio-technical approach*   43

2. **The present and the future of work**   47

A. The duality of the work universe   47
   i. *A growing gap between the quality of the world of work and economic performance*   47
   ii. *The myth of the incompatibility between the quality of life and productivity*   49
   iii. *The heterogeneity of the work milieu*   49

B. A refusal to accept the gap and the duality   50
   i. *Towards a reconciliation of the old contradictions*   50
   ii. *A twofold difficulty to overcome*   51
     (a) *Forces of inertia: education, mentality, economic interests*   51
     (b) *The necessity for change to be reckoned in economic terms*   52

CHAPTER 2 – EXPERIMENTAL SOLUTIONS   60

1. **Descriptive study: attempt at a concise typology**   60

A. The conflictual origin of the experiments   60

B. Typology of the experimented solutions   60
   i. *Timorous solutions: job-enlargement and job-rotation*   60
   ii. *Job-enrichment*   62
   iii. *Semi-autonomous groups*   63
   iv. *Diverse solutions relating to the environment*   71
     (a) *Arrangement of working-time*   71
     (b) *The decline of the payment-by-results system*   74

C. Three French examples   76
   i. *The Renault projects*   76
     (a) *The circumstances*   76
     (b) *Running the experiments*   76
     (c) *The over-all evaluation of working conditions*   79
   ii. *The Crédit Lyonnais projects*   83
     (a) *The circumstances*   83
     (b) *Two job-enrichment experiments*   84
   iii. *The BSN-Gervais-Danone projects*   86
     (a) *The circumstances*   86
     (b) *The planning of new forms of job-design*   87

D. The methods of experimentation   89
   i. *The field*   90
     (a) *The definition of the experiments*   90

    (*b*) *Experiments of a global nature*   90
  ii. *The implantation procedure*   91
    (*a*) *The up–bottom or descending procedure*   91
    (*b*) *The bottom–up or ascending procedure*   92
    (*c*) *The looping or up–bottom–up–bottom hybrid procedure*   92
  iii. *The degree of democratic participation*   93
    (*a*) *Participation by workers and their representatives
    (delegates, trade-union members)*   93
    (*b*) *Supervisor participation*   94
    (*c*) *Middle-management participation*   95

2. The factors to be taken into account in organizational innovation   96

A. The mental factor: the psychological and cultural heterogeneity of men at work   97

B. The social factor   98
  i. *The trade-union attitude in France and abroad*   98
  ii. *The behaviour of the hierarchy*   100

C. The technological factor: determination or indetermination   101

D. The educational factor: participation by interested parties in finding a solution, and continuing education   102

E. The economic factor and the power of the myth of specialization   102

F. The legal factor   106

CHAPTER 3 – THE STRATEGY OF CHANGE   113

1. The need for change   113

A. The irreversibility of the global process of aptitude enrichment   113

B. Societal development within micro-organizations   115

2. The necessity for change to be planned   115

A. The planning of organizational change; a corollary to economic and technical planning   116

B. The dangers of the non-planning of human development   116

C. The content of the planning of change   118

3. The need to evaluate change economically   120

A. The weaknesses of general and cost-accounting   121
  i. *General accounting*   121
  ii. *Cost-accounting*   123

B. Suggestions for new methods of human resource accounting   125
  i. *The criticism of attempts at accounting in terms of human
    capital and the balance sheet*   125
    (*a*) *Attempts to evaluate human capital*   125
    (*b*) *A criticism of the search for the evaluation of human
     capital*   127
    The semantic criticism   127
    The accounting criticism   127

ii. *A meaningful and useful accounting system: collection of
     the financial and real flow concerned with human resources*   128
     (a) *The differential view of the economic calculation of
          organizational change*   128
     (b) *The method of rational allocation*   129
     (c) *The adaptation of the method to the control of change*   129
iii. *Adaptations to the accounting system with a view to taking
     account of movements of human resources*   135
     (a) *Accounting for human resources — the three methods of
          allocating costs connected with human resources*   137
     (b) *Time adjustments made in the human resource investments* 139
     (c) *Cost accounting of change*   145

C. Innovation — the economic calculation   146

4. The propagation of change   148

A. External propagation of change through the market-place   148
    i.   *The market of goods and services*   149
         (a) *Organizational innovation*   149
         (b) *Factors which encourage and impede propagation*   149
    ii. *The job market*   150
         (a) *Supply and demand of working conditions*   150
         (b) *The insufficiency or non-pertinence of the analysis in
              terms of supply and demand of working conditions*   150

B. External propagation through social organization   151
    i.   *Professional organizations*   151
    ii. *Public opinion*   152

C. Internal propagation of change   152
    i.   *Management and consultants*   153
    ii. *Educators*   153
    iii. *Workers*   153

D. The specific role of public bodies   154
    i.   *The legal aspect*   155
    ii. *The economic, financial, and fiscal aspect*   155

5. A method for a socio-economic diagnosis of the enterprise   155

A. Tracing hidden costs and performances   158
    i.   *Major concepts*   158
         (a) *Expected operation of the organization and dysfunction* 159
         (b) *Socio-economic variables as indicators of structure and
              indicators of behaviour*   160
         (c) *Hidden costs linked with the company's operation*   161
    ii. *Measure of hidden costs*   162
         (a) *General methodology: experimental clinical and action
              research for tracing the costs*   162
         (b) *Principles of computation*   163
         (c) *The main components of hidden costs*   166
         (d) *Costs of regulation or of absorption of the dysfunctions
              and cost of prevention or correction*   166
    iii. *Outline of models for evaluating hidden costs and numerical
         results*   168

(a) Evaluation of costs linked to absenteeism and industrial accidents	168
(b) The quality of products	172
(c) Costs linked to turnover	173
(d) Direct physical productivity	174

B. Tools used for the socio-economic diagnosis: towards a new management analysis — 174

  i. Principle of inserting hidden costs in the new cost-accounting system — 174

    (a) Brief description of the model — 174

    (b) Relationship between the matrix for hidden costs and the matrix for visible production costs — 174

  ii. Socio-economic control system: from the control system of the personnel department to the control system of the operational hierarchy — 176

    (a) Principles — 176

    (b) Instruments — 177

  iii. Elaboration of socio-economic models for choosing investments with a view to a socio-economic strategy — 177

    (a) Implicit hidden costs — 177

    (b) Socio-economic strategy — 179

  iv. Applications of the socio-economic analysis method — 180

CONCLUSION — 187

1. The conditions for the validation of our thesis — 187

A. First postulate: the dichotomy between life at work and life outside work is pure deception — 187

B. Second postulate: social and economic organization is a rather barren idea — 187

2. A scientific questioning — 188

A. The probable obsolescence of certain theories — 188

B. The hesitant nature of the return to man, a return so often proclaimed by the economists — 189

Index of names quoted and bibliography — 191

INTRODUCTION

A. Factual Observation: a Troubled Present

i. *The Recent Disputes*

In France, especially since 1970, industrial disputes have frequently been due
to causes other than wage claims. These disputes appear in the shape of strikes or
of illegal restraint, insulting and threatening of employers or managers. The press
and recent literature can provide us with numerous examples. At the Ferodo
works an 'unskilled worker, grade 2, 47 years old, husband and father, hurled
abuse at his section head . . What was the motive for this incident, which led to
the holding of four managers and to a long strike in December 1970? The pace!
Tired, over-worked, this otherwise calm father just exploded . . . In Paris women
working at the "La Grenelle" laundry stopped work and shouted insults at the
owner . . . At the Besnier cheese factory in the small town of Domfront,
workers, whose hands were covered in deep cracks from the acid in the
camembert . . . erected barricades, knocked the owner over and drew up a list of
threats. At the Batignolles factory in Nantes the strikers ransacked the offices.'[1]

It was the strike at the Renault works in Le Mans from February to May 1971
which for many observers marked the beginning of an era in which people have
become more overtly aware of the problem posed by the working conditions of
workers in general, and particularly of the most underprivileged and under-
qualified workers, the unskilled workers. This category of worker experiences
more directly than anyone the bad working conditions which are imposed by a
certain concept of technology in an economic system of which the ultimate objective is a production objective. This is the system of our contemporary world.

It is very significant that alongside traditional – primarily economic – claims
(wage-level, working hours, holidays with pay, . . .) other claims have emerged.
They are not, of course, entirely new, but the qualitative nature, so to speak, of
such claims is being emphasized with new vigour. This evolution does not disarm
those claims of an economic nature; it clears the path for claims based on an
improvement in working conditions.[2]

The immediate advantages for the workers of the 1968 Grenelle agreements
were economic, but it is no less significant that, thereafter, French government
policy,[3] especially under Jacques Chaban-Delmas, consisted in bringing workers
and employers closer together. Their representatives had not met for several
years. By the autumn of 1969 this policy, which was instigated by Jacques
Delors, enabled an initial inventory of points for discussion to be drawn up. Two
connected points led to results, one to the law of 1971 on Continuing Education,[4] and the other to the law of December 1973 on working conditions and,
finally, to the creation of the national agency for the improvement of working
conditions, founded and directed by Yves Delamotte.[5]

The same phenomena, the same evolution in claims and social legislation, could be observed in other countries.

ii. *The Conditions of Life at Work*

The conditions of life at work can be classed as intrinsic conditions (work-content itself) and extrinsic conditions, or, to use an expression which is very much in fashion, the working environment.

Environmental conditions are first of all physical or material in nature: hygiene, safety, the framework of life at work, space, harmful effects. . . .[6] They are also psychological or moral: horizontal relationships with other workers, vertical relationships with the hierarchy, working 'atmosphere', the 'spirit' within the firm, organization of working time.

The intrinsic conditions are more directly concerned with work content: the 'intellectual' interest of the work; type of work, carrying out instructions, checking, giving orders; the nature of the work with regard to the capacity for individual or collective development; the integral nature of the work (degree of fragmentation or, on the other hand, of achievement, of accomplishment), and the level of responsibility and qualification involved in carrying out the work.

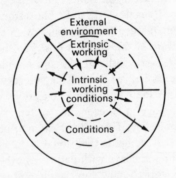

The diagram which we have constructed to show the interrelation between extrinsic and intrinsic conditions represents two wholes. The broken boundary-lines show that there is no discontinuity either between the real different milieux or between the different perceptions of these milieux by the individual. Our classification, which is of necessity an arbitrary one, does not however exclude the reciprocal and dynamic relationships, and hence dialectic relationships, which exist between all these elements. The three categories of conditions as a whole constitute an evolutive system in which the internal composition and balance depend on the possibility of carrying out the adjustments necessary for its stability.

There is a certain distinction to be made, however, because it is didactic and also because of the fact that in our study, when we talk of work or of the organization of work, or even of working conditions, we shall be alluding more particularly to the intrinsic conditions and to the first stratum of extrinsic conditions, where there is a closer connection with the former.[7]

Which exactly are the conditions that create a problem? A few examples will illustrate them best.[8]

Repetitiveness and monotony: 'Job-fragmentation? . . . that means that the workers are limited to a few movements which each last a few seconds, perhaps one or two minutes at the most. These are movements which are repeated continually for days, weeks, months, years . . . You find such fragmentation in every industry . . . Four years ago I used to stitch the whole shoe; that's all gone now; there are fifteen of us stitching now, each one does a little bit, all in a line . . . There are some workers who never stop depressing the pedal on their machine; they're on their feet all day, they look as though they're dancing; 1,760 pairs go past on the assembly line every day, 3,200 with insteps . . . For the sheets and the pillowcases . . . there's a third girl who ties the knots in the tassels . . . 1,760 knots a day! . . . At Mazda I used to solder the small plates on to the bulbs . . . I used to press the pedal 1,200 times an hour, that's 10,600 times a day!'[9]

Rhythm and pace: 'In the space of one month output went up by 15% after management had increased the pace because of an extra 15 centimes an hour they had just given us as the result of a strike. It's been like that for years! for every increase in wages there's an increase in speed! . . . At Mazda the speed of the line changed so much in one year that I just couldn't have got used to it again. . . . In November 1972 a long-drawn-out dispute was started at the SPLI company's plant in Fougères as a result of an increase in pace . . . Quality? Who cares! At Olida . . . the management told us that it was more important to work quickly than to get every last gram of meat off the bone! Everyone is on to us to increase productivity. . . . We've always got one eye on our competitors so that everyone on every rung of the administrative ladder, from the managing director of the firm down to the timekeeper, neglects the human aspect . . . they all look on the worker as a super-machine which has to achieve the same production level at the beginning as at the end of the day, at 25 as at 40, in December as in June . . . and all this according to a system which is imposed on us by the speed of the line or of the machine!'[10]

On health and hygiene: 'At Berliet . . . the noise level sometimes reaches 115 decibels, whereas the permitted level according to industrial medicine is 75 . . . At the Chausson plant in Paris men and machines are piled one on top of the other. It's a jungle; you'd think you were in a permanent fog . . . At Olida in the abbatoir some workers paddle around in the blood and offal; there are pigs which haven't been stunned properly and which put up a fight . . . most of the French workers won't do these jobs, so management, instead of giving priority to improving the machines and the abattoir, . . . looks elsewhere for immigrant labour. . . . In a metallurgical company an unskilled female worker, aged 52 and who has been with the firm for 29 years, works all day long in very unpleasant conditions:

she takes the valves soaked in oil and, using a trolley, wheels them under the blow-lamps. . . . there's this very heavy smoke which gets up my nose and burns it. . . . In the lead-shop at the Pennaroya factory in Lyons three workers remove 25 tonnes of the stuff from the furnace in eight hours. While still hot the ingots, which ought to be left for two hours before being handled, are piled up by two men. A few years ago this same job was done by five workers. The heat is so great near the furnace that it deforms the protective face-masks. This is parti-cularly hard work, since it is impossible to stop for a moment, even to take a drink. It runs counter to all the health and hygiene regulations concerning lead. . . .'[11]

The above evidence, taken from the serious press, is better than a more general description and illustrates well the working conditions which we are proposing to study. It must be made clear that we shall be looking at these conditions in the restrictive sense defined above, and that although the question of health, hygiene, and safety is a crucial point in the physical environment of life at work, it is not strictly part of our present subject.

As for finding out whether conditions have deteriorated in absolute or in relative terms,[12] we are inclined to say that this is a meaningless debate. The question has to be examined in the following light: when we consider the total economic and social evolution of a given society and the *perception* of conditions of life at work by some, if not all, workers, are these conditions bearable in comparison with what the workers have a right to expect from our current civilization, taking into account the image that workers have of it? Do workers have the feeling that technological progress for them is accompanied by new and less tolerable conditions than the ones they were used to, or than the ones they had expected from a civilization in a state of development? Is there at least a small proportion of workers who feel strongly, and more or less consciously, that there is something they have a right to expect from social progress? To what degree have their expectations been transformed in their heart of hearts into claims on the community at large, i.e. into an attitude which one day will manifest itself in the form of demands? Provided that the problem is looked at from this strictly positive angle, with no reference to any norm and to any value-judgement, it seems possible, we believe, to avoid becoming involved in the wrong argument. The wrong argument is the one in which one asks whether, on the one hand, this negative evolution of the conditions of life at work is or is not widespread, and whether, on the other hand, conditions have 'really'[13] deteriorated or only appear to have done so when reflected through the distort-ing mirror of an individual's psychology.

iii. *The Universality of the Situation*

The system known as scientific management or Taylor management[14] is wide-spread throughout industralized countries, regardless of their political, social, and economic systems.[15] The economies of the Western industrialized countries, the countries of Eastern Europe, and Yugoslavia[16] are all organized on the Taylor model.[17] In these countries the 'to have' civilization, as represented by the possession of capital rights, has not been able to satisfy workers' aspirations, for they seem rather to emerge from a 'to be' society. It is in fact more important for the worker to have his acknowledged place in the everydayness of his working life than to see himself acknowledge a patrimonial right to capital or to results. The two kinds of right are not mutually exclusive. A work-force which holds shares or receives a share of the profits *and* which enjoys good working conditions is without doubt a satisfactory and viable solution. The various types of worker-representation in decision-making, consultative, or controlling bodies within differing socio-economic systems are just as much of an obstacle to the worker who wishes to assume direct control of his own existence and destiny, to learn to take responsibility. The lack of interest which every representation system encourages – we might just as well say therefore every complex human system – seems to be a logical consequence of the various solutions tried and tested throughout history with a view to ensuring the administration of the city state.

Having put forward the *postulate of universality* it seems to us to be important to take certain precautions and to draw a provisional conclusion from it. The logical conclusion is that the form of job-design appears to be independent of *existing* political, social, and economic systems and that the management of human resources towards economic ends[18] poses universal problems in the same way that reputedly more exact or more 'objective'[19] arts and sciences do. We do not, however, say that the inverse is true, i.e. that the form of job-design has no influence on future political, social, and economic systems.

This universality manifests itself in the fact that in hybrid countries, those whose economic structure is partly capitalist and partly state-run or nationalized, the problems of life at work are the same[20] in private enterprise, nationalized undertakings, government departments, and para-administrative services. Working conditions at Renault originate from the same problems as those in any privately financed French or foreign competitors. The Crédit Lyonnais, the Banque Nationale de Paris, or the Société Générale encounter the same problems with their administrative work as those which the Union des Banques Suisses, for instance, has had to solve, or which any private French bank is trying to solve at the moment.

Overt conflict, in which workers' demands are based on an improvement of working conditions, or *latent conflict* (absenteeism, staff turnover), is similar in nature in the United States, in France, in Italy, in Great Britain under a Labour or a Conservative government, in the USSR, in Sweden, or in Norway.

Statistics are better than words to demonstrate the extent of the wastage and the established tendency of the phenomenon. In Great Britain the average rate of absenteeism runs at 9 days per annum for a man and 14 days for a woman. This represents *in toto* a loss of production of £2,000m, or 4.4% of GNP. In the Netherlands absenteeism rose from 4.9% in 1961 to 7.6% in 1969. In Sweden there was a 60% increase in the rate of absenteeism between 1962 and 1969. France is in the same position, for according to a 1964 survey carried out by the Union of Mining and Metallurgical Industries in nearly 1,300 firms and involving 700,000 workers, the rate was 6.25% in Paris and 6.9% outside Paris. In 1971 a new survey involving nearly 1,100 firms and 500,000 workers confirmed that this tendency was increasing, i.e. 7.9% for the whole of France (8.86% for workers and 5.7% for office workers). Experiments demonstrate that a reduction in hours and an increase in qualification lower the rate of absenteeism.[21]

We believe that this *universality*[22] has the advantage of freeing us from the need to choose our civilization in advance or state a preference for a particular socio-economic regime whether already in existence or yet to be established. The debate about new forms of organization for human work ought to be clearer as a result.

B. The Economic Approach to New Forms of Job-Design

i. *The Historical Precedence of the Contribution from Psychologists and Sociologists*

The economist involved in this area joins in a discussion which has already begun. He did not take part in the initial debate and consequently has to put up with certain disadvantages.

For the last few decades psychologists and, more recently, not to say more timidly, sociologists have been led to study working conditions as a result of cases of overt general or individual conflict. Either they have been consulted by company chief-executives or, more recently, they have of their own accord been stimulated by research at university level to carry out investigations. In some cases this research has been undertaken at the request of trade unions or employers' associations.

The contribution made by industrial psychology and the sociology of work can be described briefly as: to resolve disputes, to explain behaviour, to throw light on the importance of motivation, to suggest measures to prevent disputes. This is all in relation to working life, either at individual or at group level. The merit of these disciplines has been to bring out those dimensions which are normally forgotten by our technical, productivist, and progressive civilization.[23]

ii. *The Theoretical Insufficiency of the Socio-Psychological View*

The socio-psychological view results from a research bias which we do not subscribe to. It proceeds along well-known lines of thought and neglects economic factors, the very factors against which it is quite legitimately involved in fighting and with which it is unfamiliar.[24]

The socio-psychological theory[25] of working life suffers from a congenital defect, namely the exclusion of the economist from a team which has a multi-disciplinary vocation and which either analyses existing organizations or, at the conclusion of an action-research,[26] manages to promote the implementation of a new form of job-design. The consultants and researchers, whether university-based or not, seem from this point of view to be equally the victims of their own exclusive point of view.

It seems to us that this mistrust with regard to economic factors is due to a lack of information about what economics is, and to a confusion between the symptom and the deep cause of the identified evil. The belief that economic factors are ultimately responsible for the evolution of job-design results in the situation described above. According to the psycho-sociologists, the constraints of the economic system lead directly to the enterprise being obliged to look for more and more productive forms, to the detriment of working conditions. This point of view is partly accurate, but is too superficial. We shall endeavour in the course of our study to show what are the conditions for a different solution, one which is compatible with certain economic constraints.

Socio-psychological theory has made progress over the last two decades owing to the integration of technology into its field of investigation. The resulting socio-technical approach[27] offers considerable possibilities for the enrichment of research into job-design. This integration is, however, very superficial. For psycho-sociologists technology remains largely something exogenous. They assert that at the end of their procedure there is a logical questioning of existing technology, and they are not wrong in that. Yet the multidisciplinary team also suffers from the absence of the man from the world of technology.[28] It does seem, though, that from now on a place will be kept for him within the team.

The absence of the economist and, even more regrettably, of things economic from the psycho-sociological field of analysis seems to us to be more serious. Even within the socio-technical school, one can see a very clear difference of conception between those such as Cherns and van Beinum, who champion what we may call pure psycho-sociology, and those such as Davis, who try to integrate economics, or Thorsrud, who would like to do so.

We believe that this theoretical sterility leads to the presence of two major gaps in the present state of the socio-technical approach, this approach representing the most advanced state of what we have called the socio-psychological theory. The first is the absence of a complete apparatus for *measuring* the effects of new forms of job-design. The second is the exclusion from the field of analysis of economic constraints (which are occasionally only relative constraints, it is true).[29]

We are convinced that the integration of economics would serve to remind the researcher that to measure phenomena is the legitimate preoccupation of all who claim to be scientists, and that, without synthesized solutions which integrate economic variables, the experimental solutions contributed by the socio-psychologists are not viable.

iii. *The Pragmatic Insufficiency of the Socio-Psychological Method*

Certain psycho-sociologists exclude any economic constraint from their field of analysis, as do certain personnel men in the enterprise from their field of action. During our discussions it emerged that for them change should take place with complete disregard for any so-called constraints of an economic kind. We hold that this is both tactless and dangerous.

There is no worry about the incidence of new forms of organization on productivity, on cost. Van Beinum states that when there is a dispute firms are always obliged to do 'something'. When we made him see that at a given moment it was necessary to measure the effects of this something, his reply made it clear that according to him the argument had no bearing. . . . There are several explanations for this attitude, one which is in our opinion sterile. We shall take just one in order to clarify the debate, namely the confusion in the minds of certain psycho-sociologists of cause and effect, of driving-force and consequence. The search for greater productivity is assuredly not the motive that will provoke change. Nobody is going to improve work with a view to increasing productivity. At some moment, however, one will have to measure the effects of the new job-design on productivity. In the long term productivity must not be and will not be able to remain *the sole criterion* for evaluating the performance of the organization (enterprise, production unit in general) or of the entire national economic system. It is evident, however, that the choice will have to be a conscious one, i.e. made on the basis of precise information and the most accurate measurements possible.[30] Only then will it be possible to set productivity aside, if need be, or put it in its proper place as an evaluative element of economic and social performance.[31]

The attitude of certain psycho-sociologists seems to evoke a new organization which would be less efficient than the old one in terms of traditional criteria such as productivity. It is a serious mistake and one which also seems to contradict their own theory of the development of human aptitude.

There arises from this the fact that certain psycho-sociologists, researchers, experts, consultants, and also some personnel directors advocate a strategy the essence of which is conflicting. It consists of saying: 'Let us provoke change which is *outside* any preoccupation of an economic nature, and then we shall deal with it.' This head-in-the-sand policy seems to us to be doomed to failure because it is destined to run up against more structured, technologically, economically, and financially planned systems, which will create obstacles to social progress.[32]

Our position on the problem of the reality of work is fundamentally different from the socio-psychological approach. The point of departure for our study is the same — a change in job-design is *desirable* and *inescapable*. We make a prognosis which can be summed up in two propositions.

The first is that, whatever the political, social, or economic system, whatever the legal status of the organization, and independently of the solution to the conflict of interests between profit and wages in the sharing-out of the increased value, we think that no lasting change, of whatever magnitude, can take place until one has compiled an *economic dossier.*

The second is that at a certain moment during the testing of a new form of job-design its economic effects will have to be *measured*[33] and that the extension of the experiment, its application throughout the system, will depend on these results. This will take place after a selection which, because it is political in nature (at national as well as at enterprise level), will be able to integrate *new* socio-economic *performance indices* which have yet to be defined.

In short we believe that the economic analysis of new forms of job-design has to consolidate the socio-psychological analysis on both the theoretical and the operational level of change.

iv. *The Area of our Study*

There are two features to the area of our study. On the one hand there is the integration of the *economic variables* as endogenous, complete variables, which have to condition the change without our being able to prejudge their weight in the decision process. On the other hand there is the need to work out a *measuring* apparatus which spotlights the 'real and complete' comparative costs of the different forms of job-design. All change, to speak the specific language of the economist, is seen as the source and/or result of a *differential economic calculation.* The economist's legitimate research in this area is his contribution to defining and measuring the elements of the calculation, while making sure that he does not obscure social indicators,[34] i.e. those elements which economists have neglected too often and for too long.

We shall not hide our prejudice. It rests on the hypothesis that the new forms of job-design are superior to the traditional ones, *even from the economic point of view.* In this respect it is important to reassert that prejudice and value-judgement have a legitimate place in scientific investigation provided that such investigation remains open to criticism and that it allows itself to be permanently called into question. 'To believe in science is a value-judgement.' The range of specialist publications produced by men of science, the selection of the object for study, of the appropriate tool, the influence exerted by the team, one's supervisors, one's moral or political convictions are all the more reason for the man of science to believe in the modest nature of his research and its relativity. 'In the final analysis scientific research is a series of value-judgements. The fundamental motivation is the search for the universal, but the universal is waiting to be proved in order to be acknowledged. Far from being the cold robot as described by secular mythology, the man of science is above all — and most emphatically — a man.' This is the fruit of the deliberations of a number of scientists[35] at the Versailles Colloquium of July 1974.[36]

The first part of our study will be devoted to the criticism of Taylorism, to the new theories of job-design, and to an examination of the situation created by Taylorism in the current work-world. In the second part we shall attempt to set up a typology of the experiments in the new forms of job-design and an initial inventory of the difficulties encountered. In the third part we shall try to outline the dynamics of organizational change and we shall outline some proposals which attempt to perfect an accounting system that relates to human resources. Finally, in the Conclusion, we shall explain the postulates which validate our thesis.

NOTES

(1) J.-P. Dumont, *La fin des OS?*, Éd. Mercure de France, Paris, 1973, p. 7.
(2) Cf. 'Les conditions de travail des OS, extrait d'un document de la Fédération générale de la Métallurgie, CFDT', *Formation continue*, 1973, no. 3.
(3) Cf. *Le Monde*, 21 June 1974, p. 37. The Government declared its willingness to intervene in order to facilitate the implementation of certain measures, e.g. reduction of output-linked payments, night shifts, the gradual suppression of production-line work.
(4) Cf. J. Delors, 'Pour une politique du travail', *Le Figaro*, 11 & 13 July 1974, and idem, *Changer*, Stock, Paris, 1975.
(5) Cf. Y. Delamotte, 'Recherches en vue d'une organisation plus humaine du travail industriel', in *Documentation française*, Paris, Mar. 1972; cf. also G. Gorse, 'Humaniser le travail, c'est possible', *L'Expansion*, Dec. 1973.
(6) Cf. G. Roustang, B. Romagnan, M.-N. Beauchesne, F. Guélaud, 'Recherches d'indicateurs sociaux concernant les conditions de travail, 1re partie', Laboratoires d'Économie et de Sociologie du Travail (LEST, Aix-en-Provence), CNRS, Feb. 1972.
(7) Cf. Y. Chotard in *Professions et Entreprises*, May–June 1973, p. 21: 'The inquiry carried out by the journal *Usine nouvelle* revealed that the real problem was that of work, i.e. the nature of work, and not that of working-conditions, even for unskilled workers. . . . The fact that unskilled workers are industry's greatest present-day problem, even when in certain cases they are earning more than twice the basic minimum [SMIC], proves my point. A society involved in quantitative progress creates new, qualitative aspirations.'
    The same idea is to be found in J.-L. Donnadieu's final report to the Assises nationales de Caen, 'Carrefour sur les conditions de travail', *Professions et Entreprises*, forthcoming.
(8) Cf. Ph. Bernoux, D. Motte, J. Saglio, *Trois ateliers d'OS*, Éditions ouvrières, Paris 1973, and Ph. Bernoux, J. Ruffier, *Les Groupes semi-autonomes de production*, Éd. Économie et Humanisme, 1974.
(9) J.-P. Dumont, op. cit., pp. 14–20.
(10) Ibid., pp. 23–27; cf., below, the notion of *isoproductive* time.
(11) Ibid., pp. 39–44.
(12) In 1972 Christian Poncelet, then French Secretary of State for Employment, said: 'The strange thing about economic and technological progress is that, quite contrary to expectation, it has led to an aggravation of working conditions compared to what they were at the beginning of the industrial era' (cited in the introductory document to the colloquium held 8 March 1974 at the École Supérieure de Commerce de Lyon on the theme of working conditions and social relations).
(13) A. Touraine, *L'Évolution du travail ouvrier aux usines Renault*, CNRS, Paris, 1955, talks of 'the decadence of the professional manufacturer' (p. 57) and 'the disappearance of trades' (p. 66). D. Dautresme, in an interview with H. Savall, asserts that administrative work in banks has decreased in absolute value as a result of the introduction of computers. Cf., below, pp. 20 and 83.
(14) Cf., below, p. 18, the distinction between Taylor's theory and the specialized organization which we are familiar with nowadays and which is quite wrongly called Taylor organization.

(15) Cf. G. Fiori, 'Lavorare stanca – Da necessità a virtù?', *Mondo economica*, Milan, 14 Apr. 1973.

(16) Cf. A. Meister, *Où va l'autogestion yougoslave?*, Paris, Éditions Anthropos, 1971, pp. 341 ff. Cf. also three articles by the same author in *Le Monde* 1, 2, and 3 July 1974: 'Autogestion: les équivoques de cas yougoslave'. In the second (*Le Monde*, p. 38) we find the interesting idea: 'Whatever the chosen form of self-management, the instigators always believe that the suppression of class conflict as a result of the socialization of the means of production would suffice to clarify, to transform working relationships. People have, however, been forced to admit the existence of other forms of conflict which previously tended to be hidden by the conflict between employers and workers. Once formal equality has been achieved, natural inequality appears all the more vociferously and it is this which gives birth to a new form of stratification which is sometimes every bit as odious as that based on money.'

(17) The ILO has given technical assistance to countries such as Bulgaria, Hungary, Romania, and Poland to set up productivity and management-training centres based on modern management techniques taken largely from Western countries (cf. *Le Monde*, 2 July 1974, p. 15, 'Une interview du nouveau directeur général du Bureau international du Travail, M. Francis Blanchard').

Cf. also M. de Montmollin, 'En Chine, une nouvelle morale industrielle?', *Le Monde*, 11 Mar. 1975. In the course of his visits to factories in various regions of China de Montmollin observed that: 'Work is very often fragmented. Safety equipment is virtually non-existent. It is a surprise, perhaps even a disappointment, for a Western specialist full of ideas on economics, job-enlargement, job-enrichment, and job-design to discover that these preoccupations seem totally absent in Chinese firms.' It is true that premiums have disappeared since the cultural revolution and that establishing work-norms is part of the discussion of the plan at all levels.' The author thinks he has 'identified . . . a few significant *indications* [our italics] of a really new concept of the division of labour and of social relationships in [Chinese] industry'. De Montmollin doubts, however, whether it will be possible to achieve the objectives which are on display everywhere in the factories – 'quantity, speed, quality, economy'.

(18) J. Marczewski, in *Crise de planification socialiste?*, PUF, Paris, 1973, analyses the causes of the relative ineffectiveness of planned economic systems. Among these causes he points to the non-existence of strikes which would be a way of getting to the root of a problem and bringing about reforms and reorganization which, amongst other things, would result in economic efficiency.

(19) Our position is therefore very close to the concept of 'generalized economics' as 'communal research which is above systems' as developed by F. Perroux in *La Coexistence pacifique*, PUF, Paris, 1958, vol. i, p. 192, and later by P.-L. Reynaud in *Économie généralisée et seuils de croissance*, Génin, Paris, 1962.

(20) We are referring to *intrinsic* working conditions as already defined. It could be quite a different matter where extrinsic or environmental conditions are concerned. Because nationalized companies are freer with regard to constraints of profitability they could in certain cases be more efficient and insistent about respect for safety norms, for example, and factory legislation in general.

(21) Taken from E. Galnier, 'Pourquoi s'absentent-ils?', *Usine nouvelle*, June 1973 (special number).

(22) Cf. F. Blanchard, director general ILO, loc. cit.: 'Everyone wants the ILO to deal with it urgently; because, way beyond ideological opposition, there exists a most interesting area of exploration and action between countries with differing political regimes. It is the kind of subject area where we could easily bring East and West European countries together and create a common front, in order to find answers.'

The universality thesis is supported in the report on an international colloquium held in Czechoslovakia. Cf. *Intersocial*, no. 55, 1 June, 1973, p. 13: 'Trade unions have to pay systematic attention to protecting the environment, both inside and outside work. They have to make sure that any measures taken to protect the environment are not detrimental to the workers' economic and social interests. . . . All participants were adamant about the international aspect of the problem of the environment; there is a need to establish, at international level, widespread co-operation between trade unions, especially where the working environment is concerned.'

(23) In the strict etymological sense as used by G. Friedmann. For a term which is as heavy with emotional or political overtones as 'progressive' it might be a good thing to substitute 'expansionist'.

(24) It has to be admitted that the opposite has often been found to be true. Cf. P.-L. Reynaud, 'Économie politique et psychologie. Contre-rapport au Congrès des économistes de langue française', *Revue d'économic politique*, May 1968, in which the author deplores the insufficient inter-penetration of the economic, psychological, and sociological disciplines, in spite of the interdisiciplinary progress already made in these areas.

(25) The use of the singular should not be taken as an attempt to conceal the diversity of the theories and the nuances between various schools of thought.

(26) Action-research is a method which brings together consultancy work and the search for new theoretical materials. Cf. O. Ortsman, 'Le Tavistock Institute, son rôle dans la conception et la diffusion de nouvelles méthodes d'organisation du travail', *Enseignement et gestion*, no. 6, Nov. 1973; P. A. Clark, *Action Research and Organization Change*, Harper and Row, London, 1972; A. Cherns, P. Clark, W. Jenkins, *Action Research and the Development of the Social Sciences*, Tavistock Institute, London, Aug. 1973.

(27) Cf. p. 43.

(28) Davis himself criticizes psycho-sociological analyses which either forget to take account of technology or regard it as unalterable.

(29) P.-L. Reynaud, *Précis de psychologie économique*, PUF, Paris, 1974, insists on the need for qualitative measures for psycho-sociological phenomena, and quantitative measures for economic phenomena. In our method for calculating human resources we suggest that both be incorporated (cf., below, pp. 125 ff.).

(30) It is significant that American work on the progress of government social measures since the creation of the Union shows the importance of social indicators: 'Social indicators are used more and more to give support to political programmes' (J. Delors, *Les Indicateurs sociaux*, Paris, Sedeis, 1971, p. 359); cf. also Olson Committee Report, 'Toward a social report', Washington, DC, 1969. It should be emphasized that the first of numerous precise proposals made in the Sudreau report (cf. 'Rapport du Comité d'étude pour la réforme de l'entreprise présidé par Pierre Sudreau', *La documentation française*, Feb. 1975) consists of 'drawing up an annual *social balance sheet* from *indicators* which are representative of a firm's social situation and working conditions' (p. 55; our italics). A law passed on 12 July 1977 makes it compulsory for French firms with more than 300 employees to draw up a social balance sheet. For the time being, until 1981, this will be restricted to companies employing more than 750 people. The social balance sheet will comprise the main employment statistics, wages, hygiene and safety measures, other working conditions, training, employees' professional relationships and living conditions.

(31) Cf. H. Tézenas du Montcel, 'Les performances sociales des organisations', complementary thesis (unpublished) in economic science, University Parix IX–Dauphine, 1973.

(32) It is significant that the trade unionists do not fall into the same trap as the psycho-sociologists whose analysis we challenge. In effect, workers and their union representatives are careful to make sure that any measures adopted with a view to improving extrinsic and environmental conditions 'are not to the workers' economic and social detriment' (cf. n. 22). It is clear that in workers' minds pay could never be dissociated from other working conditions, nor could it be sacrificed to them.

(33) Since 1977 two groups of experts set by ANACT, to both of which the author belongs, have been devoting their energy to working out a methodology for evaluating the experiments from the sociological, ergonomic, organizational, and – particularly – from an *economic* point of view.

(34) It is worthy of note that out of 158 indicators selected in the American work on illustrating society's progress, 70 are non-economic in nature.

(35) It is also worthy of note that participants included G. Balandier, A. Lichnerowicz, François Perroux, and that the title of Perroux's last series of lectures at the Collège de France (March–April 1974) was 'L'Économie de la ressource humaine'.

(36) Cf. O. Postel-Vinay, 'Colloque, Science et jugement de valeur', *Le Monde*, 14–15 July 1974, p. 13.

THE PROBLEM OF JOB-DESIGN

1. THE HERITAGE OF THE PAST

A. The Dominant Theory Questioned

i. *Taylorism and its Substitutes*

(a) F. W. Taylor's theory

F. W. Taylor, born in 1856 near Philadelphia, gave up his legal studies (his father was a famous jurist) to be apprenticed as a pattern-maker. He was attracted by mechanics and was working as a manual labourer at the age of 22. Six years later he became chief engineer, having moved up through all the ranks of the hierarchy and having successfully passed his certificate examinations. Finally he became the first consultant engineer in the field of organization, a profession he was engaged in until his death in 1919. He was therefore a practical man who constructed the first theory of scientific management and who successfully put it into practice.

His approach is part of a macro-economic view. Of the cotton workers in Manchester in 1840 who were violently opposed to the introduction of power looms, he says: 'I cannot help but feel a certain sympathy for men who believe, with absolute certainty, that their means of livelihood is being taken away from them . . . [but] any truly labor-saving device will win out. All that you have to do to find proof of this is to look at the history of the industrial world. . . . let us see what happened from the introduction of the power loom in 1840 . . . In Manchester . . . in 1840 there were 5,000 operatives and today there are 265,000 . . . has the introduction of the power loom, has the introduction of labor-saving machinery thrown men out of work? . . . the fundamental meaning of increase in output [is] that additional wealth is coming into the world. Such wealth is real wealth, for it consists of those things that man needs for his everyday happiness, for his prosperity, for his comfort.'[1]

This confidence in technological progress is the manifestation of great perspicacity, the intuition of a process of growth and development which the political economists of the time had left largely unexplored. We agree[2] with Coriat[3] who maintains that Taylor's theory goes beyond the framework of scientific management, having its real roots in a genuinely economic concept.

Could we say of Taylor that he was Keynesian before Keynes? Taylor asserts: 'Whenever a worker increases his output and gets higher wages as a result . . . boards of directors will say "We are spoiling the labor market in this part of the country by paying such wages." What they fear is . . . that they will be unable to compete . . . the foreman, acting on the orders of the board of directors, cuts the price per pen down until the workman finds himself turning out 20 pens per day when before he only turned out 10 and is receiving . . . $2.50 [as before] . . . Under those conditions it would take an extremely broadminded man to do any-thing else than soldiering as his permanent policy.' He concludes: 'this restriction of output . . . this going slow on the part of the workmen is an almost universal fact in this country, . . . from the workman's point of view there is ample justi-fication for the policy which, in the main, they have adopted.'[4] It is worth underlining that the policy of low wages and the concept of balance denounced here are somewhat analogous to the famous general theory of employment, interest, and money which has too often been described as original and in-novatory.[5]

Which objectives does Taylor in fact set himself in order to attain prosperity through the growth of productivity? A policy of high wages, accrued profits, of low costs and selling prices may doubtless appear naïve and *a priori* incompat-ible. History has, however, never formally given the lie to his optimistic view. This visionary reasoned implicitly in terms of a non-zero sum game and hence from a dynamic standpoint of growth where the interests of the three parties which he wishes to satisfy — the workers, the employers, and the consumers — are not necessarily incompatible in the long run. It was a premonition of what has come about, especially since the Second World War. What is more up to date than his identification of man's enemy: wastage — wastage of natural resources (a matter of burning topicality since 1973). He adds to this: 'But our larger wastes of human effort, which go on every day through such of our acts as are blundering, ill-directed, or inefficient . . .'[6]

Taylor's most positive ideas are contained in four propositions:

1. Scientific management implies a *'complete revolution of one's state of mind'*. This revolution of reciprocal attitudes between workers, foremen, techni-cians, engineers, and employers will be made easier by a better flow of in-formation, by an increase in and delimitation of responsibilities. 'Scientific management . . . has for its very foundation the firm conviction that the true interest of the two are one and the same; that prosperity for the employer cannot exist through a long term of years unless it is accompanied by prosperity for the employé, and *vice versa*; and that it is possible to give the workman what he most wants — high wages — and the employer what he wants — a low labor cost — for his manufactures.'[7]

2. For *work* to achieve the desired degree of efficiency it has to be subject to *'prior scientific* investigation of all stages of execution'. This statement of the necessity to analyse and prepare work, the application for the first time of scientific method to industrial work, denotes in our opinion the principal base of Taylor's contribution. However the *unicity* of the optimal solution pro-claimed by Taylor can be criticized; scientific organization of work should not be incompatible, *a priori*, with the plurality of optimal solutions.

3. The employer (let us add 'the hierarchy') has a duty to give *technical*

assistance to workers at subordinate levels. Taylor saw clearly the role of the hierarchy as being that of transmitting knowledge at work by means of the optimal utilization of competence. In the light of lessons drawn from current teaching one can reproach Taylor with having conceived this dichotomy[8] between two categories of men, definitively condemned, some to an active role, the others to a passive role — the helpers and the helped. Such a concept has to be rejected nowadays. In Taylor's defence, however, we have to admit that it has taken us a long time to discover this.

4. One has to look for *team spirit*: teaching work methods leads to the creation of a team spirit between a group of men, where each one has his own specialized task. In this way work becomes a co-operative venture. On the other hand, though, specialization takes place in the same way, whatever form of management is used. This idea and the pages which follow in Taylor's work reveal a great misunderstanding between what, on the one hand, we are accustomed to calling Taylorism and, on the other hand, Taylor's expression and implementation of his own ideas. It has to be observed that, historically, specialization within the production unit *preceded* Taylor's ideas. He does not condemn such specialization but neither does he make it a condition for the existence of the scientific organization of work. On the contrary Taylor declares that specialization is a *neutral* element in scientific management. He replies to a question on this subject: 'I think this tendency to training toward specializing the work is true of all managements, for the reason that a man becomes more productive when working at his speciality, and while it is deplorable in certain ways (*there is no question about it, there are various elements in this specialization that are deplorable*) still the prosperity of the world and the development of the world . . . [are] due to a certain extent to just this very specialization.'[9] Taylor is not stupid; the division of labour does have its inconveniences which he deplored even in his day. It does not contradict scientific management but neither is it a product of scientific management.

The following quotation shows clearly that Taylor has a good idea of the possibilities arising from work done in a team and that he *condemns the splitting-up* of the workshops: 'I think this operation performed by eight or ten men, all co-operating, working as a team is very different from giving the molder one thing to do in one department by himself and the machinist another thing in another department.'[10]

Scientific management as conceived by Taylor can be defined thus: 'the system of scientific management of businesses is only the equivalent of the organization of the economics of labour; it is nothing more than that. It is a way, and a very efficient way, of making men more efficient than they are at present without giving them more work to do.' For management it consists in: (1) 'the development of a science to replace the old rule-of-thumb knowledge of the workmen'; (2) the 'scientific selection and then the progressive development of the workmen'; (3) 'the bringing of the science and the scientifically selected and trained workmen together'.[11]

In spite of this partial rehabilitation, there are three grounds for complaint against Taylor. He believes that work can be rationalized by reducing or suppressing initiative and stimulants (except wages), thereby ending up with another variety of a familiar monster — *homo economicus* at work[12] and thereby plagiarizing one of the most sterile creations of political economy of the last two centuries.

He has too optimistic a view of the possibilities of co-operation and a certain naïveté concerning the resources for social harmony which his system would contain. He believes that the impersonalization of the finality of work — productivity equally shared — should resolve *sui generis* the difficulty of social co-operation. Taylor, like the classical and neo-classical economists, is mistaken about the notions of the *equality of the exchange* and of the *degree of freedom* of the different actors in economic life. On the question of the sharing of productivity Taylor had the following question put to him by the President of the Commission of the House of Representatives (January 1912). It was about a method of bricklaying which one of Taylor's disciples, Gilbreth, had perfected: 'Do you contend or state that $6.50 for laying 2,000 bricks is a proper division, as against $5 for laying 960 bricks?'[13] Taylor replied:

He reduces his motions from 18 movements per brick to 5 per brick,[14] so that the workman himself was working less hard than he formerly did. The workman voluntarily chose his own pace. Mr. Gilbreth did not tell him how fast he must work. He did not have to lay 2,800 bricks. The workmen, of their own accord, laid 2,800. There was no limit put upon them. They were merely told by Mr. Gilbreth, 'Use my methods and the moment you use my method I will pay you $6.50. That is all I ask of you, to use my methods.'[15]

Taylor goes on to explain that certain accessories and the bricklayer's mate are cost elements of the new method which reduce the possibility of a higher wage increase. Taylor thereby conjures away the question of the bases for sharing the increased value and sacrifices it to the needs of his demonstration. He thereby lays himself open to the Marxist criticism based on the illegitimate appropriation of surplus value by capital.

(b) Scientific management or the classical school of organization

The classical school, as it is called by the great majority of Anglo-Saxon authors, was born with Taylor, established with H. Fayol, and carried on until R. C. Davis.[16] It is based on a collection of concepts:

1. The *scalar* concept or the hierarchical principle. The firm is a collection of rungs arranged in sequence. Authority descends from the highest rung to the base, which has no authority. The continuous chain of command is made up of superior–subordinate links.

2. We owe the principle of the unity of command to Fayol. In fact Taylor, claiming that it was impossible to find a universal superior, had suggested that each worker should obey eight functional bosses. E. Rimailho was the first to formulate a compromise — *organisation à la française*. More widely known under

the Anglo-Saxon name of *Staff and Line*, this is an amalgam of functional and hierarchical relationships, the latter always taking precedence over the former. The principle of the hierarchical organization is very deep-rooted.

3. The principle of *organizational specialization*, which was asserted more in Taylor's work than in Fayol's. The latter admits a growing polyvalence the higher one rises up the hierarchy. The principle of specialization, however, remains entrenched, particularly, but not exclusively, on the lowest rung.

4. The applications of *scientific method*. As a first attempt at a scientific analysis of the organization Taylor's theory presents the defects of its qualities. Whilst it is a laudable attempt at scientific construction over and against the pragmatism which had for thousands of years ruled over job-design, Taylor's scientific organization conjured away a great number of problems from within the field it was aiming to cover, i.e. human problems. It is however right to quote it when dealing with industrial theory and practice.

5. The *materialist* concept is what characterizes Taylor's philosophy of man. Capitalism and Marxism are, moreover, two equally materialist systems.[17]

B. Lussato[18] has extracted the implicit hypotheses which scientific management is based on. We shall list them all because they are nearly all called into question in the most recent theories of scientific management.

The *mechanistic* postulate: efficiency can be measured in terms of productivity, irrespective of human factors.

The *rationalist* postulate: men behave logically and sensibly.

Detailed supervision: men need to be subject to detailed supervision because they cheat.

The principle of the *narrow definition of tasks*: tasks have to be strictly defined and must not overlap one another.

The *materialist* postulate: the worker looks for security and the clear definition of the framework of his job. There will therefore be a convergence between his behaviour and his motivation, on the one hand, and the demands of the system of production, on the other.

The postulate of the *closed system*: the firm is a closed system[19] which can be wholly analysed.

The principle of *formalization*: the only exchanges between individuals which one has to concern onself with are official or formal.

The principle of *impersonalization*: activities have to be defined in an objective and impersonal way (depersonalization of functions).

The *economic* postulate: wages are workers' only motivation. To obtain cooperation it will be enough to work out an equitable system of remuneration.

The *natural laziness* of man, which implies strict supervision.

The principle of *centralization*: co-ordination has to be imposed and controlled from above.

The *up-bottom* principle: the delegation of authority takes place from the top downwards.

The *specialization* postulate: simple tasks are easier to assimilate; hence one should instigate the finest possible division of work in order to increase productivity.

The *universality* postulate: based on experience it is possible to extrapolate universal principles which are valid for all men and in all situations (even if these principles cannot always be applied).

ii. *The Criticisms*

(a) *Taylorism and its deviations or caricatures*

It would appear to us unfair to put the blame for all the faults in the organization of work, as it is practised in economic reality, as it is still taught, as it is still preached by method-men in firms, on to Taylor alone,[20] or even on to his disciples or followers.

An observation of life at work today often provides the spectacle of a caricature of the implicit principles and postulates listed above. Before beginning a criticism of Taylorism,[21] we should look for extenuating circumstances and make a distinction between what can be attributed to Taylor himself and what can be attributed to those managers, organizers, and teachers who, while quoting Taylor as their authority, have deformed his theory in their respective spheres.[22]

The scientific organization of work has made possible an increase in productivity and in the quality of life by means of the rationalization of movements, the study of time and motion, and the study of elementary tasks. It has enabled us to invent and perfect tools[23] and thereby to increase productivity. This, it would seem, is undeniable. Marxist doctrine tends sometimes to confuse the explanation of the division of labour within the firm with that within regional, national, or international confines. It gives us an explanation, frequently a tempting explanation, for certain historical coincidences, for example, the development of Taylorism concomitantly with the recrudescence of economic imperialism at the end of the last century. It is certain that Taylorism is part and parcel of a historical reality characterized by the great expansion of industry and employment, by the scarcity of skilled labour, by the appetite for gain and particularly for profit. We think, however, that to ascribe to Taylor the Machiavellian intention of increasingly and deliberately enslaving the worker exploited by capital, is to ascribe to him ambitions of a theoretician of political economy which he in no way had and which do not really go with the high-wage policy he advocated.[24] We believe, rather, that, on the one hand, Taylorism is based on an economic system which is above all concerned to reduce costs, with no thought as to who profits thereby, and that, on the other hand, Taylorism in practice has been used to facilitate in a certain way the exploitation of workers. Has not Taylorism contributed to the renewal and aggravation of crises of overproduction because of the great increase in productivity which it has made possible? Could it be responsible for the survival of capitalism? We doubt this for two reasons: firstly, because fifty years after the first implementation of Taylor-type organization, a certain kind of flamboyant capitalism died in 1929;

secondly, because Lenin, writing in *Pravda* in 1917, held that scientific management was the way to economic progress which the economic organization of life at work ought to follow.[25]

(*b*) *The effects of Taylorism*

We see two principal aspects of the effects of Taylorism on the organization of work — the dehumanization of work and technological hegemony.

The instrumental concept of man at work. The dehumanization of work can perhaps be stigmatized in the following terms: 'Scientific management according to Taylor rests on a very restrictive concept of the worker, who appears as a rudimentary composition of laziness and hunger for gain. Man in the organization is treated as an automaton and this entails the definition of rigid and rigorous work-norms and an extremely strict system of authority'.[26]

This concept is not new, nor is it unknown to economists. Adam Smith had already written:

A man who spends his life carrying out a small number of very simple operations with perhaps the same effects, has no room to develop his intelligence or to stretch his imagination so as to look for ways of overcoming difficulties which never occur. He thereby loses quite naturally the habit of using these faculties and, in general, he becomes as stupid and as ignorant as it is possible for a human being to become.[27]

Such a concept[28] does not conform either to a certain individual or social ethic which we accept, or to reality as currently observed. Nowadays the preparation for one's professional life is long, rich in cultural contributions, often rich in technical knowledge, so that right from the start of his professional life the worker does not conform to the Smith or the Taylor canon. In addition, life outside his place of work has a great impact on the worker's behaviour, for this life is rich in opportunities to develop intelligence, to use imagination, to reflect on the considerable gap between life at and life outside work. The tendency to become 'stupid' and 'ignorant' which Smith indicated or to become the 'automaton' subject to an extremely strict system of authority, as seen by Taylor, is not very plausible — or at least it does not have much chance of lasting — in our post-industrial society. We shall have occasion to speak of this again later.

Technological hegemony. Taylor's fragmented analysis of work prepared for or facilitated the mechanization of work[29] and the advent of a much bolder all-prevailing technology in the whole production goods or services. Such a system is all-powerful in the allegiance which it imposes on everyone — workers, directors, managers, foremen, operatives. Let it be noted, however, that production-line work and the hegemony of the machine preceded Taylor theory. Marx[30] established opposition between the manufacturing and the industrialized process:

In the manufacturing process the social grouping is purely subjective. It is a combination of fragmented workers. Under the industrialised system heavy industry possesses a form of production which is absolutely objective, which the worker finds already prepared and which appears as a material condition of production . . . The co-operative character of the work process now becomes a technical necessity, imposed by the very nature of the means of work.[31]

This evolution is consistent with progress, intrinsically consistent both with a desirable economic evolution (productivity is increasing) and an ethical evolution (arduous work has decreased over-all).[32] There would be grounds for self-congratulation if this evolution had not been seized on and contorted by an overwhelming belief in science and an excessive application of technology which have led to an impoverishment of the content of *human* work. Of course the man–machine combination has seen its productivity increase; in terms of power of consumption the worker has partially benefited from this evolution. Nevertheless, the result of a comparison between the content of work before and after the increase in mechanization is frequently negative as far as human work is concerned. In a large bank such as the Crédit Lyonnais, the work of the 10,000 administrative personnel (out of a total staff of 45,000) was affected in this way as a result of computerization.

The logical outcome to the evolution of our technical society is the supremacy of technology, the mental and even intellectual enslavement of man to technology and to the machine, whatever his level in the hierarchy of the organization may be, and often, whatever his intellectual and mental capacity may be. Such a situation is dangerous for obvious non-economic reasons but – and here lies the paradox – it even comes up against elementary economic finality. This technological hegemony deforms and deprives one's capacity to judge its simple common sense. During the setting-up of new forms of organization, particularly of semi-autonomous work-groups, it has become clear that certain technical processes, certain kinds of equipment, certain tools,[33] have been questioned by the people carrying out the work, and that simple common sense should have enabled work-study experts to put forward of their own accord the solutions suggested by the workers.

Economists themselves have been deluded by the belief that mechanization is only the replacement of human work by a machine. The famous on-going debate about the substitutability or the complementarity of the factors rests implicitly on this dual conception of the organization of work – man, like the machine, is an instrument of labour, and whenever possible the machine can advantageously replace man.

Pushed to the limits of absurdity such ways of reasoning have often misled the best economists into fruitless areas of research into the functions of production, one of the implicit bases of which is not only the substitutability but also the *independence* of the two factors capital and labour.[34]

The reasons for progressive deviationism. How can the deviations from the system conceived by the classical organization theorists be explained? We see three converging explanations. The first is based on the development of material need and the convergence of workers' interests with those of the firm. Guaranteed employment, wage-level, and therefore consumption level and the worker's short-term fate, all depend on the fate of the firm in a market economy. In a planned economy the reforms undertaken in the management of firms over the last decade and the Yugoslav system are leading progressively to the same results. The 'fate' of the worker is thereby identified with the fate of the firm, which results in an objective alliance that facilitates the race for productivity.

The second results from the development of international competition, the opening and interpenetration of economic regions, which have intensified the search for productivity. War economy – the Second World War, the Korean war – and more recently the energy-shortage economy in Great Britain show clearly that in absolute terms over-all productivity can be pushed to very wide limits.[35]

The third is due to the evolution of the production system itself. The rationalization of work leads to technological progress, to the search for more automated processes, to the invention of the right machine for the job. Production tends to become more costly in terms of initial investment than does a labour-intensive process. This capitalization of production – the future effects of which ought logically to benefit, under certain conditions, the workers – brings with it the search for increased profit or self-financing capacity and, consequently, the worker's 'objective' approval. It would seem that this is the partial explanation for the search for productivity at all costs which is frequently imposed by the directors of firms and frequently accepted by the workers. It seems to be possible, because of the vividness of a mirage which has sometimes become reality for a fraction of workers – those whose conditions of work have, if anything, improved – namely the illusion that today's increased effort will be rewarded by a more agreeable and/or better-paid life at work tomorrow. This conflict of intrapersonal interest between the present and the future is well known to economists, even though, as we believe, it has often been wrongly interpreted.[36] In the field of work, as in that of energy, the classical lessons of political economy are flagrantly contradicted. E. Malinvaud, for example, who was in our belief wrong in keeping too many links with the function of production,[37] has meanwhile clearly perceived the necessity for appreciating the future,[38] and not the contrary, as is so frequently asserted, in the name of a traditionally wrongly-interpreted time preference.

(c) The Taylor paradox and the internal contradictions of Taylorism

Once again we wish to make it clear that use of the adjective Taylor or of the noun Taylorism corresponds to the system of scientific management as it has developed and become established historically and not to Taylor's original thought. Lussato seems to admit the importance of this reservation when he shows that the ideas of Taylor and Fayol represented a historical innovation to the age in which they were born, for he says that: 'to criticize him [Fayol] would be as absurd as to reproach Lavoisier for not having foreseen the transmutation of the elements'. What is more serious according to Lussato is the survival of company directors and even organization specialists for whom the organization is identified with classical concepts.[39]

All theory and all decision intend to supply the necessary explanation and solution to enable us to cope with a given situation. They generally provoke undesired effects which diminish or cancel out the positive effect of the original decision. Thus monetary devaluation is accompanied by pernicious effects which frequently cancel out the expected advantages. In the same way Taylorism has brought with it perverse effects, particularly a waste of human resources such that current organization of work has become a system wherein entropy prevails.

The development of the perverse effects of Taylorism. The assertion of the scientific nature of the preliminary study of the job, of the rigidity of the operational modes which were envisaged as correct and unique, the dichotomy between planners and operators, have all brought about effects which are contrary to those sought. The principal positive long-term consequence has been that the analysis of work done by man has made its transfer to a machine easier. This has happened to such a degree that, paradoxically, Taylorism, the theory of scientific management of human organizations, is claimed to have had its greatest positive effect in the *development* of mechanized work by means of the induced perfection of tools, while it makes the organization of men, on the other hand, *sterile.*

Is the increase in productivity due to organizational performance in terms of an adaptation of man and of the organization of men to the process of production? Or is it due to the development of a use of machinery? We will not let ourselves be drawn into the trap of the (for our subject) sterile argument about the appropriation of productivity. Productivity, in our view, functions as an ambi-system[40] man–capital or human work–machine work and the worker must be pre-eminent. This important question is only raised here as a reminder of the difficulty of dissociating the two factors of production and of the fact that in every analysis of this kind the point of view of the complementarity of the factors has to be given priority.

Therefore, rather than helping us in developing human resources at work, Taylorism is said to have made us discover more technical or material resources. It seems that this type of organization has had more of an inhibiting than a developing effect on the former area.

Unavoided wastage.[41] Taylor had the sensible idea of attacking wastage[42] — wastage of matter, of time, of movement. He said that his system had been conceived as the economizing of work. The emphasis on ergonomics, economy of movement and human strength, the search for a reduction of the arduousness of a task, the idea of time standards, all show clearly the orientation of his theory.

Current observation, however, reveals that numerous unskilled workers cannot keep to the imposed work-rhythm and this tends to invalidate the programming of work-time. It reveals that many of them resort to absenteeism and job-turnover as a temporary respite from the fact of being programmed. It reveals that the increase in occupational illness, especially nervous illness, or in fatigue away from work (but in this case the fault lies with the system of urbanization and transportation) tend to increase down-time and wasted time.

There is no prevention of material wastage either. This takes the form of a deterioration in actual quality compared with standard quality, an increase in rejects and returns, an increased need for after-sales service owing to insufficient quality control, all of which can be analysed in terms of loss of time, of material, of productivity, and, consequently, of income.

Open conflicts and their consequences are a waste of time which can be calculated in units of millions[43] of work-hours wasted and in large-scale loss of production.[44]

But even in the eyes of the economist this strictly material wastage is perhaps not the most acute one. About forty years ago the struggle used to be against underemployment in terms of unemployment, because of the implied economic social and moral consequences. What we are seeing nowadays is a more subtle form of underemployment, one that is being tolerated less and less.[45] It is the underemployment of individual ability,[46] the repression of workers' natural gifts, the sterilization of human competence and resources. It is the lack of fulfilment of hopes, expectations, and ambitions — in the most noble sense of the words — at all levels of the hierarchy.[47]

Is this what Taylor wanted? Of course not. Yet at whatever level of the hierarchy a worker may be, structuring, partitioning, demarcation, analysis, and preparation have all impoverished his human potential.[48] For work has lost the need for qualifications, whether it be a question of the overworked, under-informed manager who is the mere tool of some distant directive or the method-study man who, like the worker, is the victim of the system which it is his job to put into operation.

The entropy of the work system. Taylor wanted social harmony, solidarity between workers and bosses, the common search for material well-being, the advent of a team spirit for production workers. This was to be possible because of high wages and low costs, highly increased production, and the recognition of common interests by all socio-economic partners. The results are remarkable in many technical, economic, and material respects. On the spiritual, human, and intellectual side, the result, when looked at strictly within the field of work, is unconvincing and is perhaps even negative in certain cases.

From the point of view of human resources, whether in the strictly economic sense or in the broad sense of the term, there is a word which has become more than well known, not only by analogy but also as a synonym — entropy. This word describes perfectly the past and present evolution of job-design. Entropy has three connotations: the *degradation* of human energy by a synchronic comparison between potential and reality; the *irreversibility* of the tendency towards a lowering of the quality of work — irreversibility as understood diachronically within the existing organizational system; increasing social *disorder* resulting logically from the first two tendencies.

The system has therefore had to discover ways to reduce entropy without however calling into question its own general philosophy.

iii. *The Palliatives*

If it is to survive, every system must resolve the difficulties it encounters. When the search for solutions takes place within the system, within the framework of its constraints, the latter are rarely questioned. The 'natural' evolution of the Taylor system has taken three directions: that of compensations-deviations, that of the increasing incorporation of poorly qualified workers and, finally, that of different procedures which aim to make meaningless work bearable. We are only going to look at the first two here.

(a) *Compensations-deviations*

As his work is felt to be more and more depressing, qualitatively poorer and poorer, the worker develops the natural reflex to escape and to spend as little time as possible at it.

This escaping takes on a variety of forms: the sly desire not to be very productive, the refusal to take on responsibilities, little industrial accidents, sick-leave, absenteeism in all its forms, claims for a reduction in working hours, difficulty of integrating young people and interesting them in their work. In short, it is the refusal to identify one's fate, one's career, with that of the firm. It is the search outside work for compensations necessary for one's mental, intellectual, and moral stability. It is the concept of work as drudgery, a constraint which is only tolerable when seen as a way to earn one's living and the money to pay for interesting activities outside work.

The debate is both economic and philosophical. From the economic point of view the search for non-work is a catch, in so far as it is accompanied by a desire to reduce activity at work. In effect, on a collective level, the development of outside leisure and cultural activities implies increased production of goods and services.[49] Travel, sport, and cultural activities require an infrastructure and a working system which are *costly* in terms of *social product*. The freedom of choice for certain people, with a relatively high personal income, to reduce time spent at work is hardly valid for the mass of workers, unless they renounce totally our form of civilization. Thus we are imperceptibly brought back to the philosophical debate. In other words, if we remain within the framework of our present-day civilization,[50] even if it were to be vastly improved thanks to the development of outside activities and to respect for the imperatives of our ecological and social environment, the *development of man* demands totally, globally, *the development of his economic activity*. But this is the fruit of the combination of the factors of production, and a large reduction in working time appears improbable in the short term, in spite of the predictions of J. Fourastié and of H. Kahn.

Despite the importance of the philosophical debate, we do not intend to become involved in it because it is an area where only value-judgements can decide and a value-judgement alone is not scientific. J. Delors[51] defends the idea that 'work is always at the centre of our lives. All the prophecies about the exclusive reign of the leisure civilization will not change anything in this.' He is confident that it will be possible to make of work: 'not only a means of earning one's living but also an end-state – that of living one's life successfully'. The opposing theses will not be developed here, but we should like to emphasize the doubts felt by certain members of the National Plan study-groups researching into work in the future about the cogency of J. Delors's thesis. We shall refer to this important question in our conclusion.

Be this as it may, it is possible to organize work-time in a way that is both more rational and more consistent with the free hopes of men.

Time spent at work and productivity. The working week can be noticeably reduced without changing the level of over-all production. Numerous experiments prove this point.[52] The figures below are those quoted in the LEST study[53] and we shall show diagrams and tables based on them.

Figure 1.1 shows an experiment carried out in Britain:

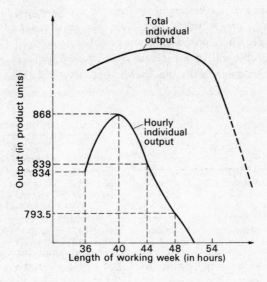

Fig. 1.1

When the production objective is given, it is advisable to look for the optimum complement to give a working week of as near as possible to 40 hours. If the labour market is tight, it will be advisable, whatever the circumstances, not to exceed the 54 hours seen to be the threshold beyond which weekly production and, *a fortiori*, individual output decline. It is interesting in this experiment to notice that wage progression, the rest being equal, is linked to a system (production level, complement, working week) which produces a solution for this latter variable as near as possible to 40 hours.

E. Grandjean[54] shows that according to an inquiry carried out in several factories by the American Department of Labor, a reduction in the number of hours worked by the men per week from 48 hours to 40 hours brought about an average increase in output of 14%. The author concludes that: 'since the reduction in the working week was 16% there was a total production deficit of 2%'. It should be noted that this figure is wrong and that Table 1.1 shows the correct calculation.

Table 1.1

Working week	Individual hourly productivity index	Individual weekly productivity index	Number of workers for same level of production	Employment Index $n' = f(n)$
40	114	4560	n'	105.263
48	100	4800	n	100

Let us assume that the effects of the reduction of work on productivity are lasting and that a generalization of the experiment described leads to results similar to those recorded for the whole of the economy.

Different possible employment and working-week policies are outlined in Table 1.2, for example, with the chosen objectives-constraint of a 40-hour working week.

Table 1.2

Policy	Production level	Employment level	Wage level	Probable short-term economic effect
A (extreme)	maintain at 4800 n	increase of 5.263%	rise of 14% (index 114)	increase in demand → pressure on the level of production (inflationist).
Z (extreme)	reduce to 4560 n	maintain at n	rise of 14% (index 114)	as above; inflationist pressure probably stronger.
K (intermediate)	4560 $n < P_k$ $< 4800 n$	$n < n_k < n'$	$100 \leqslant s_k$ < 114	increase in demand lower than D(A) and D(Z). Less inflationary pressure + able to be stopped progressively via a policy of investment, the capacity for auto-investment being equal to $(114 - s_k)$ per manpower unit and higher if workers' savings permit external financing.

In spite of the criticisms that can be made of such a simulation, we think it interesting to start from a productivity gain and show that the range of

employment, wage, and production policies is wide and that the probable economic effects — all else being equal — are a constraint which influences the decision
as to the most appropriate policy in view of the state of the economy. In the
long term a mortgage, because of the foreseeable inflationary pressure, influences the degree of freedom of choice in all types of policy between A and Z,
with one exception — let us call it I.

I is the policy which puts into operation an ideal combination of the three
variables (production, employment level (complement, working week), wage
level) which allows a sufficient level of auto-investment so that the increase in
final demand is reduced and that the technical progress incorporated as a result
of the investment allows a modification of the function of productivity for the
following period and a production increase without raising either the level of
employment or the number of hours worked.

This simulated example, however, calls for some comments and some reservations.

(1) To be really significant the measure of productivity has to refer to a
homogenous population. Hence no *single* productivity index will be obtained
but a matrix of different productivity indices. In an analysis at the level of the
micro-organization, the matrix will correspond to a division of the production
unit into workshops or sections. On the macro-economic level the indices will
correspond to measures taken in different sectors of activity. This complicates
in a singular way our determination of policy I.

Table 1.3

Sections or sectors of activity	Hours worked h_1	h_2	h_3
s_1	i_{11}	i_{12}	i_{13}
.	.	.	.
.	.	.	.
.	.	.	.
s_n	i_{n1}	i_{n2}	i_{n3}

(2) The measure of *differential productivity* ($i_i = 114$ for $h_1 = 40$, against
$i_2 = 100$ for $h_2 = 48$) has to be carried out under conditions which neutralize
all effects other than those which one is trying to measure. In the American
example (and the others also) quoted by the psycho-sociologists, the latter do
not trouble to point out all the details of the experiment — length, technological
change or improvement carried out, the coefficient of productive capital per
worker, production and employment policy, the situation of the labour market,
organizational details, etc.

Without this information we can only make a rather vague statement about
the 48-hour experiment and the 40-hour one: a 14% increase in productivity
concomitant with a reduction in working hours from 48 to 40 was observed,

but it is not possible to state that the latter was the cause of the former and, *a fortiori*, that it was the only cause. This comment shows clearly the need to be careful about the conditions under which measures are taken and the need to draw up a *complete set of apparatus of quantified observations*. Without this, experiments in the social sciences lose a great deal of their validity.

(3) It is therefore important to make precise observations which show that a reduction in the working week brings with it an increase in hourly productivity, and which measure the size of this variation. We have to be very precise as to the combination of conditions required for this cause to produce this effect. Fortunately, recent experiments have led to such conclusive results that we can state that, although a reduction in the length of the working week is not the *only* cause of an increase in productivity, it is at least possible to organize production and work in such a way that the same level of production can be obtained in a reduced number of working hours, *and* under unaltered or unimproved working conditions. This was Taylor's mistake, this is the mistake of all time-and-motion-study men[55] – they argue in terms of *isoproductive* time.[56]

(4) Finally it must be remembered that production cannot be strictly measured in terms of *isoquality*. The average quality of a batch of items machined or assembled by one worker during a 40-hour week is higher than a batch completed during a longer working week.[57] One may hesitate to argue in terms of average, but this is not really troublesome. It would be possible to take a sample of workers, measure their total production for a 40-hour week, and classify it by order of quality in '*n*' categories. The same experiment could be carried out based on either a sample of workers selected as having a level of productivity very close to that of the first group and working 48 hours over the same period, or even the same sample working 48 hours during a week offering approximately the same working and economic environment.

Empirical observation[58] has shown that quality improves when the working week drops from 48 hours to 40 hours and that a reduction in hours is accompanied by a resorption of the absenteeism which disorganized work and brought with it a loss of production.[59] A reduction in hours between these two limits produces cumulative effects: quantitative increase and qualitative increase in production by unit of time. On the basis of these findings we can reaffirm our initial statement: there exists a solution which enables one to achieve production objectives at the same time as reducing the number of working hours.

Reduction in the number of hours worked – a necessary and insufficient condition. A reduction in the number of hours worked is possible over-all,[60] yet there are cases where it will be difficult to achieve this.[61] For structural reasons the number of hours worked is long where there is a chronic shortage of skilled workers or when there is a desire to avoid working nights or to shorten the length of the working week (in these two cases the length of the working day is affected). For economic reasons – a rush of orders at certain times of the year, or just before taking on new workers – firms increase the number of hours worked. There is also a veritable store of overtime which gives the organization greater flexibility either because the rush is temporary or because the tightness of the labour market makes taking on new workers more expensive and/or more problematical than the cost, albeit higher, of overtime.

A reduction in the number of hours worked has effects which are sometimes beneficial, sometimes harmful: 'In certain cases it will enable the system of team-work to be extended, which will, in turn, entail an improvement in the way equipment is used and therefore an improvement of the over-all productivity of the firm's production factors.'[62] Team-work, when the teams work in relays, entails a desynchronization of activities and rhythms of life (in France 20% of workers are affected by this problem).[63] There is another effect which is both beneficial and unfortunate: according to an inquiry carried out by INSEE in 1969,[64] the number of hours worked would probably result in an acceleration of investment by firms. This acceleration of investment should lead to a more rapid incorporation of technological progress and an increase in productivity from the man–machine combination. It does, however, require considerable prior financing. Such an evolution is only possible in stages. We have to remember, however, that it is difficult to treat all firms in the same way and that the most rapid progress can only be made in certain sectors of economic activity.

In conclusion let us look at the paradoxes – the incompatibility of carrying out simultaneously certain improvements in the field of work time. In order for it to be compatible with the lowering of the retirement age, a reduction in the length of the working week can only take place by stages. A shortening of the working week (experiments into a 4-, 3½-, or 3-day week[65] are being carried out in the United States) corresponds to a need for whole days which can be given over to leisure activities, but it implies a lengthening of the working day. Will this be compatible with the above analysis into productivity?

A reduction in the number of hours worked is equally necessary because of the increase in time spent travelling from home to work.[66] The Gruson report suggests that travelling time should be included in time spent at work.

A reduction in working hours is, however, insufficient. Apart from the difficult choices which it leads to, it does not solve the basic problem of job-content, motivation, and the aspirations of the man at work. In this sense it appears as a cover-up, at best as an incomplete solution.[67]

(b) *The incorporation of categories of less-qualified and/or more docile workers*

The growth of industrialized countries has always been accompanied by a need for a new labour force, which is drawn from the rural, or the so-called non-working population, or from abroad. The need for a highly qualified work-force, scientists, managers, technicians, results in migration between countries which have reached a certain level of development. The so-called brain drain from West Germany and Great Britain to the United States, and nowadays the brain drain from India, is taking place alongside the more organized, more official forms of migration in the shape of technical aid to developing countries. Worker migration has always taken place. It has advantages for individual and national development and involves all manner of professional qualifications to differing extents. It is a general phenomenon and is strongly induced by economic and technological development and growth.

We shall pay particular attention here to two 'migratory' movements which have a very direct bearing on our central theme — the organization of work. While facilitating growth, scientific management has revealed pockets of man-power shortage centred on jobs involving intrinsically and/or extrinsically the worst working conditions. These are jobs which had been left vacant or refused by male indigenous workers and for which it became necessary to incorporate foreign or female workers who were 'happy' to find a job, even at the expense of their physiological or moral equilibrium. This is an accompanying phenomenon to scientific management. The rationalization of movements and work so planned that no professional qualification is necessary have enabled us to incorporate an unprepared and unqualified work-force. It is not part of our brief to show that this historic process has perhaps contributed to the economic development of countries or sectors which profit from the contribution made by foreign or female workers, as well as to the rapid development (under certain conditions) of those countries supplying manpower and, in spite of reserves, to the *material* improvement of their families. What we want to bring out are the defaults of such a situation, the incomplete, provisional, and doubtless ephemeral nature of this palliative solution, the harmful effects of which are nowadays admitted by the majority of opinion.

Because of job mobility which has been made easy by economic growth, and because of trade-union protection, job-design has vacated the boring, tiring, or dirty, and often badly paid jobs. In place of unskilled nationals we see immigrant workers who 'like what they do', who 'ask for nothing', who 'don't want to change their job, even if it is hard, because they've got used to it', who 'are quite trusting because they can't read', who 'are quite happy to work on the line because they can do it without thinking, they don't think and they manage to gain a bit of time, . . . a few seconds . . . gained so as to be able to relax . . .', who, because they do not have to think 'don't suffer from it . . . , whereas your Frenchman does. Those who suffer from the monotony don't stay . . .' This foreman's view of 'his' unskilled workers[68] sums up quite well the use people make of the docility of immigrant workers. Without scientific management, without analysis, work-preparation, without the breaking-down of tasks, it would be much more expensive to incorporate this labour force. It is true that a less developed economic activity would not necessitate the employment of such a labour force.

The docility, manual dexterity, and lower wages of immigrants is also a feature of female work. The 1971 CNPF report on unskilled workers says: 'We have seen how women seem to be able to put up with the boredom of certain jobs better than men can. We have therefore to ask ourselves if there is not good reason to encourage their employment.' Fortunately this opinion is not shared by all French employers and, fortunately too, France seems to make proportionally less use of female labour on production-line work than do other countries, notably Japan.[69] However, the proportion of female wage-earners in France is higher than in neighbouring countries (36.3% as against 23.4% in Luxembourg, 25.7% in Italy, 29.9% in Belgium).[70] The comparison between men's and women's wages in the six founder members of the EEC is significant.[71]

Table 1.4
Average hourly earnings, by sex, in the whole of industry in October 1970
(in national currency)

	W. Germany	France	Italy	Netherlands	Belgium	Luxembourg
Men	6.76	6.19	6.82	5.24	69.02	88.18
Women	4.65	4.82	5.06	3.10	46.83	50.27
Women's earnings as a percentage of men's earnings	68.7%	77.8%	74.1%	59.1%	67.8%	57.0%

Source: Office Statistique des Communautés Européenes.

In general women at work are known for their dexterity and constancy. Absenteeism and instability of employment are not the attributes of women at work. Studies of absenteeism[72] have destroyed the myth of women's 'biological' absenteeism. As for the instability of female labour, this decreases rapidly as qualification increases, as indeed is true for the whole of the working population, irrespective of sex. Does under-qualification explain the fact that 75% of women employed in West German industry are manual workers, or that 39% of unskilled workers in Denmark are women? Why is it then that industries with a large female work-force (clothing, shoes, . . .) have large percentages of skilled workers when it is here that the lowest wages are to be found.[73] There is, however, disagreement as to the degree of interest which unskilled female workers take in their work compared with their male counterparts.[74]

In spite of this pessimistic picture, some progressive factors can be shown. An evolution is taking shape in the recent strikes at Renault by unskilled immigrants, female workers, and employees. Young people seem to be playing a significant role in the evolution of work[75] in no matter what country.[76] We shall come back to the rejection of the present system in the next chapter.

Taylorism has succeeded in establishing itself very widely in industry. It has enabled a large increase in production to come about, albeit to the detriment of the quality of life at work. The negative effects of Taylorism have inspired new theories. The oldest of these attempt to complete the Taylor organization, the most recent to question it totally. These new theories were initially spurred on by the human sciences and have followed recent developments therein.

B. The Theories Inspired by Human and Social Sciences

i. *The Amendments to Taylorism*

The first ways in which human sciences were introduced into scientific management did not question Taylorism, but aimed rather at completing it, at filling in the gaps.

(*a*) *The need to understand the enterprise in its entirety, as a really living being*
The enterprise is a being with its own finality and cohesion. Survival is its primary aim. The condition for survival is financial equilibrium rather than profit as P. Drucker and Lussato state.[77] Two instincts balance each other: conservation and expansion. The enterprise has a hierarchical skeleton, a physiological mechanism consisting of flows of material, energy, and formal information, and of a psychological apparatus which results from the psychicism of its members. This psychological system, which has only recently been recognized — the work of March and Simon dates from 1958 — 'is animated not only by the motivations, drives, sympathies and other behavioural traits of emotional existence, well known to specialists in human relations, but also and above all by the cognitive, perceptual and decision-making processes which form the principal link between man and his work, between the "psychological" and "physiological", between individual desires and the execution of a task. . . .[78]

'Therefore it is necessary first of all to resolve the problems raised by communication between man and the artifical world surrounding him. Systems theory offers some hope of success here, provided that we avoid concerning ourselves exclusively with the information circulating in machines, and give very close study to its influence on human recipients.'[79]

The partitioning of the enterprise into three areas according to objectives: intrinsic, mixed, extrinsic, allows us to understand the opposition between the optimistic thesis of the classical writers on organizations, such as Max Weber, and the pessimistic thesis of C. Argyris. Max Weber regards man at work as an emotionally ascetic being, whose personal motives coincide with the objectives of the enterprise. Argyris is passionately opposed to this position, when he says: 'The formal constraints of the principles of organization are incompatible with individual needs, which necessarily leads to frustrations and conflicts.'[80] One has an idea that the effort of imagination required for the creation of new forms of job-design has precisely to be used to try to make these two constraints compatible. It is remarkable how the history of the science of organization runs parallel to that of economic science, albeit with a certain time-lag. The coincidence which the classical writers on political economy decreed between private interests and those of the community, their simplistic theory of equilibrium which aims implicitly at justifying individualism, their *homo economicus*, all have a striking resemblance to certain features of the classical organization theory worked out half a century later. Lussato's diagram (Fig. 1.2)[81] throws a clear light on the idea of partitioning.

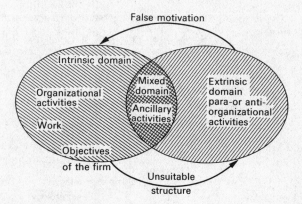

Fig. 1.2. Interactions between domains; an unsuitable structure (intrinsic domain) can engender conflicts and motives opposed to the firms, which nevertheless counter-react on the latter obliquely through false motivations (from the Eng. trans. (pub. Macmillan) of Lussato's op. — see p. 279).

Figure 1.3, also borrowed from Lussato,[82] illustrates usefully the place of organization theories inspired by the human sciences in the different schools of thought.

(b) The school of human relations

The behaviourist or human relations school took its inspiration from the psychological theory of behaviourism. Once again there is a very clear parallel between economic science and the science of organization.

It studies the behaviour of men at work and leads to a methodical search for motivations and ties which ensure the group's adaptation to the set objectives. It looks at the phenomena of co-operation and conflict and at the barriers to communication.

It studies and suggests different types of non-authoritarian chains of command, either participative or co-operative, but other styles are also admitted. It advocates seminars on communication as one way to get people involved in breaking down communication barriers.[83] In addition to the founders[84] E. Mayo[85] and F.-J. Roethlisberger, whose ideas were brought to France by G. Friedmann and J. Lobstein, the contemporary representatives of this school are C. Argyris and R. Likert in the United States and J. Woodward and E. Muller in Great Britain.

The behaviourists's contribution consists of spotlighting innovatory ideas in the matter of management: the decentralization of decisions, the efficiency of confidence over authority, responsibility rather than external control. It gives to one's superior a role of communicator between and with the group, rather than that of the representative of authority. It chooses the group and not the individuals as the area for study.

In spite of this school's incontestable contribution, which marks the transition

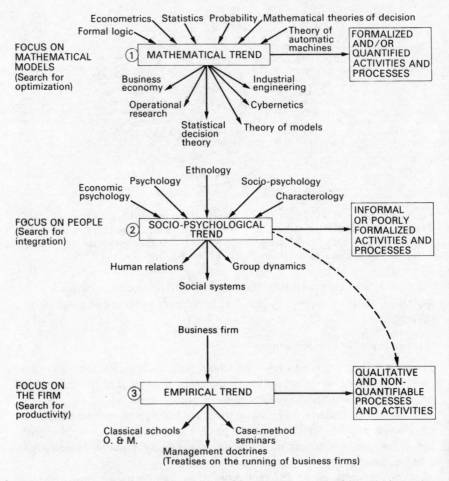

Fig. 1.3. Relationships between the three trends — mathematical, socio-psychological, and empirical (experimental, pragmatic) — and the three zones of formalization (from — see above, Fig. 1.2)

to the modern movements, it has to be noted that the theory's operational virtues are weak. Co-operative and friendly behaviour is not enough to stimulate people to exceed themselves, to raise the efficiency of the group. The human aspect, when thrown into relief, takes on too exclusive a role[86] to the detriment of the other ingredients of management, namely the economic constraint. H. Koontz[87] puts the problem in a nutshell when he says: 'To identify the field of human behaviour with management is the same as calling cardiology the study of the human body.' What is remarkable, in addition, is that in spite of the exclusivity of the human relations point of view, it nevertheless does not succeed in destroying the Taylor system, it does not really call into question its techniques, and especially not the fragmentation of work.

(c) *The social systems school*

Lussato sums up the concept this school has of the enterprise as a co-operative coalition which is viable so long as it can provide its members with sufficient satisfaction to encourage them to continue to make their contribution. It is founded on the Gestalt theory developed by Köhler and Lewin. The accent is on the notion of *structure*. Taking the opposite view to the Cartesian method, it opposes dissociative analysis which destroys or conceals the relationships which order the groups within a whole.

The social systems school, born of C.-I. Barnard, is represented nowadays by H.-A. Simon, J.-G. March, I. Ansoff and R.-M. Cyert. Starting from the premiss of the Gestalt theory, it 'intends to study the psycho-sociological and decision factors, the interdependence of which facilitates mutual adjustment and the conformity of the activities of the enterprise to its objectives. It does so while stressing the extrinsic and mixed domains and the socio-psychological theory of decision.'

The social systems school does not refute the foundations of Taylorism, it reformulates them in the light of the contribution of sociology. The bases of the command unit, the extent of subordination, and centralization, are not called into question. Certain contributions from the human relations school are integrated into the social systems school. Barnard considers the system of communication and information to be essential. March and Simon[88] underline, for example, the unfavourable effect of centralization on motivation. These two authors have made a particular study of the decision process and have shown the importance of the degree of motivation, of the way the economic environment is perceived, and of the distortions in this which depend on the role and place in the structure of the man who decides. The analyses made by March, Simon, and Crozier allow us to see the enterprise as a group of *systematic relationships* in terms of the power which each person acquires from his *place in the structures*.

The essential contribution of this school in this area can perhaps be briefly summed up in the following proposition: conflicts are not necessarily born of poor human relationships or of incompatibility between individual motives and the objectives of the organization, they are all the more dangerous and more difficult to resolve when they are due to *differences in perception* of the environment.

The social systems school can be reproached on two counts: for not having integrated the elements necessary to the completion of its theory — cultural habits and semantics; and for not being a true *management theory* (H. Koontz's criticism), integrating material, procedural, and engineering constraints. It has, however, rendered great service to the study and prevention of industrial disputes. The latter reproach is the one generally levelled by practitioners against theories inspired by the social sciences, up to and including the socio-technical approach, in spite of the progress it enables us to make.

In this brief review of theories we can only touch on the neo-classical or empirical school, represented by Drucker and O. Gélinier, because from a strictly theoretical point of view the school appears to be a rearrangement — albeit important and effective — of the classical theory corrected by a few contributions from the human sciences. It is an amendment to Taylorism, which is why it is mentioned here, but it has no theoretical orginality. Let it be said in passing that it has penetrated numerous enterprises, notably Anglo-Saxon enterprises, and that it forms the basis of contemporary American management.

The richness of the general theory of systems goes beyond the framework of our study and has little to contribute to the problem of the organization of work in its strictest sense.

ii. *Taylorism Overtaken*

(a) *The French forerunners*[89]

Before the Second World War the Frenchman H. Dubreuil,[90] worker, trade-unionist and sociologist,[91] promoted the idea of restructuring the enterprise in autonomous economic cells, of self-managed production groups within the enterprise, in order to add to the economic viability of the Taylor enterprise a socio-psychological viability founded on the accomplishment needs of the workers. E. Rimailho, who 'saw no contradiction in being both a disciple of Taylor and concerned about workers' aspirations',[92] was associated with this concept and published a book in collaboration with H. Dubreuil.[93]

Dubreuil's[94] concept is based on the findings of the cultural duality of workers, the criticism of alienation of the wage-earning classes and that of the bureaucracy, on the denunciation of wrong steps and wrong solutions, those which endeavour to situate the problem on the over-all level of the economic system in its entirety. His concept is based on the co-operative system. The cultural duality exists between, on the one hand, the thinkers who never actually face the obstacle of the matter involved and yet who allocate themselves the task of conceiving the products, the material, the tools, the organization of work and, on the other hand, the workers who are refused the right to participate in this conception, in spite of their know-how. This duality secretes bureaucracy. As for the wage-earning classes, bureaucracy adds to the line-workers' inhibition and to the inhibition of the worker in general. It cuts him off from the rest of the economic system.

Dubreuil makes suggestions which have sometimes been successfully carried out experimentally[95] but they have never been applied at large. This reconstruction of the enterprise rests on the following bases: the worker has a certain living-space and, to a limited degree, it is advisable to circumscribe his field of action (the group), to let a certain number of initiatives and responsibilities 'descend' to that group so that the group has a system of relationships based on semi-autonomy which are different from those emanating from Taylorism. The learning of not merely technical but also management skills ('to know is to be able') and the reaffirmation of the close relationship between wage and productivity are brought into relief ('it is along the path of decreasing people's alienation that we have to look for the secret of productivity'). All these suggestions lead to a subdivision of the enterprise into semi-autonomous cells.

Debreuil makes very precise propositions.[96] There would be three sorts of groups inside the enterprise, 'planning, producing, and selling groups'. The author is very concerned with the first two and especially with the way the production groups function.

The production sector[97] of the firm breaks down into production units (plants, factories) which are economically and technically viable, without exceeding a certain size. The production units are in turn subdivided into groups of 30 workers. The group is at one and the same time a production and an accounting centre -- an autonomous accounting section (it should be noted that at the time the method of homogeneous sections and cost accounting was flourishing).

The production group has as leader a sort of artisan combining moral qualities with technical ability, but above all competent at accounting and pricing. The leader would be a provisional head until the workers in the team become really adult in H. Ford's sense, i.e. able to organize their own work and take initiatives. The head's role as an educator would be pre-eminent; it consists in promoting individual technical and management skills. The result would be the greater efficiency of the team's work.

The group can subcontract part of the work either internally or externally and can itself act as a subcontractor. External relationships are a way to test internal work prices in the market-place. In this way the enterprise is regarded as a federation of subcontractors.

The planning group has the role of conceiving products and analysing the work *without any hierarchical authority* over the production groups. It takes on one of the aspects of the management function in the Taylor concept: that of technical assistance.

The technical assistance would be ensured by the creation at a national level of trade institutes, taking their inspiration from the French optical industry. This opening-up of the groups to the world outside the enterprise is a guarantee of progress and a stimulant. It is a pledge of psycho-sociological, economic, and technical autonomy.

Figure 1.4 shows the organization chart of the Dubreuil enterprise. The group head, who has become the leader at the end of the period of evolution described earlier, does not give orders but prepares the work. The content of the work is such that each person has a principal task which best corresponds to his aptitudes. There is organized job-rotation, and everyone offers help to and receives help from other members of the group. Finally, everyone carries out the tasks necessary to the main production task -- servicing, stocking-up, stock control . . . Under such a system a man's worth no longer appears to be linked to his promotion but to the amount of help he gives to others around him, and to his capacity to increase and improve the economic efficiency and the socio-psychological life of the group. This is the meaning of the 'elevation' of the individual of whom Dubreuil speaks.

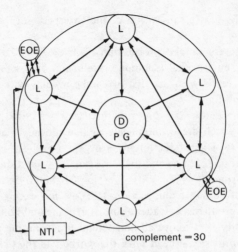

Fig. 1.4. The enterprise (and/or the establishment) = federation of small enterprises of 30 workers. L = leader of the production group. D = director of the enterprise (or the establishment if there are several). EOE = the enterprise or the outside establishment (in the case of subcontracting with another enterprise or another establishment of the same enterprise). PG = planning group. NTI = National Trade Institute.

Without knowing it, Ford came to the rescue of Dubreuil's ideas on various points.[98] Let us mention a few: (1) on the optimum size of the enterprise (or of the factory): 'the idea that it is necessary to concentrate industry is in my opinion unfounded. This necessity only corresponds to a stage of industrial development . . .' Thus here is confirmation by premonition of the *unstable* nature of large organizations.[99] (2) On the diversity of job-content and the sharing-out of tasks: 'when a mechanic finishes his work in four hours he finishes the rest of his day at whatever other job can be assigned to him.' (3) On the pseudo-necessity of constraints: 'we shall never be quite civilized until we have abolished the treadmill of discipline in manual labour.'

We shall not undertake a critical analysis of the system advocated by Dubreuil because we shall have occasion to show the difficulties of putting it into practice during the second part of this study, when dealing with experiments into semi-autonomous groups.[100]

G. Friedmann, the famous French industrial sociologist, occupies an important place[101] amongst the forerunners because of the accuracy of his descriptions of the world of work, of the pertinence of his analyses, of the way he strongly asserts the necessity for job-enrichment, of his renewed faith in autonomy, and of the doubt that he has helped to sow about the limits and harm of technically-based rationalization. He does not, however, escape from the criticism levelled by practitioners and management theorists against psycho-sociological theories, namely their incomplete and, in certain aspects, extra-company nature, and the absence of any proposal for a new *integral* system. This criticism cannot be levelled against Dubreuil. Yet we must not minimize the contribution, even if it

is purely intellectual, of thinkers, of those who, in the absence of suggesting operational solutions, stimulate us to think and thereby to work out practical solutions.

The evolution of Friedmann's thinking has been marked by three successive
stages: at first in favour of task-restructuring, he next advocated a compensation
system such as leisure activities; finally he now extols automation. We believe
that automation, seen from man's horizon, does not imply a very noticeable and
generalized reduction in working hours, but rather a transfer of some sections
and categories of human work. Automation has to lead to an increase in professional qualification, but it leaves pockets of poor or impoverished work which
only new forms of organization could reduce.

(b) The dichotomy of motivation to work: F. Herzberg

F. Herzberg, Professor of Psychology at Western Reserve University, USA,
has in his principal works[102] contributed a theory of motivation to work which
can be exploited in the organization of human work.

The point of departure of Herzberg's theory is a triple objection:
(1) indirect work-incitement methods: reduction of work-time, wage rises,
hygiene or atmosphere (= part of the physical environment, in Herzberg's
terminology), interest, development of human relationships, group dynamics,
communication, dialogue, participation, job-counselling are *insufficient* and
inefficient.
(2) Constraints which are *external* in origin cannot but give mediocre results. We
have to discover the *internal* motor, man's motivation to work.
(3) There is no symmetry between satisfaction and dissatisfaction. There is
dichotomy between the different factors which condition work-life: the factors
which cause job-dissatisfaction are different from those which cause satisfaction:
satisfaction is not absence of dissatisfaction.[103]

The author defines six factors of satisfaction:
1. 'Achievement' of the individual and his task.
2. Esteem or 'recognition' by the group of the individual's qualities.
3. The 'work itself' or work-content.
4. 'Responsibility'.
5. 'Advancement' or 'promotion'.
6. 'Possibility of growth — the fringe factor, difficult to code.'[104]

These factors are called 'motivators' and are the opposite of 'hygiene factors'
which are a cause of dissatisfaction. This idea is close to the overlap shown in
our introduction[105] concerning intrinsic and extrinsic conditions. It is work in
its internal structure which motivates the worker. Environmental conditions
(factors of hygiene or of atmosphere) enable the worker to *put up with* life at
work not to *take it on* fully and develop it. The efficiency of environmental
conditions is ephemeral. They should not be neglected but one should not look
to them for the key to the solution of the organization of work. Taylor organization is criticized in the following terms: 'In effect, man's inherent ability to
realize his potential solely by his own efforts seemed to be denied him', or

again: 'the creative man has been restricted and channelled to serve narrow and specific[106] purposes of the company.'[107] The author calls on the important notion of psychological growth based on 'knowing more', 'more relations in knowledge', 'creativity', 'effectiveness in ambiguity', 'individuation', and finally on 'real' (as opposed to imaginary) growth.[108] This notion has been borrowed by present-day researchers apropos of different types of employment which are classified according to the degree of development that they offer.[109] The nature of man at work is characterized by its duality: on the one hand, Adam (the animal aspect) urges man to escape from the evils of his environment, on the other, Abraham (the human aspect), by means of his achievements, shows his aspirations for development.

Figure 1.5 reproduces the diagram suggested by Herzberg in *The Motivation to Work*. Figure 1.6 sums up the results of a study carried out by M. M. Schwartz of Rutgers University using Herzberg's theory.

A temporal dimension is added to this duality. The factors do not last for an

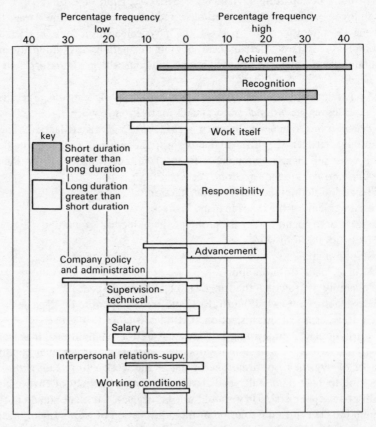

Fig. 1.5. Comparison of satisfiers and dissatisfiers (from F. Herzberg *et al.*, *The Motivation to Work*, John Wiley and Sons, New York, 1959)

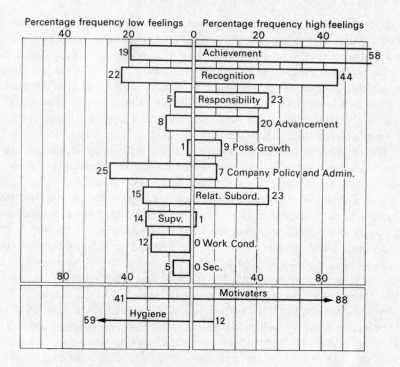

Fig. 1.6. Comparison of satisfiers and dissatisfiers: lower-level supervisors in utility industry (from F. Herzberg, *Work and the Nature of Man*, World Publishing Co., New York, 1966)

equally effective period and so it happens that of the five motivators it is the work itself, responsibility, and advancement which have the three longest-lasting effects.

'The factors listed are a kind of shorthand for summarizing the "objective" events that each respondent described. The length of each box represents the frequency with which the factor appeared in the events presented. The width of the box indicates the period for which the good or bad job attitude lasted, in terms of a classification of short duration and long duration. A short duration of attitude change did not last longer than two weeks, while a long duration of attitude change may have lasted for years.'[110]

P. Froidevaux[111] has drawn attention to the little-known works of the fore-runners J. Plaquevent and J. de Monès[112] which, as often happens, the Anglo-Saxons, among them C. Argyris in America and E. Jaques in Britain, took up with much furore some ten years later. These works developed a theory of four needs: biological and motor activity (physical environment), psychological, intellectual (job content), self-fulfilment.

Froidevaux adds a fifth need: the 'societal' or work-organization need which makes the group dimension appear. According to him, job-enrichment is not only an individual affair but also a question of organization. 'Experience[113] shows that an improvement in the production structure also brings with it at one and the same time a decrease in the number of rejects, greater precision, a decrease in manufacturing time, and positive satisfaction for those taking part.' Froidevaux's thesis, which starts from Herzberg's analysis, aims to integrate the communication structure and the gathering of information, an interest which was manifested by the social systems school, into a more integral cybernetic concept which is close to the general theory of systems.

The *internalization* of motivation to work realized by Herzberg's theory has enabled us to take a decisive step in the science of organizations. The theory has brought about numerous criticisms, which will not be dealt with here.[114] To sum up, there is an initial category of counter-arguments. Firstly, the method is above all psychological and the criteria are too subjective for us to validate the results or transpose the experiments. There is a second series of arguments in the ambiguity of the concept of satisfaction. The radical separation between the factors of hygiene (negative) and those which are motivators (positive) appears more didactic than real. Finally, this theory leaves the traditional *power* in the enterprise intact.

We shall not defend Herzberg's theory as the search for a psychological truth because this would pose difficult conceptual problems (what is *satisfaction*? Is the psychology of all individuals constructed on the same dichotomous model of motivators–hygiene?). The opponents of the theory have not omitted to raise these questions. We, however, will credit Herzberg with having made a considerable contribution to the science of organizations, namely a simple but operational schema which, if put into practice, should avoid bewilderment and waste: 'Hygiene acts like heroin — it takes more and more to produce less and less effect.'[115] In this way Herzberg concludes *implicitly* that the marginal productivity of investments made with a view to improving these 'hygiene' factors (in his terminology) is inversely proportional because of the low degree of efficiency of these investments and the 'insatiability of hygiene needs'.[116]

In this way light is thrown on the failure of research exclusively into the conditions of work-environment and based on a 'light-headed symptomatology'.[117] The solution to the problems of life at work consists *principally* in enriching job-content and restructuring the entire organization (Herzberg does not insist on this second structuring, although he brings it up in his work in conclusion), and *secondarily* in improving the environment and not the reverse. It is paradoxical that, because the improvement of the environment is more expensive and less effective, nobody has tried to make an effort to apply *imagination*, especially in the field of intrinsic factors. Job-enrichment is not a simple enlargement or quantitative and horizontal regrouping, but rather the giving of internal motivation and the surpassing of oneself at and through work. It is the system which requires the operator to exceed his routine capacity and in which work becomes a motivating source of interest.

Friedmann's judgement[118] seems to us rather harsh: 'basically Herzberg's theory tries to give the capitalist economy a second wind rather than solve the human problems which it implies.' Herzberg himself[119] endeavours to show the validity of his analysis under different political and economic regimes: 'This past summer, I received an invitation to lecture in Budapest to the Society of Engineers and found, to my delight, that a "motivation-hygiene" study was being made on a group of engineers . . . The Hungarian study seems to be evidence that the pattern of job attitudes in one Communist society is no different from that in the Western nations.'

In the same way he quotes Soviet studies of his theories: 'The Soviet investigators conclude that these results indicate that the most effective and the most important attitudinal factor for effective job performance is satisfaction *with the kind of work.*'[120]

We retain the idea that the interest of the theory from a strictly economic point of view is to show that an increase in productivity is compatible with job-enrichment and that this increase depends first and foremost on the increase of internal motivation.

(c) A synthetic vocation theory: the socio-technical approach

The socio-technical theory was born of the meeting of three currents of thought: the psychologists and sociologists of the Tavistock Institute of Human Relations, London, those of the Oslo Labour Institute, and the American 'engineers' tired of human sciences.

The first step taken by the researchers at the Tavistock was a classical one, purely socio-psychological in inspiration. It ended in failure on the experimental level, but also in a new concept: the socio-technical approach, a theory developed mainly from the successful experiment carried out in the British coal-mining industry around 1950.

The enterprise is conceived as an *open system*[121] composed of a technical system (technical and economic) and a social system. The socio-technical concept aims at optimizing jointly these two systems in the conception of the equipment, organization of production, and the structure of the enterprise. It leads to an upset of current practices. It is an empirical theory, the fruit of on-site research and action,[122] and of experiments carried out by the Tavistock researchers in association with the Norwegians (E. Thorsrud), the Americans (Davis), and the Dutch (Van Beinum). The 'classic' experiments are the Glacier Metal ball-bearing factory (E. Jaques), a single system in a coal-mine (E. Trist and H. Murray), a textile factory in India (Rice), Norwegian wood-pulp, wire-drawing, and fertilizer companies (F. Emery and E. Thorsrud), the British Shell project (Tavistock researchers in association with other Europeans and the American, Davis).

The Norwegian contribution consists essentially in the *industrial democracy* project carried out in the work-place itself, as a corollary to political democracy. Thorsrud is director of both the Oslo Work Institute and the Programme for Industrial Democracy in Norway, under the aegis of the trade unions, the employers' federations, and the government. The originality of the Scandinavian approach to the reform of work-organization lies in a close relationship between the political, ideological, and social factors at the national level and the variables which are to be given preference in the setting-up of new forms of job-design at production-unit level (participation, relative autonomy).

As for Davis,[123] he sets forth the anti-Taylor principles of 'the' new American school:

(1) accomplishment of economic aims depends on the survival of the production process
(2) the production process is in danger of collapse because of random events
(3) the prevention of random events implies men's involvement, each to his function
(4) economic constraint or economic motivation (wages) are both powerless to provoke involvement
(5) the structure must provoke individuals' involvement by means of autonomy, decentralized or auto-regulated planning at the job level.[124]

The socio-technical approach was born in the first instance of a negative finding based on its original socio-psychological specificity. It is not enough to concentrate efforts at reorganization on interpersonal and inter-group human relationships. E. Trist[125] was 'the first to discover that there was in fact a more general problem to be solved, that the numerous problems which people had sought answers to in terms of the social system of the firm or of the psychology of the workers, were in fact rooted in the technological system: *the job-design itself.*[126] In factories it is *the human tasks themselves*[127] which led to the constraints and to the pressure on the social system. In one sense the new evolution of the social system could only achieve its aim by taking the technological system into account, i.e. the real economic demands.'

As for exclusively socio-psychological solutions, Murray condemns them[128] by saying that: 'If the organization of labour fails to respect the technical interdependence of the tasks, great difficulties can occur in the production system and in working relationships.'[129] For Emery and Trist[130] this taking into account of the technical aspect optimizes the psychological results. The multi-disciplinary approach advocated by the author[131] marks a considerable step forward with respect to the post-Taylor theories. 'In all cases it appears that a socio-technical approach requires managers to be both expert social scientists and engineers. When analysing the demands imposed by technology it is necessary to know which are the variables involved in the technical details of the material, the factory, etc. so as to be able to forecast human reactions and to estimate whether the combination of the two will lead to results. It is at this point that one realizes that the task has to be adapted to the social system, that it is possible to try and organize all tasks in such a way as to maximize the use of resources and potential inherent in the social system itself.'

The socio-technical approach is confident that those carrying out the work will discover the optimum operational modes.[132] 'In fact, the very complex, well-adapted job-design model which is constantly developing is not one which has been worked out by management, but by the workers themselves.' The role of management is thereby better delimited, its competence is more specialized and it is no longer universal and exclusive: 'Management's role was clearly defined as being to keep the rules of the game running (e.g. making sure that supplies are available, that coal is extracted, that outside disturbances do not interfere)[133] . . . Management delegated to the team and the team accepted the responsibility of organizing itself, depending on which tasks had to be performed. This gave the group a remarkable degree of autonomy, responsibility, and creativity.'

The group dimension does not follow the rules laid down by human sciences: *There is an optimum grouping level which can only be worked out by analysing the demands of the technological system.*[134]

The socio-technical theory objects to grouping by affinity. 'Putting together workers who feel a need for friendship at work does not mean that their basic psychological needs are fulfilled (as is sometimes claimed by those who advocate better human relationships at work). Grouping produces its principal psychological effects when it leads to a system of *roles at work*, in such a way that the workers are above all held together by the demands of production and by task interdependence. Once the general orientation has been fixed, the worker should find himself working at a suitable task, fulfilling a mutually supportive role with respect to the results. Such reciprocal help enables the constraints which result from work to be removed.'[135]

The psychological needs on which the theory is based hardly differ from those studied by Plaquevent and de Monès or by Herzberg. As formulated by Emery[136] and recapitulated by Murray,[137] the individual needs are:

(1) work content which demands more than physical effort and which is varied in aspect,
(2) to learn a job, to renew the learning process, and to have a certain degree of liberty in carrying out the work,
(3) to have power of decision in an area, no matter how small, which implies one's individual judgement,
(4) to have social contact and some consideration at the job,
(5) to be able to explain what one does and produces during one's life in the work community,
(6) to feel that the job is leading to a desirable future.

The criteria to be taken into account for job-analysis and restructuring correspond to the seven following concrete questions:

1. Is there an optimum variety of tasks within the job being considered?
2. Is there a meaningful task model which gives each job the appearance of a single and complete job?
3. Is there an optimum length to the job cycle?
4. Is there room for the application of standards of quality and quantity, and efficient feed-back on the results obtained?

5. Does the job have to include preparatory and auxiliary tasks?
6. Does the task involved in the job imply a certain level of care, dexterity, knowledge, or effort — of everything that is necessary for respect in the community?
7. Does the job enable the worker to see at all the usefulness of the product to the consumer?

The enterprise is defined as: 'an open socio-technical system which acts in relation to an environment. It receives various things from this environment (raw materials, equipment, money, personnel). It uses what it receives in different sorts of conversion processes and then sells the goods and services which are the result. The open socio-technical system is basically self-regulating.'

Auto-regulation implies that the personnel have

(1) a sufficiently rich information flow,
(2) a certain statutory autonomy to be able to choose.

With this information the groups must exert pressure on the hierarchy and this simultaneously provokes and implies *role-enlargement*. The creativity of management and of the groups is interdependent and reciprocal.

The socio-technical theory is a synthesis of different angles which result more in an approach than in a 'rounded' theory.[138] From the start it aims to include the human and the social dimension. This is a preoccupation which is already fifty years old, but the socio-technical theory considers that to achieve this aim one has to take into account a technical system with technological, organizational, and economic components, without which the attempted inclusion is abortive. Finally it is part of the modern movement of cybernetics, and it contains an embryo of systems theory[139] by dint of the function it allocates to information as an element which feeds motivation. In this respect it is curious that Lussato does not give it a place among the modern schools inspired by systems theory.

The criticisms which can be made are of insufficiencies rather than errors in orientation. The ambiguity of the technical system is obvious in certain researchers in this theoretical movement (Cherns, Van Beinum). What do they define as technical content, are they as assertive as Murray, Trist, Emery, or Davis on the role of economic constraint in the technical system and on that of the technical system in the socio-technical system? There are important divergencies which show up the heterogeneous and even ambiguous character of 'this' school. So much so that contact with these theories made us want to develop the concept of the socio-economico-technical system. Froidevaux develops[140] and defends this concept by advocating a tripolar socio-technico-economic system. Finally we yielded to J.-D. Reynaud's objections. He considers that the economic system is an analytical system which is not on the same level as technical and social systems, which are 'real' systems. We accept this idea, although this conceptual hierarchy is not evident in certain socio-technical tenets. Is it even rejected, perhaps? Another apparently less pertinent argument consists in embodying the economic concept in the technical concept. Murray does this, as do certain consultants or personnel men in the enterprise. Such a confusion — simplification is always tempting — is not made up of the right ingredients to satisfy the economist, who is always at pains to escape from the confines of the point of view of the technician *stricto sensu*.

The socio-technical 'theory', inasmuch as it is an approach that is open to all solutions which are compatible with its principles, inasmuch as it is the opposite of dogma, is an attractive approach. We are bearing in mind especially its *omni-methodological*[141] aspect, the fact that it has the merit of attracting the attention of organization specialists and the fact that it has resulted in positive and viable experiments.

The history of the theory of job-design is new ... It is marked by successive contributions from, for the most part, the social sciences. Its progression marks the growing globalization of the analysis of and solutions to the organization of work. Simplified to the extreme, this historical path reveals primarily a concern to add socio-psychological motivation to the economic motivation which Taylorism favoured (the school of human relations). Only with the social systems school does one perceive the deep ramifications of the organization of work within the organizational structure of the enterprise in general at the micro- and macro-social levels. A movement which is more and more autonomous has separated itself from this school, the socio-technical approach. It is better able to promote change than to describe the functioning of existing systems. The most recent theories show clearly via their explanations and propositions that it is not sufficient to increase psycho-sociological motivation and that the *entire* organization has to be reshaped so as to make the largest possible number of workers *participate* in the elaboration of the solutions.

We shall now study the features of the current work world and the factors of evolution.

2. THE PRESENT AND THE FUTURE OF WORK

A. The Duality of the Work Universe

i. *A Growing Gap between the Quality of the World of Work and Economic Performance*

The cultural level of the population is tending, by and large, to rise. This is the result of the development of organized teaching both in and after school and university. It is the result of the development of an informal parallel form of teaching and of economic development which enables an increasing number of individuals to improve their lives as consumers. Continuing Education should accelerate the development of skills.

This development — let us call it cultural — is characterized by a development of abilities and, as a corollary, by a development of expectations. The first is the direct result of the formal or informal 'institutions' mentioned above. The second is the indirect result of this, the subsidiary but powerful effect.

The development of expectations, which is simplified by economic theory in the form of the development of needs, is a powerful reservoir of stimuli for ensuring the development of a civilization based on consumption-production.

Not only has the workers' perception of what their working conditions are declined, but also in certain cases the conditions themselves have declined. Such cases are doubtless more frequent than one imagines them to be. There has been a decline either in comparison with the earlier conditions or in comparison with what a worker has the right to expect from a civilization in which, as both a citizen and a consumer, he is respected and sought after.

There is therefore an apparently increasing gap between the quality of life at work for a particular individual and his life outside work. In the same way it is possible to identify the co-existence of a duality between certain workers whose working conditions have not deteriorated or which may even have improved, and those whose conditions have worsened, having been affected by different factors: an increase in rhythm, technological evolution, routine, lack of interest owing to a decrease in the right to take decisions and initiative at their post, even at some of the highest posts in the hierarchy. This duality is a supplementary source of inequality between individuals.

Evidence from workers, trade unions, middle managers, and employers' groups is sufficiently concordant on this point to assure us that we are not becoming involved in empty polemic where the facts are concerned. The development of education in general, at whatever level, and the setting-up of procedures which encourage people to undertake professional training are very powerful factors *in accelerating the enlarging of the gap* between working life and professional, intellectual, psychic, and human ability. There is a risk that the gap which exists between those who have and those who have not yet found equilibrium in their working life will increase. The number of people dissatisfied is likely to increase to the detriment of the rest. Even if the phenomenon of dissatisfaction remains a minor fact, it is the *tendency* which is significant from this point of view. Delors[142] admits that one should not generalize and we should not believe that numerous workers expect nothing more from their work than their pay, or that certain young people are impatient to begin their working lives.

We must anticipate this evolution and its social, economic, and organizational implications. There is the example of the manager who finds himself back at his office desk after some exciting seminar on communications or some other subject likely to nurture hope and illusions of changes in the organization; not to mention secretaries who are expected to be increasingly qualified and who are in fact given merely routine jobs.[143] Dissatisfaction is more widespread than one imagines. Even the 'pressurized' top managers from flourishing national or multinational companies are rarely exempt.

In France at the present time a system has been set up which compels companies with at least 10 employees to devote a relatively large fraction of their total salary bill to the continuing education of all personnel.[144] This legal obligation has the merit of encouraging a desirable development of workers' attitudes. If, however, everything else remains the same, and particularly the present organization of work, job-content, and job-definition, it is easy to foresee that the *conflict situation* of man at work will rapidly become *explosive*. It is impossible to demand with impunity higher and higher qualifications and offer jobs which are as empty as ever.

The present evolution, if it were to continue, would tend to convert work into a foil for contemporary man.[145] Anything would be acceptable which would take his mind away from work, allow him to escape, to put on to the community at large the economic and moral task of taking care of his physiological and psychological health. The economic system would have added a *supreme* paradox. The technical and economic performance of the system would be inversely proportional to the human and social disappointment, *the system would evolve towards its own destruction.*

ii. *The Myth of the Incompatibility between the Quality of Life and Productivity*

Is the economic performance of the present system the inexorable cause of this evolution? We could reply superficially that this is so and thereby humour a delight in paradox.

However, both psychological analysis and on-site experiments lead to the conclusion that performance *vis-à-vis* the stated evolution is neutral. The search for productivity would not in itself be harmful if it did not take place to the detriment of working conditions. Let us quote a personnel director on this point:[146] 'The problem now is to correct our scale of values. Efficiency is not incompatible with solidarity. Solidarity is not opposed to the extension of responsibility and self-fulfilment. Man is not at one moment a worker for whom we have to organize working conditions "as best we can" while he is in the factory, and at the next moment, away from work, someone who is free to organize his own time, leisure and cultural activities.'

Now Dubreuil's experiments, those of the Tavistock Institute and its foreign associates, the success of the new forms of job-design which have been carried out on a large scale, especially in Scandinavia — all agree that the direct *productivity* obtained from restructuring increases.

Why have enterprises invested enormous sums on improving the working environment without, at the same time, including 'lower' categories of workers in this, instead of enriching the job-content itself? Our suggested reply in the following study has perhaps little to do with the pursuit of economic performance.

iii. *The Heterogeneity of the Work Milieu*

Our deep conviction must not conceal other observed behaviour: more or less conscious resignation and scepticism about the possibility of reforming the present system. In this area we come up against the difficulty of discovering workers' opinions about present-day reality, about the outlook for work. We come up against the ambiguity between opinions of the moment and behaviour observed over a period. We can only note that many workers indubitably fit into the present system very well, that a certain number would agree to work under another system in time, but that others would muster the considerable power of *inertia* against this.

This heterogeneity is natural and is not specific to the area being studied. It is indeed an obstacle to any reform, but it is a human factor which is constant, which must not be overestimated, and which cannot be used to justify inaction.

B. A Refusal to Accept the Gap and the Duality

Young workers play a prime role in the rejection of the world of work. This rejection assumes different shapes: strikes,[147] job instability,[148] or even the refusal of certain jobs. Employers are more unhappy about the appearance of the two last forms of rejection than they are about the first one. The *shortage of young, skilled labour* in certain jobs is a fact which is making them think (this is what is generally believed to have decided Volvo to undertake its job-structuring.) According to a recent inquiry,[149] 28% of young workers between 16 and 21 years of age have already had two employers, and 27% three; 12% have already been unemployed. National and company employment policy, the short-fall in supply and demand are also responsible for this situation. According to the inquiry quoted, only 32% of all those holding a basic job qualification are taken on as skilled or semi-skilled workers. The rest are taken on as unskilled workers. The implications of this situation are worrying officials:[150] 'There is a certain disaffection on the part of young people in particular to be found with respect to numerous jobs in industry. We are very preoccupied with this situation because there is a danger that it will compromise the [French] government's planned industrial development policy.'

The nature of this rejection can be shown from certain figures.[151] In 1969 and 1970 in manufacturing industries there was one unfilled vacancy for every two job-hunters. In service industries the supply–demand ratio was inverted and higher: for one job-offer 7–8 unsuccessful candidates. In February 1971 the French Ministry of Labour offered a guaranteed employment pre-training scheme in enterprises in 26 regional departments. For 8,000 jobs offered only 4,000 applications were received.

The proportion of the working population looking for another job (instability index) is, for the under 25s (7.4%), almost double that for the working population (3.9%) and therefore more than double in relation to the over 25 working population (3.025%). The under 25s represent 19.8% of the working population which itself makes up nearly half of the total working population (47%).

i. *Towards a Reconciliation of the Old Contradictions*

According to one manager,[152] the level of discontent is just as high for managers ('we're only intermediaries, carrying out instructions . . . in a lot of cases we cannot take decisions . . . to my way of thinking relationships have deteriorated . . .'). It is not only the problem of workers who are employed at a level below that of their qualifications but also the problem of those who are under-qualified and who realize the need to develop their abilities. They want priority given to their training. 'Very early on, young people manifest a need to be given responsibility and more interesting work.'

This pressure exerted by young people at all levels of the hierarchy can be *salutory* for the organization if the latter equips itself with the means to reply, if it is made up of *plastic structures* and not of totally rigid ones, so as to be able to make the appropriate adjustments.

A. Mayer[153] attributes the adoption of this truculent stance to the evolution of men in general. He analyses it in terms of *demands*: 'Man today has become more demanding in terms of his existence. The same is true for men *vis-à-vis* the enterprise.' Speaking of top managers (there is a remarkable parallel with the demands made by the young unskilled workers above), he declares: 'They no longer want merely to work. They want to be able to carry out an important task successfully, a responsible and progressive task. They want to become experts and to advance further and further. Instead of being congratulated on their work, they want to be in control of it themselves. They want enormous demands to be made of them so that they can prove their ability, knowledge, and initiative . . . professional work must be a challenge . . . For them financial enouragement, social advantages, and fair treatment have lost the stimulant effect they once had.'

There is a widespread desire to transfer to work a part of what is needed for man's development. The seeds are everywhere. It is up to the State, to trade unions, to researchers, to act as a catalyst for this movement and it is up to management to make organizational structures more supple in order to enable people to make the desired changes.

ii. *A Twofold Difficulty to Overcome*

To assert that we must reform work is to have a *normative* conception taken from a positive analysis of reality. Is such a conception scientific? Not in the current state of our study because it is necessary to add guarantees taken from a prospective analysis into the conditions and effects of putting reforms into practice.

(a) *Forces of inertia: education, mentality, economic interests*

The introduction of change runs up against and imperils the status quo. It creates waves of anxiety within the organization. The history of work shows that workers have in the short term frequently borne the negative effects brought about by changes, for the unions are vehicles of tradition. This explains their circumspect attitude to the question, especially in France. Change is a painful moment in the setting-up of a new form of organization, even supposing that this is accepted and wanted by everyone.

Change is all the more intensely felt and upsetting in that it is organizational and in that technology in a way is no justification for innovation.

It leads to doubt about foreseeable performances. The Taylor organization is very robust in this respect in that it offers the misleading guarantee of a 'successful' experiment. The men who are usually given the responsibility, if not for planning then at least for implementing the new form of organization, are nearly always the existing organizational specialists, trained in the Taylor school. They manage to create such a force of inertia where change is concerned that a leading director of a large nationalized company in the tertiary sector told us that the organizational specialists in the firm would be kept well away from the implementation of the new form of job-design and given other tasks.

The taste for risk and innovation is sufficiently rare for economic theory not to make the entrepreneur the pivot of the functioning and progress in a market economy, for management not to be concerned with looking for creators and with developing a spirit of creativity.[154] The more or less conscious taste for inertia is certainly one of the things most widely shared between men. History has taken on the task of teaching us the cost of change in terms of violence.

Let us remember the fear that is so firmly rooted in every actor on the economic stage, the fear of seeing one's standard of living or, for some, one's power deteriorate. Who could in fact state that change would not be followed by a modification of the economic advantages which each individual had previously enjoyed?

(b) The necessity for change to be reckoned in economic terms[155]

For the moment we will limit ourselves to raising a few questions on this subject. Is the implementation of new forms of work organization costly? How far does it imply new investment? Does this investment have a lasting effect? When does it have to be repeated? What is the repercusion of this cost on the cost price of goods and services in the short, medium, and long term? Can this cost be borne in all sectors of the economy, in all enterprises, whatever their profitability and their size? Must the community at large intervene in order to facilitate the financing of this implementation? Must it give priority to the more underprivileged enterprises?

What does this new organization yield? What will the non-economic advantages be in the future? Can they be translated into economic terms? How are the advantages and the yield to be evaluated? What will an evaluation system cost? How long will it be before the cost–advantage balance becomes a positive one? If the balance is negative — both on the sectoral and a fortiori on the national level — are individuals and the community at large ready to pay the price of comfort at work? To reply to the last question, it is interesting to note that the energy crisis is opening up new choices and revealing a flexibility of thinking that can be provoked by certain de facto situations. In this respect the implementation of new forms of job-design poses problems analogous to those posed by energy.

The experiments which we shall study in the second part will give a series of replies to some of these questions. It is, however, the extension of these experiments rather than their results that is more problematical. In the third part we shall attempt to outline a possible strategy for change in the organization of work.

NOTES

(1) Taylor, *Scientific Management*, Harper & Row, London, 1964, 'Testimony Before the Special House Committee', pp. 16 ff.

(2) With certain reservations, cf. below.

(3) B. Coriat, *Science, techniques et capital*, Seuil, Paris, 1976.

(4) Op. cit., pp. 23 ff.

(5) Elsewhere we have added a great name to Keynes's forerunners; cf. H. Savall, 'Avant Keynes et au-delà: Germán Bernácer, économiste espagnol', *Mondes en développement no. 5*, ISEA, June 1974; H. Savall, 'Germán Bernácer, économiste espagnol (1883–1965). Une théorie générale de l'emploi de la rente et de la thésaurisation', thesis, University Paris – II, 1973; H. Savall, *G. Bernácer. L'hétérodoxie en science économique*, Dalloz, Paris, 1975.

(6) Op. cit., 'The Principles of Scientific Management', p. 5.

(7) Ibid., p. 10.

(8) R. Sainsaulieu speaks of an élitist concept: 'Now (with Taylor) competence is something which will be reserved for certain people only . . . On one hand there will be those who implement, on the other hand there will be the objects of rationalization, who no longer have any power over their own work.' (*Formation continue*, no. 3, 1973, p. 21.)

(9) Op. cit., 'Testimony Before the Special House Committee', pp. 204 f., our italics.

(10) Ibid., p. 203.

(11) Ibid., pp. 41 f.

(12) J.-L. Donnadieu uses the expression 'homo mechanicus' in 'La révolte contre l'efficacité', article in *Le Monde*, 5 Sept. 1972.

(13) Op. cit., 'Testimony Before the Special House Committee', p. 228.

(14) Taylor implicitly adopts the concept of *work as a commodity*.

(15) Ibid., pp. 228 f.

(16) Not to be confused with L. E. Davis.

(17) G. Bernácer (cf. above), a Spanish theoretician, forerunner and contemporary of Keynes, fixes his 'New Economic System' at a point equidistant from these two opposed *materialist* systems.

(18) Cf. B. Lussato, *Introduction critique aux théories des organisations*, Dunod, Paris, 1972, pp. 60 ff.

(19) This same postulate has been implicitly denounced in our introduction (cf. diagram p. 2).

(20) Both Donnadieu (cf. above) and H. Douard, in *Formation continue*, no. 3, 1973, p. 32, in an article on new forms of job-design, adopt the same point of view.

(21) Taylorism in the broad sense (= all Taylor's principles + all the principles stated by others who use his terminology for reasons of facility of expression) and as deformed by application in practice.

(22) Taylor condemned both Ford's and Renault's system of industrial job-design (cf. P. Fridenson, *Histoire des usines Renault. Naissance de la grande industrie* (1898–1939), Seuil, Paris, 1972).

(23) Touraine, *L'Évolution du travail ouvrier aux usines Renault*, p. 25, calls Taylor the father of 'improving the design of tools . . . [which] have enabled us to determine working methods mathematically'.

(24) Cf. however Coriat's thesis, n. 3 above.

(25) Touraine, op. cit., p. 115, evokes the importance of 'human relations, communications, informal organization, i.e. the worker's social adjustment within the enterprise'
as a way of creating allegiance to the Taylor form of organization. He makes no
difference between the USA and the USSR. He goes on to say, 'As in American personnel management, an appeal to *social motivational factors* is at the centre of the
Soviet Union's labour policy – build up Socialism, defend the Soviet fatherland, raise
the standard of living of the Soviet people. These are social objectives which are supposed to give *meaning* to a fragmented and monotonous way of working which, on a
technical and professional level, cannot have any meaning. Both the USSR and the
USA recognize the importance of the social aspects of work as far as production is
concerned.'

(26) Roustang *et al.*, 'Recherches d'indicateurs sociaux concernant les conditions de
travail', p. 30.

(27) *The Wealth of Nations*, Book V, ch. I, section 3.

(28) There is a striking convergence of ideas between Smith and Taylor. Cf. Touraine,
op. cit., p. 53: 'Taylor summed up this evolution brutally when he said to the worker
Shartle, "You're not being asked to think; other people are paid to do that." ' This
appears to corroborate our judgement of Taylor and his disciples, for Touraine adds,
'certain of Taylor's disciples have only seen this aspect of his work'.

(29) We support the thesis that Taylor has had an extremely *positive* historical role by
encouraging indirectly but firmly the development of the machine tool through his
advocacy of *an analytical study* of human *work*. Taylor's methodological approach
was then further developed by inventors of production materials. This is Taylor's
fundamental contribution to technical and economic progress and it *partly* compen-
sates for the distortions suffered by the very work which he has helped to impoverish.

(30) Quoted by Touraine, op. cit., p. 41.

(31) K. Marx, *Capital*, Book I, ch. XIII.

(32) However, surveys reveal that in certain areas of the economy the work-load, even
from a psychological point of view, has increased with technological progress (cf.
Laville's and Wisner's surveys carried out for the Conservatoire National des Arts et
Métiers). The dispute between the supporters of these two opposing theses about the
evolution of the work-load can doubtless be explained by the unequal nature of
situations which involve different sectors of the economy.

(33) Cf. the Thompson–Brandt experiment in Lyon, Chapter 2 below.

(34) The criticisms are too numerous to list. We should like to cite Perroux's lectures
at the Collège de France (*Annuaire du Collège de France*, 1965–66) and A.
Bienaymé, *La Croissance des entreprises*, vol. I, *Analyse dynamique des fonctions de
la firme*, Bordas, Paris, 1971, pp. 39 ff.

(35) Cf. *Bulletin intersocial*, 5 Apr. 1974, 'De Londres bilan de la semaine de 3 jours',
p. 15: 'The threats to employment have contributed greatly to reducing absenteeism
and have led to a degree of enthusiasm which in turn has allowed firms to maintain a
remarkable level of productivity during the period. . . . The 3-day week has given
people ideas; already several unions are thinking of asking for a 4-day or a 34-hour
week.'

(36) Cf. Bernácer's interest theory based on the rejection of time preference.

(37) Cf. J.-J. Carré *et al.*, *La Croissance française. Un essai d'analyse économique causale
de l'après-guerre*, Éditions du Seuil, Paris, 1972; cf. also F. Perroux in *Mondes en
développement*, no. 2, 1973, p. 237.

(38) Cf. three articles by E. Malinvaud, quoted by T. de Montbrial, 'Programmes d'expan-
sion et taux d'intérêt', *Econometrica*, vol. 27, 1959; 'The Analogy between
Atemporal and Intertemporal Theories of Resource Allocation', *Review of Economic
Studies*, 1961; 'Interest Rates in the Allocation of Resources', in *The Theory of
Interest Rates*, ed. Hahn and Brechling, Macmillan, 1966; cf. also T. de Montbrial,
'Intertemporal general equilibrium and interest rates theory', and 'Reformulation et
généralisation de la théorie néoclassique de l'intérêt', *Économie appliquée*, 1973,
pp. 877 and 919.

(39) Lussato, op. cit., p. 67.

(40) The ambi-system, an expression used by E. Morin, is a system composed of two

elements, each having its individual characteristics but also common inseparable characteristics.

(41) F. Herzberg, *Job Attitudes. Motivation to work*, Wiley, New York, 1959, mentions current wastage: 'there is the additional damage of sloughing off too much of man's *creativity*' (p. 170) and past wastage: 'From the first orientation to the farewell party, the history of work careers is a history of human waste. What a *paradox* we face!' (p. 176, our italics.)

(42) The theme of waste, brought to the fore by a growing interest in ecology and catalysed by the energy crisis, has many and varied aspects. Government bodies are very interested; cf. the inter-ministerial report of the Gruson committee on the environment: 'La lutte contre le gaspillage: une nouvelle politique de l'environnement' in *Le Monde*, 6 July 1974, p. 24. Of the concrete proposals made we would mention the need to include travelling time when calculating the working week and the retraining of engineers, architects, and town-planners in the management of resources. We would add that organization and methods specialists should also be subject to this retraining.

(43) Cf. *Le Monde*, 24 July 1974, p. 22: 'Employment, 3,910,000 working days were lost because of strikes in 1973' (figures supplied by Ministry of Employment). In 1972 = 3.7m. in 36,000 enterprises. Between 1959 and 1966 the average was 2m., the lowest figure being 1m. in 1965, the highest 6m. in 1966. In Italy 24.26m. in 1973, 16.82m. in 1972; in Great Britain 7.17m. in 1973 against 22.77m. in 1972; only 0.56m. in West Germany in 1973.

(44) Cf. *Bulletin intersocial*, no. 53, 1 May 1973: 'De Paris, Renault: la fièvre est tombée'. The one-month strike by unskilled workers paralysed 90,000 employees and led to a loss of production of 60,000 vehicles.

(45) Cf. R. Mahaux, *Le Gaspillage du capital humain dans l'entreprise*, Éditions Marabout, Verviers, 1974. This survey carried out on 1,200 managers and 300 directors reveals that the majority condemn the fact that their ability is not used to the full and reveals that, in addition, 80% are not happy in their work.

(46) A Gallup poll in the United States shows that on average 57% (between 43% and 72%, depending on age and type of activity) of workers questioned gave an affirmative answer to the question: 'Could you produce more if you wanted to?' (Cf. *Problèmes Économiques*, 11 July 1973, p. 5.)

(47) According to a survey carried out by the Institut Français d'Opinion Publique in October–November 1973 for the CGT, the majority of young workers have few qualifications and are poorly employed.

(48) Cf. H. Levinson, *Emotional Health in the World of Work*, Harper & Row, 1964.

(49) Cf. D. F. Johnston, 'The future of work: three possible alternatives', *Monthly Labor Review*, May 1972, pp. 3 ff. The author predicts three possible scenarios for the future of work. In the green scenario a few cybernetic engineers will organize and carry out production for an army of consumers. The blue scenario would maintain a demand for work because the reduction of development costs would require labour-intensive methods. The author seems to prefer the intermediate turquoise scenario whereby the demand for work is maintained as a result of an increase in personnel required in the leisure industry. This increase would absorb the spare labour generated by automation. Like Delors he asserts that 'work is probably destined to conserve its traditional position as the determining factor in the individual's orientation in society.'

(50) Delors, *Les Indicateurs sociaux*, p. 349: 'It is certain that at the present time workers' claims for a reduction in hours are eclipsed by the need to increase income. Consumer society leads to this choice.'

(51) Delors, 'Gagner sa vie ou réussir sa vie', *Le Figaro*, 11 and 13 Feb. 1974.

(52) Cf. R. Normann, F. Maier, *La Psychologie dans l'industrie*, Marabout, Paris: J. Tiffin, E. J. McCormick, *Industrial Psychology*, Allen & Unwin, London 1952.

(53) Cf. Roustang *et al.*, op. cit., pp. 42 ff.

(54) Grandjean, *Précis d'ergonomie. Organisation physiologique du travail*, Dunod, Paris, 1969.

(55) Cf. 'Les conditions de travail des OS', *Formation continue*, no. 3, 1973, p. 42.

(56) We have coined this neologism without, however, being certain whether or not it has already been used. The idea contained in the word is interesting. The concept of iso-productive time results from the hypothesis which states that work *can* be carried out at a constant pace within a given period (hour, day, week, month, year). This idea does not take into account the productivity distortions caused by (the sometimes sizeable) fluctuations in the pace of human activity.

(57) Cf. p. 67 the three categories of thread at Rhône-Poulenc-Textile, 1st grade, rejects.

(58) Grandjean, op. cit.; Normann and Maier, op. cit.; cf. also work carried out by the Max Planck Institute, Dortmund, quoted by J. Barraux, 'Pour une usine plus humaine', *Entreprise*, 8 June 1973.

(59) Roustang *et al.*, op. cit., p. 48, quote the case of Norway, the surveys carried out by the French Ministry of Employment in 1948 and 1951, and the work of G. Lehmann (the increase in productivity depends on the level of the number of hours worked from which the reduction takes place).

(60) By 1977 the effective length of the working week in France was 40 hours. This meant that she had caught up with her neighbours. The average length of the working week fell from 46.1 hours in 1961 to 43.8 hours in 1972 (cf. art. cit. by J. Barraux in *Entreprise*).

(61) Cf. W. Grossin, *Le Travail et le temps*, Paris, 1969.

(62) Cf. Roustang *et al.*, op. cit., p. 49.

(63) Cf. Barraux, art. cit.

(64) Cf. Roustang *et al.*, op. cit., p. 49.

(65) Cf. *Bulletin intersocial*, 15 July 1973, p. 13: 'Conditions de travail, USA'.

(66) Cf. INSEE survey in cities, quoted by Roustang *et al.*, op. cit.

(67) Cf. p. 71 below, however, arrangement of working time.

(68) 'Un contremaître et ses OS', *Formation continue*, no. 3, 1973, pp. 19 ff. This household electrical goods company employs 200 unskilled workers, of whom 100 are foreigners, 50 women (average age = 25). The work is clean but very simplified and involves several production lines. 'You can learn the work after a few hours on the job.'

(69) Cf. *Bulletin intersocial*, no. 74, 15 Apr. 1974; 'les femmes remplaceront-elles les immigrés à la chaîne?', interview with P. Guest.

(70) Cf. M. Gazzo, 'L'Européenne au travail', *30 jours d'Europe*, Nov. 1973.

(71) Cf. O. Rigoir, 'Revenues et Salaires. CEE', *Les Cahiers français*, no. 151, Nov.–Dec. 1971, note 2.

(72) P. Froidevaux, 'Étude sur les facteurs d'absentéisme et le façon dont ils sont perçus par l'encadrement d'une entreprise', Social Science doctoral thesis, University Lyon II, 1971.

(73) E. Sullerot, *Les Françaises au travail*, Hachette, Paris, 1973.

(74) Cf. 'Un cadre parle de ses OS', *Formation continue*, no. 3, 1973, the manager in question notices considerable malleability amongst female unskilled workers compared with male unskilled workers. On the other hand there is less desire for promotion, less interest in the work. It should, however, be remembered that this is a man talking.

(75) Cf. article quoted in *Formation continue*, no. 3, 1973, pp. 39 f. (extracts from a document produced by the Fédération Générale de la Metallurgie – CFDT) which throws into relief the role of young people in the origin of current conflicts.

(76) P. Guest, art. cit. n. 69 above, went on a world tour of the car industry observing young people's reactions: 'In no country do they want to be subject to bureaucracy, authority, and technology.' Speaking to factory managers in Yugoslavia about work problems he finds that 'they are very concerned by the consequences of alienation, especially on young workers'.

(77) This appears to us to be clearer in a general theory of organizations. In effect they have very varied legal and social statutes, very varied economic and political ends. They cannot all be analysed in terms of profit.

(78) Lussato, op. cit., p. 4.

(79) Ibid., p. 12.

(80) Ibid., p. 43.

(81) Ibid., p. 43. It is possible to bring this diagram closer to the one we have already suggested (cf. above, p. 2) by replacing respectively our 'extrinsic' and 'outside work' areas by Lussato's 'mixed domain' and 'extrinsic'.

(82) Ibid., p. 49.

(83) On informal communication and authority structures see J.-D. Reynaud in G. Friedmann and P. Naville, *Traité de sociologie du travail*, A. Colin, Paris 1961, vol. II, pp. 73 ff.

(84) We must also add the name of K. Lewin who, before the Second World War, analysed group effects and the possibilities of the informal group. He invented the concept of research-action.

(85) During experiments carried out in the Western Electric Company near Chicago (1927–32) a decisive variable was isolated: the *Hawthorne effect*, 'according to which it turned out to be enough to co-operate liberally with the personnel so that, all else being equal, productivity could increase at no extra cost and with no extra effort'. (H. Douard, 'Nouvelles approches de l'organisation du travail', *Formation continue*, no. 3, 1973, p. 33.) The Hawthorne effect had been known intuitively for many centuries and has been applied whenever certain people were of the opinion that it was more efficient to use cunning than to use force to get others to accept projects and ideas.

(86) R. Sainsaulieu (art. cit., p. 25) uses an expression which sums up the human relations point of view: 'An enterprise which works well on the human relations level has to function in a system of complete harmony', or again, 'one tends to modify working relations without changing the way the work is organized.'

(87) H. Koontz, *The Management Theory Jungle*, 1961, quoted by Lussato, op. cit., pp. 70 f.

(88) J. G. March, H. A. Simon, *Organizations*, Wiley, New York, 1958. These authors influenced M. Crozier's concept of *power* in the enterprise.

(89) It is significant that Dubreuil's solution in the article in *Hommes et Techniques*, Aug.–Sept. 1967, p. 657, is introduced by a translation from Aldous Huxley's *The Ends and the Means*. This is a good illustration of a widespread habit of looking abroad (preferably to the Anglo-Saxons) for a scientific guarantee for our forerunners. Huxley sums up Dubreuil's book *A chacun sa chance. L'organisation du travail fondée sur la liberté*. Grasset, Paris, 1935. In Chapter II, 'Le problème de la liberté ouvrière est étroitement lié à celui de la rémunération du travail', pp. 46 ff., there is the outline of the thesis to which we subscribe about the *interdependence of economic and socio-psychological motives.*

(90) See bibliography.

(91) Douard, art. cit., p. 34.

(92) Cf. Donnadieu in *Le Monde*, art. cit.

(93) E. Rimailho, H. Dubreuil, *Deux hommes parlent du travail*, Éditions B. Grasset, Paris, 1939.

(94) P. Froidevaux, 'Le travail et l'homme. Un retour aux sources du "job-enrichment"', H. Dubreuil: un précurseur de l'organisation socio-technique du travail', *Bulletin de L'IRAS*, no. 26, Sept. 1973.

(95) Dubreuil himself tried out these solutions; see *A chacun sa chance*, pp. 85 ff. and 142 ff.

(96) Cf. ibid., pp. 99 ff. and 197 ff.

(97) In its widest meaning. Since 1972, at the Crédit Lyonnais, for example, all the administrative procedures (10,000 employees out of 45,000) go under the name of 'Production'. According to our definition one should also add the commercial sector.

(98) Cf. H. Ford, *My Life and My Work*, London, 1922.

(99) Cf. article by M. Hannoun in *Économie et statistique*, Jan. 1974, p. 29. Between 1962 and 1965 more firms with more than 100 employees disappeared than were created (246 disappeared, 155 were created). The inverse was true for firms with fewer than 100 employees (344 created, 204 disappeared). Later the author says (ibid., p. 37) that 'in place of the optimum plant-size in car production we have the concept of optimum production size for a gear-box assembly unit, an engine unit, etc.'; cf. also S. Wickham, *Concentration et dimensions*, Flammarion, Paris, 1966.

(100) There exists a 'Comité Hyacinthe Dubreuil' (82, rue de l'Hôtel de Ville, 75004 Paris) for the development of autonomous groups in factories. The committee publishes a quarterly information bulletin and tries to propagate Dubreuil's updated ideas and encourage experiments in firms.

(101) Cf. in *Production et gestion*, BTE Formation Promotion, Paris, May 1973, 'Dossiers des OS' a table which sums up and compares the relative position of the social partners and the 'experts', Taylor, Friedmann, Herzberg.

(102) Cf. Herzberg, *Job Attitudes. Motivation to work*, 1959; *Work and the Nature of Man*, World Publishing Co., New York, 1966.

(103) Herzberg, *Work and the Nature of man*, ch. 4.

(104) Ibid., p. 127.

(105) Cf. diagram, p. 2.

(106) *Work and the Nature of Man*, p. 20.

(107) Ibid., p. 170.

(108) Ibid., pp. 57 ff. Cf. 'One of the highest levels of psychological growth is becoming an individual – desocializing and separating the individual from his environment, as his organic condition suggests is a natural thing to do. This means a man's having, in addition to what the socialization process makes of him, his own feelings, beliefs, values, judgements, ideas, and behaviours, as a mark that he himself, exists and not merely as a protest to society.' (p. 67.)

(109) Interview with J.-L. Jacquet of the Institut Entreprise et Personnel.

(110) Herzberg, *Work and the Nature of Man*, pp. 92 f.

(111) In *Bulletin de L'IRAS*, Jan. 1972.

(112) Cf. in *Économie et humanisme*, Mar.–Apr. 1954, 'Problématique des besoins'.

(113) The author has directed research-actions into task motivation within enterprises in and around Lyon.

(114) Cf. C. A. Lindsay, 'An examination and test of a modification of the Herzberg theory', *Dissertation Abstracts*, 1966, no. 26 (11), pp. 6873 f.; C. Rodney, *Personnel Administration*, 1967, 30 (2); pp. 23 ff. of 'Wage and Salary Manager', Martin, Baltimore.

(115) Herzberg, op. cit., p. 170.

(116) Ibid., p. 172. We suggest the expression 'trapdoor for hygiene investments' to put over the idea that the marginal effectiveness of improving hygiene factors decreases rapidly and that because of this certain investments are virtually luxuries and do nothing to solve the basic problem of job interest.

(117) Ibid., p. 190. We have already indicated the uselessness of solutions based on a confusion between the symptom of the illness and its true cause.

(118) Cf. Friedmann, *Le Monde*, 21 Mar. 1974.

(119) Cf. Herzberg, op. cit., pp. 116 f.; Froidevaux, 'Les modèles de travail et la satisfaction dans un kibboutz en Israël. Un test pour l'hypothèse de Herzberg', *Bulletin de L'IRAS*, May 1974.

(120) Herzberg, op. cit., p. 164.

(121) Cf. Emery, Trist, article quoted no. 139, below.

(122) Cf. O. Ortsman, 'Le Tavistock Institute – son rôle dans la conception et la diffusion de nouvelles méthodes d'organisation du travail', *Enseignement et gestion*, no. 6, Nov. 1973: 'In this way research and action feed off each other. Intervention in the enterprise leads to research which, in turn, leads to more refined ways of intervention elsewhere.'

(123) Cf. Douard, art. cit.

(124) Cf. L. E. Davis, article on job-design and productivity in *Personnel*, Mar. 1957, translated into French as 'Conception du poste de travail et productivité' in *L'Étude du travail*, Nov. 1966.

(125) H. Murray, 'An introduction to socio-technical systems at the level of the primary work group', Tavistock Centre, London, Oct. 1970, para. 20.

(126) Murray's italics.

(127) Ibid.

(128) Ibid., para. 36.

(129) Cf. pp. 80 and 82, an example of a job-interdependence matrix.

(130) Article quoted, n. 139 below.

(131) Murray, op. cit., para. 37.

(132) Ibid., para. 38, our italics.

(133) The author is referring to the experiments carried out in British coalmines.

(134) Ibid., para. 39; Murray's italics. Cf. also Emery and Trist, article quoted no. 139, below.

(135) Cf. J.-D. Reynaud in Friedmann, Naville, *Traité de sociologie du travail*, A. Colin, Paris, 1962, vol. II, pp. 69 ff.

(136) Cf. Ortsman, art. cit., p. 10.

(137) Cf. above.

(138) It should be noticed that in general we speak of a socio-technical *approach* and not of a *theory*. An approach is above all a way of analysing a problem. It comprises a body of methodology and of variables, to be taken into account. A theory goes further and suggests an explanation.

(139) Cf. Emery, Trist, *Socio-technical systems* (1960), reprinted in Emery, *Systems Thinking*, Penguin Modern Management Readings, 1969, p. 281.

(140) 'Rapport sur la réunion d'experts des 17–19 octobre 1973: l'absentéisme et la rotation du personnel' (OECD, 15 May 1974).

(141) Our expression: omnimethodology is an approach which is open to all methods and does not exclude, *a priori*, any method which accepts all contributions from different origins which are likely to enrich and clarify the analysis.

(142) Cf. article in *Réalités*, 1973, p. 50: 'Changer le travail pour changer la vie. Le diagnostique de Jacques Delors'.

(143) 'Une OS des bureaux', *Formation continue*, no. 3, 1973, pp. 5 and 14.

(144) This sum is equal to 1% of the total salary bill.

(145) Cf. Herzberg, op. cit., p. 189.

(146) Donnadieu, *Le Monde* article quoted above.

(147) Delors, art. cit., p. 53, points to disputes born of, amongst other things, 'confrontation between employees within the same union where those who are in their 20s rebel against the way their elders pass on orders or directives'.

(148) Cf. above, article in *Le Monde*, 6 July 1974.

(149) Ibid.

(150) Cf. J. Montel, 'L'emploi industriel et les jeunes', *DIS*, Jan.–Feb. 1972.

(151) Ibid.

(152) Cf. article in *Formation continue*, no. 4, 1973, p. 15: 'Ils [unskilled workers] ont des réactions que je comprends mal.'

(153) Cf. 'L'évolution de l'homme', *Personnel*, Oct. 1969, p. 14.

(154) Cf. Sudreau, quoted above.

(155) Between the first and second editions (1974–8) this idea made headway. It was developed by various organizations in France such as ANACT, FNEGE, GETAM, Secretariat of State for the Condition of Manual Labour.

EXPERIMENTAL SOLUTIONS

1. DESCRIPTIVE STUDY: ATTEMPT AT A CONCISE TYPOLOGY

A. The Conflictual Origin of the Experiments

Experiments into the setting-up of new forms of organization or improving working conditions are rarely generated spontaneously. History's lesson is that more often than not — perhaps always? — management agrees to think about reorganization in order to settle a dispute.[1]

Disputes can be overt or be a sign of something deeper.[2] Strikes based on a claim for an improvement in working conditions (hours, hygiene, and security), or the rhythm, or based on payment systems linked to production, are not the only forms of conflict.[3] We should point out that production-linked wages are tolerated less and less and that the French government is considering introducing legislation which will drastically reduce this system of wages.[4]

Absenteeism, rotation of personnel, recruitment difficulties which force employers to take on female and foreign labour on a large scale, the drop in the quality of products, job-changes brought about by the refusal of certain tasks, the necessity to develop a system of financial stimuli and punishments (premiums, fines)[5] — all are symptoms of conflict on the individual or group scale.

These indicators of social tension attract the attention of researchers, employers, and workers. Absenteeism and turnover are the areas which generate the most studies.[6] Alongside external factors which lead to absenteeism, such as shortage of labour, the level of unemployment benefit, increasing taxation, the role of doctors, and the efficiency of social security checks,[7] the emphasis is put, of course, on the internal factors which we have already spoken of. Froidevaux's proposed diagram (Fig. 2.1)[8] suggests how to calculate the gap identified between objective and product. The definition of the objective has to take into account[9] the existence on the one hand of the incompressible and 'natural' absenteeism which the new forms of organization will not be able to reduce.

Experiments into new forms of job-design have therefore a therapeutic end because of the conflictual nature of their origin. This is what differentiates them from, for example, a reorganization based on Taylor's original aims.

B. Typology of Experimented Solutions

i. Timorous Solutions: Job-Enlargement and Job-Rotation

Job-enlargement is a horizontal regrouping of tasks — generally of the same nature — which lengthens the cycle and moderately reduces monotony. The

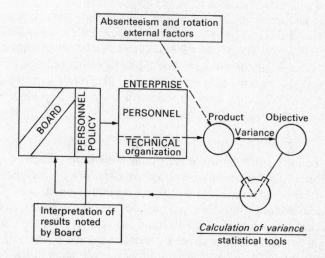

Fig. 2.1. (From Institut de Recherche Appliquée de Sociologie (IRAS), 1973)

effects have not been measured very well but it seems that the advantage of a longer and less rhythmically measured task is partly cancelled by a greater *necessity to memorize.* This is what puts off certain workers who, on the whole, prefer short cycles.[10] A job-enlargement experiment carried out at Ciapem-Thompson-Brandt in Lyon at the beginning of 1972 was a failure.[11] When carried out in isolation job-enlargement appears to give temporary relief, but there has been no large-scale work-reorganization which has formed the pivot of any experiment. It should be noted, however, that Saint-Gobain-Industries seems to rely on this technique.[12]

From the ergonomic point of view, however, job-enlargement must be regarded as positive. Nervous fatigue is greatly reduced, which leads, among other things, to a considerable increase in productivity. At the Renault works in Le Mans and Choisy the increases in direct productivity were surprising. A reduction in the under-involvement of direct labour is seen to be accompanied frequently by a reduction in indirect labour.

Job-rotation consists in making the personnel change jobs when certain fixed tasks are too arduous or monotonous, in order to avoid any worker spending too long a time exclusively on any one task of this sort. This solution is adopted also in warehouses and supermarkets and is a stop-gap measure which seems to have been introduced in the short-term by Saint-Gobain[13] and the Société Générale de Fonderie.[14] The latter does admit, however, that the unskilled workers demand more autonomy to enable them to rotate. When this technique is adopted in isolation it appears to be insufficient. To be efficient it requires a polyvalence[15] on the part of the workers and work in groups. Saint-Gobain is aiming at constituting work groups.

Although these are unadventurous solutions from the psycho-sociological professional and intellectual point of view, they do have the merit, in addition to the positive effects which they engender, of being able to be applied without greatly distorting the status and roles of the personnel. In particular they do not affect the role of the foreman. The choice of new forms has, however, to be made with a long-term perspective in mind. This leaves a certain degree of freedom in spite of the momentary inconvenience created by more ambitious solutions than job-enlargement and job-rotation.

ii. *Job-Enrichment*

This is a vertical regrouping of the main tasks involved in the work process and one which is tree-like when it incorporates supplementary tasks (maintenance, adjustment, repair, alteration . . .) at different stages of the work.

In tobacco factories there is a plan to give unskilled workers maintenance and repair jobs. In one of Saviem's factories an experiment into job-enrichment linked with an increase in professional qualification has been going on since the beginning of 1974 and should end up with a reduction in the number of manufacturing workers and an increase in the number of skilled workers. In a pharmaceutical firm a recent reorganization, in which the operating procedure was modified, has made it possible for the same person to carry out all the operations. There was a 28% productivity increase owing to the elimination of waiting-time between jobs and the reduction of micro-movements during product-conditioning. In addition to the productivity increase the advantages of this reorganization are a better distribution of work ('it is much easier to get 5 people together instead of 12 to plan the work') as well as an improvement in working conditions (operator's feeling of freedom and autonomy both in respect of others and of the product — auto-organization of the work rhythm). The only inconvenience observed is that of additional handling and longer delivery time, because of the need to allow for supplementary warehousing. In other cases it is possible to observe, on the contrary, a shortening of the manufacturing cycle.

In a firm responsible for the administration of blocks of flats,[16] job-enrichment, which has been in existence for ten years in one of the decentralized co-operatives, consists in giving each person complete responsibility for a whole sector of flats. The other co-operatives meanwhile were organized horizontally and by function: letting, notice, payments.

At the Kodak-Pathé factory in Châlon-sur-Saône,[17] the reorganization plan aims at suppressing monotonous or arduous jobs and at moving towards job-enlargement. This will include running the machine, adjusting, small administrative tasks, or even selective destruction tests of 1 in every 100.

Another type of enrichment is the example given by W. Paul,[18] one of Herzberg's collaborators, concerning the postal and shareholder information department of a large American firm. Each unit had an expert allocated to it whom the employees could consult on complex questions, while they themselves were authorized to sign all letters. Subsequent checks were reduced from 100% to 10%, the post went out direct without going through the manager's office, and the employees were encouraged to reply in a more personal way instead of using standard forms. Finally, each employee was held personally responsible for the quality and precision of the letters. Two diagrams show the performance-index evaluated in terms of precision and speed of reply to shareholders' letters (Fig. 2.2) and attitude towards work (Fig. 2.3). The first two months are the period of the setting-up of the pilot group. Productivity is lower than that of the control group working to traditional norms.

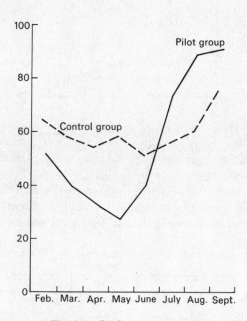

Fig. 2.2. Performance-index

In a large European chemical plant (probably ICI where Paul studied function-enrichment) the author gives another example which this time concerns sales representatives whose sales were dropping seriously, in spite of the high level of salary and of ability. Systematic written reports were stopped, the representatives were free to determine the frequency of their visits and to have direct access to the technical assistance department. It was left to their initiative to settle customers' complaints. Sales rose by 19% compared with the same period the preceding year, while in the control group they fell by 5% over the same period.

Job-enrichment implies nearly always — concomitantly or *a posteriori* — a restructuring of the social sub-system and the emergence of group-work.

iii. *Semi-Autonomous Groups*

The need to move the decision-centre to the job, to ensure task-interdependence, and role and information co-ordination, which is associated with a job-

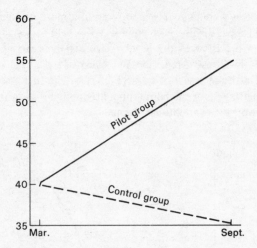

Fig. 2.3. Positive attitudes towards work

enrichment objective, gives rise quite naturally to the concept of the semi-autonomous group.

There is an empirical procedure which enables us to illustrate task-inter-dependence[19] and show how it implies the creation of small work-groups. A partially automated workshop consists of four posts and a storekeeper (truck

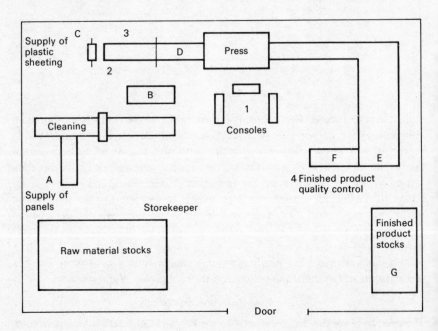

Fig. 2.4

driver): a charge-hand who, amongst other things, controls the console of a laminated panel press (post 1), his deputy (post 2) who checks the register and positioning of the plastic sheets, his assistant has a storekeeping role (post 3), the quality and quantity inspector (post 4) (Fig. 2.4).

The interdependence matrix (Fig. 2.5) reveals that certain functions are highly interdependent and that they are carried out by operatives of whom we note that there is no joint responsibility in their work. The poor quality of the products comes from this. Within the 'operations' frame of the matrix, the numeral 1 represents interdependence at the level of information between the oprations. This numeral is situated at the intersection of the line and the column of dependent operations. The numeral 2 represents a functional interdependence. The vertical and horizontal lines separate the operations carried out by two different operatives. The reorganization solution appears in Fig. 2.6 and is represented by a new matrix (Fig. 2.7). The matrix can be read line by line from right to left, starting from the bottom. For example the 'order quality' is functionally dependent (numeral 2) on 'loading', on 'handling, storage' on 'binding panels', on 'finished panel quality', and has an information relationship (numeral 1)

				Operations	Operative
				□ Customer order	
				□ Panel quality on reception	
				□ Handling, unloading panels	st.kp. 1
				□ Panel storage	st.kp. 1
				□ Quality of rolls of plastic sheeting on receipt	
				□ Handling, rolls	st.kp. 2
				□ Storage, rolls	st.kp. 2
				□ Handling, supply with panels	st.kp.
				□ Handling, supply with rolls	2 + st.kp.
				□ Quality control, panels	2 + 3
				□ Removal defective panels – loss of wood	
122		2	22	□ Wood quality	2 + 3
				□ Unroll plastic sheeting	2
				□ Quality control, plastic sheeting	2
				□ Sheet cutting	2 + 3
				□ Removal defective sheeting – loss of plastic	
	122	2 2222		□ Quality control, plastic	2 + 3
				□ Sandwich alignment	
				2□ Quality control, sandwich	
				□ Check mould cleanliness	2
				□ Check press opening	1
				□ Press	1
1		22	22	□ Quality control, panel at press exit	1
		2	2	□ Stop press	1
				□ Sort panels by quality	1
				□ Removal defective panels	4 + 1
	22	2	2212	□ Quality finished panels	4
				□ Bind panels	4
				□ Handling, finished panels (storage)	4 or st.kp.
				□ Loading	st.kp. 3
				□ Invoicing	
1		1 2222	2	□ Quality order	
1				□ Customer complaint	Sales dept.

Fig. 2.5. Analysis of operations

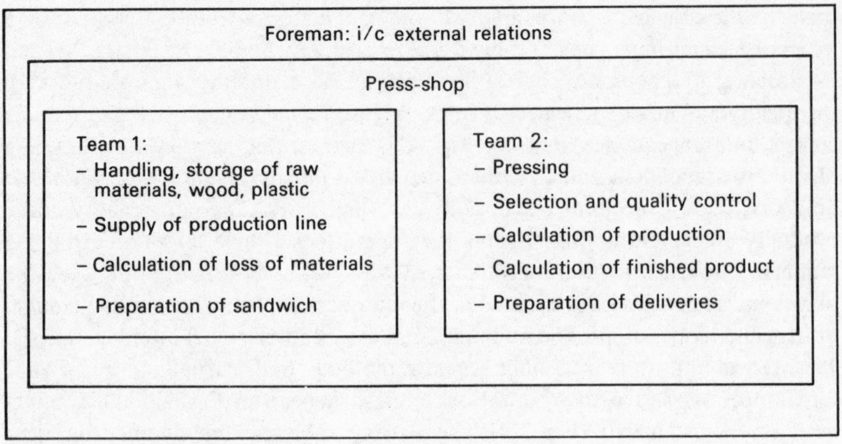

Fig. 2.6

Operations	Operative
□ Customer order □ Receipt of wood ⟶ raw material log □ Receipt of plastics (quality & reserves) □ Invoice on delivery □ Customer complaint	F
□ Panel handling □ Panel storage □ Handling, rolls □ Storage rolls □ Supply panel line □ Supply rolls plastic sheeting to line □ Removal defective panels 22 2 2□ Wood quality □ Unroll plastic sheeting □ Quality control, sheeting □ Sheet cutting □ Removal defective sheets 2222□ Plastic quality □ Sandwich alignment	Team 1
2 22□ Sandwich quality □ Check mould cleanliness □ Check press opening □ Press 22 2□ Quality control, panel at press exit 2 2□ Stop press □ Sort panels by quality □ Removal defective panels 22 22 12□ Quality finished panels □ Binding panels □ Handling, storage □ Loading 2222□ Quality, order	Team 2

(left margin markers: 1 … 11)

Fig. 2.7. Analysis of operations: press-shop

with the 'invoice on delivery' and the 'customer complaint' which are dealt with by the foreman (F).

Analysis of the interdependencies allows us to justify theoretically the constitution of the group. The group corresponds to a structure which covers complementary functions and tasks which have an over-all pertinent meaning. *Marginal internal polyvalence* must rule within the group.[20] Each operative must be able to carry out in the immediate environment of his principal customary post all the operations which the group has taken on. These are allied tasks requiring 'marginal' polyvalence. This brings with it a flexibility in the daily organization and planning of the work, increases the group's adaptation to variations which are external in origin, and gives the group greater autonomy *vis-à-vis* its own members, notably in case of absence.

The first of Rhône-Poulenc-Textile's experiments in the north of France goes back to 1969.[21] It took place in a thread-shop which has a manufacturing process that does not require a man to do anything except at the point where the thread emerges from an automated line. (There are no immigrants.)

The experiment was introduced for two principal reasons: (1) to work out a flexible organization that would allow development to take place and to ensure permanent adaptation to these developments and to technical difficulties; (2) to minimize physical and psychological personnel costs.

The workshop has a threefold objective:
to obtain the highest possible proportion of top-grade thread, the lowest possible proportion of 2nd grade, and *a fortiori* the minimum of rejects;
the smallest number of hours per tonne of 'good' production;
the lowest possible consumption of material, packing, and energy.

Since output from the machine is constant, the first two objectives depend on the man's speed when the thread breaks or during machine breakdowns (outside the operator's control), or during the bobbin change, output measurement, or the thread changes, as the case may be. Under the traditional form of organization, the time allowed and the breaks were strictly laid down, as were the operative modes, in purest Taylor fashion. The workers were simple operatives, the charge-hand looked after the very short-term planning as well as the checking, under a foreman.

The restructuring into semi-autonomous groups eliminated the function of the charge-hand and divided his tasks among the workers' groups and, in part, the foreman. It was based on the model suggested in L. E. Davis's *Design of Jobs*.[22] The objectives are fixed annually by the department head, planning takes place monthly or weekly in agreement with the foreman. The division, ordering, and determination of the work-load, as well as the checking, are all carried out by and within the groups. The internal composition is modified by the groups themselves. Management has kept for itself the power to appoint the foreman, to recruit new workers, and to apply sanctions. The results in 1971 and 1972 were a drop in absenteeism and in personnel rotation, an increase in the amount of top-grade and a decrease in the number of hours per tonne.

Table 2.1
Figures 2.8 and 2.9 illustrate clearly the economic results

	Pilot workshop (semi-autonomous groups)	Other shops (traditional organization)
	$(x - 2)\%$	$x\%$
Absenteeism average duration of individual stability	21 months	8.2 months
Turnover numbers leaving (for 62 taken on)	15	29

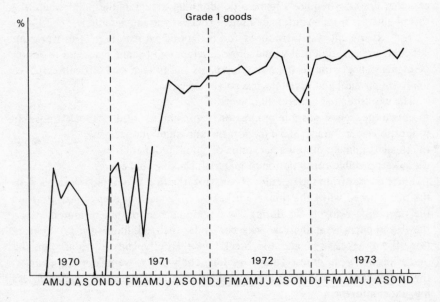

Fig. 2.8

The example at Ciapem, a Thompson-Brandt subsidiary,[23] is equally signifi-cant in that the personnel in this case consisted of immigrants (50%) and women. An initial experiment, at the beginning of 1972, into job-enrichment concerned nine women working on production and was a failure. Two job-enrichment experiments in the assembly shop were successful. One began in September 1972, the other in 1973.

The first experiment involved a group of six volunteers (two French and four foreigners) whose average age was 24. A three-week training period was necessary, followed by a seven-week running-in period before the productivity

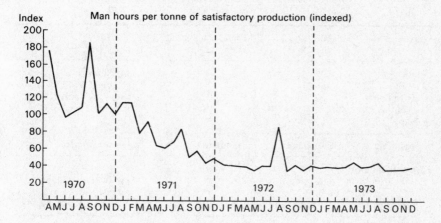

Index   Man hours per tonne of satisfactory production (indexed)

Fig. 2.9

level of the autonomous unit had reached the production level of the traditional line. The volume of productivity stabilized at this level, but it was found that absenteeism had fallen from 8% to 0.5% and that quality was higher. The inconvenience in the experiment as in the others was that the initial investment cost was higher than on the line, because of the necessary increase in floor-space and handling and assembly equipment (conveyors, automatic screwdrivers). It should, however, be noted that in the Atelier Fil Textile experiment the reorganization was accompanied by new equipment,[24] while the Ciapem-Thompson-Brandt experiment used the same technical conditions, traditional tools, and material. These ought, on the contrary, to have been adapted to the new autonomous-unit organization (the automatic screwdrivers ought to have been standardized). The cost difference due to the initial investment would thereby have been smaller. The second experiment (six workers: three French and three foreigners whose average age was 26) led to a relatively high number of candidates in spite of the secrecy surrounding the experiments. There were 20 candidates for six jobs. The training and running-time was reduced from ten to seven weeks and the results of the first experiment were confirmed.

The reorganization of work into small groups, compared with the traditional line, enabled different techniques to be integrated (Table 2.2).

The balance between constraints imposed by management and those brought about by the necessity to motivate the workers is ensured by the fact that management demands a certain production level and that it guarantees promotion in exchange. The group notifies absences and fills in production and control forms. The modest size of the experiment in this example (12 workers out of 440 assembly workers and out of 1700 in all; 70 machines per day out of 2000) means that it can be called a laboratory experiment. As with numerous other experiments, even when they concern a large part of the factory, it is remarkable that neither management nor unions try to extend the experiment rapidly in the

Table 2.2

Parameters	Traditional line (A)	Semi-autonomous groups (B)	Variance (B) − (A)
complement	109	6	suppleness
assembly	86		self-organized job-
repair and poly- valent work	10	6	rotation → polyvalence, job-enrichment
checking	13		
average cycle	51 seconds	16 minutes	job-enlargement
daily production collective	600 approx.	33	productivity volume maintained
individual	5.5 approx.	5.5	different models possible
absenteeism	8%	0.5%	reduction of lost production person absent does not disrupt work of 109 workers on line

enterprise, in spite of the positive and convergent results from the different areas. At Ciapem trade-union expectations are demanding; the social climate has not been improved; the unions have not demanded an extension in spite of the satisfactory results of the first two experiments. Prudence on the part of management and unions[25] which can be seen in all French enterprises[26] without exception does not, however, bring with it complete immobilization. At Ciapem an experiment involving 40 female production workers got under way in 1974 and the management has set up a specific system which aims to reform certain command concepts. Side effects develop from all the experiments, successful or not: at Rhône-Poulenc-Textile, line work is not quite the same as it was before the appearance of autonomous teams. Certain points have been borrowed from them. Thus the formal extension of the experiments has not been carried out on a large scale, but these experiments *induce* new forms of organization or of hierarchical behaviour which could well be the prelude to more major restructuring. From the point of view of the *strategy* of change this kind of preparation of the ground is not negligible.

Even in France, where there seems to be a certain backwardness in this area, examples of semi-autonomous groups abound. Seita is involved in a project. Renault, the Crédit Lyonnais, and BSN have all carried out projects. Different enterprises dealing in electrical material and apparatus have done so (Merlin-Gérin and others), Saviem, Moteurs Leroy Somer, and Le Carbone Lorrain[27] (where the groups of workers include two charge-hands, one foreman, and one engineer, 29 people altogether). Abroad there are Atlas Copco,[28] Olivetti,[29] and Saab-Scania. All these experiments are taking place in enterprises in very different sectors and of very varied size, using very different technology.

Sometimes they concern a few people, sometimes a few hundred, sometimes more than a thousand. The solution of the semi-autonomous team appears as the synthesis of job-enlargement and enrichment, requiring rotation, polyvalence, and secondary factors, e.g. accounting, programming, and the decentralization of certain responsibilities at the level of the small group.

iv. *Diverse Solutions Relating to the Environment*

The reorganization of certain types of work and the difficulty of restructuring the job-content itself impose priority measures, either on account of their urgency or because they can be applied more easily. We do not discount an improvement in factors such as hygiene or atmosphere, to use Herzberg's terminology, but they are not part of our study in the strict sense. There are many factors that should be remembered, for example, the suppression of arduous or monotonous tasks, safety improvement, the reduction of shift work, of night work,[30] the inclusion of journeys to work and long breaks in the calculation of work-time,[31] ergonomic improvements and improvements in the physical environment, which sometimes require very costly investment,[32] the creation of opportunities for change or promotion (mobility within the enterprise, an internal labour exchange at BSN), flexible working hours.

There are risks of errors, however, in this area which we would like to indicate. Kodak-Pathé's new headquarters in Paris were designed to have 20% of open-plan offices in a first building and the whole of a second and as yet unfurnished building to have exclusively open-plan offices. It is, however, interesting to note that after a survey carried out using all the techniques in the book, 66% of the people working in open-plan and in traditional offices are against the former, although they admit than an open-plan office is very conducive to team-work, pleasantly decorated and comfortably furnished. The employees were very sensitive to the fact that *individual efficiency* was lower in an open-plan system, that the air-conditioning was not very popular . . . Perhaps a better and less expensive arrangement of traditional offices would have better matched the employees' expectations as regards conditions for administrative work. This example seems also to corroborate Herzberg's theory that it is not by increasing investment − often very expensive investment − in order to improve atmosphere factors that one raises satisfaction and efficiency at work.

There are, however, two solutions where the cost is nil or low and which appear to offer the possibility of partial lasting solutions.

(a) *Arrangement of working time*

Diverse experiments, the latest of which took place on a large scale, tend to show that the over-all productivity of the economy is not in direct proportion to the time spent at work.[33] Two and a half months of energy restrictions in Great Britain supplied the proof that with a three-day working week the economy did not lose 40% of its weekly productivity compared with a five-day working week, but much less (20–30%).[34]

It is true that the exceptional circumstances: 'contributed largely to reducing absenteeism and reinforcing a zeal which enabled a remarkable level of productivity to be achieved during the period. . . . The three-day week gave rise to ideas. Several unions are already thinking of incorporating the four-day or 34-hour week into their policy'.[35] The four-day week operates in some 90 American enterprises to everybody's satisfaction.[36]

Arrangement of working time can take place within the framework of the day, of the week, of the year, or even of one's life. We shall touch on G. Rehn's futuristic view of the possibility for people to have freedom of control of 'drawing rights' over the way their individual lifetime is allocated, i.e. allocate working time in such a way as to arrange freely the time which one wants to devote to work, to education, to leisure.[37] The arrangement of time within an annual framework is already familiar to certain categories of workers in the form of holidays-with-pay over two or more periods, the possibility of educational leave under different economic regimes.[38]

The most recent projects cover short periods, i.e. the day, the week, the month. We have already indicated the shortening of the working week which implies a lengthening of the working day, which is sometimes harmful, as we have seen in terms of productivity or health. Certain authors,[39] who are sensitive to constraints imposed by productivity, see above all the advantages of the four-day week, i.e. a reduction in absenteeism of from 6% to 1% in an American firm. Others[40] bring out time-table difficulties or the conditions imposed by the American unions for paying overtime whenever the legal 8-hour day is overstepped, or the dissension provoked between categories of personnel when, as is nearly always the case, certain categories cannot benefit from these measures. In conclusion: 'For some employers, the 4-day week reflects an attempt to deal with work dissatisfaction shown by high absenteeism, turnover, tardiness and low efficiency, while for others the primary aim is cost reduction through better utilisation of plant, equipment and time. It is a combination of these motives that makes the 4-day week just one of the many scheduling possiblities.'[41]

The arrangement which is destined to be the most widespread seems to have to be flexi-time. For the enterprise flexi-time consists in fixing a period of time (9.30 hrs–16.30 hrs) or two periods (9.00 hrs–12 hrs and 14 hrs–17.00 hrs) each day when the whole of the personnel has to be present, and two or three mobile periods (8.00 hrs–9.30 hrs and 16.30 hrs–18.00 hrs or 8.00 hrs–9.00 hrs; 12.00 hrs–14.00 hrs and 17.00 hrs–18.00 hrs) during which the personnel are free to be present or not, subject to the following constraints:

to complete a certain number of hours per week, per fortnight, or per month (40 hrs, 80 hrs, 173 hrs);

not to exceed a cumulative credit or deficit (e.g. ± 5 hours per week or ± 10 hours per month, depending on the period of reference chosen by management and personnel);

not to exceed a certain length of working day (e.g. 10 hours).

This system was introduced in Switzerland at the beginning of the 1960s, then in West Germany, and now it operates in numerous countries.[42] In 1972 the French employers' association Entreprise et Progrès[43] recommended its introduction after preliminary research had been carried out by J. de Chalendar.[44] As of May 1973, 30 companies were running experiments and 19 others were preparing to launch one. Others have since followed these examples. There is a shadow, however — namely the difficulty of applying flexi-time to production personnel (two enterprises out of the thirty quoted above have done so completely and two others partially). The cost of setting up the operation includes a study of possible job-modifications; supplementary energy costs because of the increased opening hours; above all, there is the cost of the installation of timer clocks and hourage calculators when a check is kept by automatic counting machines. Required investment per worker is about 200 francs. The survey carried out at Sommer S.A. gives an inventory of the advantages to the workers benefiting from the new system; advantages in terms of transport (90% of responses), in terms of private life (88%), in terms of the family and in terms of organization (74%). The firm benefited from a reduction in absenteeism and turnover which could be observed after the introduction of flexi-time. In the same way the rate of personnel change at Messerschmitt (6,000 employees) went from 13% in 1966 to 11% in 1967, when the system was introduced. It dropped again in 1968 (9.2%). Even larger drops were identified at Assmann (9.5% to 5%) and Migros (9% to 4%).[45] The consequences for recruitment of personnel are positive.

In France the organization known as Catral[46] brings together representatives of government, employers, and employees' organizations and specific associations. It aims through its work to study and promote an arrangement of working hours which will improve the quality of life at work at the level of the individual. It does so while taking account of the economic constraints on the community at large which result from the changes.

The French trade unions[47] are favourable, subject to finding a solution to the difficulties raised by the calculation of overtime. For the reaction of the personnel, we have as yet only the results of a few surveys carried out in France. Those carried out at Sommer S.A. and the Biscuiterie Nantaise show that 74% and 85% of their respective personnel regularly make use of flexi-time, 20% to 13% make use of it occasionally, and 2% never.

We must note that the positive co-operation of the parties concerned often enables flexi-time to be reconciled with constraints of opening hours[48] or of a more technical nature. This augurs an extension of the formula (in other countries enterprises use differentiated flexi-time systems for all personnel, including production personnel).

Certain enterprises attach the same importance to the factors related to improving the environment that they do to those related to the job-content itself. They often intend to carry out improvements in both,[49] especially enterprises with arduous work.[50]

(b) *The decline of the payment-by-results system*

The payment-by-results system is very much called into question nowadays, as is the system of job-classification.[51] The French government is intending to introduce measures to reduce it.

Payment-by-results rests on a double postulate: productivity varies in direct proportion to the size of the variable part of the wage; a fixed wage is not a stimulant.

The challenge to this is based on two aspects:

(1) payment by results implies a perfect measure of production. There is, however, great arbitrariness and imprecision in measuring. We may cite the anecdote told by P. Viaud at a conference of the French Federation of Cardboard Manufacturers' Associations[52] concerning the precision of timing. In about 1950 an experiment carried out by Renault showed a film simultaneously to 27 time-keepers who were known for their professional competence. They were asked to calculate the time. All the results were different, which is not abnormal in itself. The spread of results was, however, abnormal, ranging from 80 to 130 . . .

(2) payment by results has a low differential efficiency in comparison with other systems of remuneration. Numerous experiments lead to the conclusion that *average differential efficiency* is only 8%. Is it not possible to make up this productivity deficit by other forms of incitement, for example, job-restructuring, especially when one considers that the cost of running this system of remuneration implies an exhaustive measuring and checking apparatus? An increase in quality and better use of equipment by the worker who is freed from the constant constraint of output must facilitate this compensation.

The evaluation chart that we can expect once payment-by-results has been abandoned in favour of a fixed-salary system can be expressed as shown in Table 2.3.

Table 2.3

Criteria	Inconveniences	Advantages
economic performance	direct-productivity deficit	lower wage-preparation cost (material, personnel) lower quality-control cost lower retouching cost lower equipment cost
social and organizational performance with economic repercussions		ease of employment ease of negotiation for job changes, change of operational modes, equipment . . . flexibility of posting less sensitivity to technological progress
social performance		better relations between foreman and operatives better social climate

Viaud advocates a method of individualized performance evaluation with which he has experimented. It is based on an 'objective performance evaluation' and, by means of a systematic salary review twice a year, it enables account to be taken of observed lasting improvements. The evaluation of the performance is 'objective' and must not be confused with the much criticized job-classification in that it only takes unambiguous definable and measurable criteria. To evaluate professional knowledge, for example, one of the questions could be: 'what is the number of posts which the worker is capable of filling?' or again 'is he able to adjust his machine?' 'can he carry out simple repairs to his machine?', etc. The weighting can vary, depending on the profession and on the results sought. For certain jobs, for example, the quality of the work will be given priority.

Example:	quantity of work done	30 points
	quality of work	20 points
	absenteeism	20 points
	professional knowledge	10 points
	team spirit	20 points
		100 points

Payment-by-results is still applied to 20% of workers in France, and it seems possible to suppress this system in a fairly short space of time.

It is desirable to replace the payment-by-results system for two reasons. First of all it would lead to a less distorted pattern of individual and social behaviour and it would appear thereafter as the corollary, or rather the condition, for applying the solutions studied above. Under this double heading such a substitution could be introduced in two phases, the second phase being the reorganization of the work itself. The first phase has implications as far as the training of the foremen is concerned, and these implications would prepare the ground well for the introduction of the second phase.

It seems that, of all the solutions put forward, those which involve an improvement of the extrinsic working conditions are more readily accepted by management and unions. Amongst the intrinsic solutions job-enlargement and rotation are the easiest solutions and the ones least likely to lead to objections either from management or from workers. The more audacious solutions such as job-enrichment and semi-autonomous groups remain the most difficult ones to put into practice. Experience shows that job-enrichment leads logically to a calling into question of inter-personal relationships, and more often than not brings about quite naturally the creation of semi-autonomous groups. We shall see from the three selected French examples discussed below what kind of difficulties were encountered and what results were obtained (pp. 76 f.) according to which plans and procedures the experiments were carried out (pp. 89 ff.), and finally which are the variables that have to be taken into account after we have evaluated all the experiments carried out hitherto (pp. 96 ff.).

C. Three French Examples

We have chosen three French projects which are likely to develop even further. They correspond to different approaches, different sectors of the economy and different structures. Experiments in other countries which the French press reports on tend to encourage the belief that what happens abroad cannot be transposed into France because of socio-cultural differences. These are often used as an alibi for inaction.[53]

i. *The Renault Projects*[54]

The Régie Nationale des Usines Renault, to give it its full title, is a social point of reference in France. It is an enterprise which is a power-house when it comes to social projects (holidays-with-pay, workers' shares) and also when it comes to industrial disputes. It is also an enterprise which is a point of reference for union-led industrial struggles, and this special place in French industry gives it a sort of goodwill or good intentions commission when it comes to solutions to industrial problems. The modest results achieved in certain cases are a measure of how extremely difficult it is to introduce a restructuring of work. In the same way the positive nature of the results and the determination and tenacity of a certain number of the firm's managers are the sign that the path is clear in France for large-scale projects in this area.

(a) The circumstances

An almost fortuitous prior experiment into task-enrichment had begun in 1952, a time when, as a result of absenteeism and of knowledge acquired on the job, the adjustment of machines was gradually being done by the operators rather than the fitters. This reached such a point that half the unskilled workers were doing their own machine adjustment themselves. Almost twenty years later a specific experiment into job-enlargment (2 min 8 s–10 min) on the car seating production line at Billancourt demonstrated the irreversibility and the positive nature of this way of working. All this created a precedent which led part of the management hierarchy to look with favour on the idea of introducing ideas from other experiments abroad. As the result of a strike in 1969, an experiment into hourly rotation over 2 or 3 posts involved a third of the personnel (two-thirds in 1971). In April 1971 a second strike by 82 unskilled workers paralysed the whole group (70 000 production workers). In spite of the context of the factory, which favoured, if anything, the status quo (skilled labour, rural in origin, very stable – turnover and absenteeism in the order of 3%– no immigrants, high wages), more determined experiments were started in January 1972. It is significant that the beginning of methodological experiments followed the crystallization of disputes concerning working conditions.

(b) Running the experiments

The first experiment of the new period concerns the front-axle assembly of the R 5. It began in January 1972 and consisted in *job-enlargement* accompanied by *a certain autonomy* with regard to rest breaks and work rhythm. The production line was not discontinued but each worker worked at each post in succession and thereby carried out the complete assembly of a sub-unit. Productivity increased compared with the classical production line because of the elimination of time lost between two posts. Difficulties arose because the management demanded an increase in production without making any immediate counter-offer and because the foreman had to adapt to the new organization of the work. In spite of these hitches, both the workers and their delegates wanted to continue the experiment, and at the end of six months the criticisms had disappeared.

In July and then in October 1972 the same sort of experiment was carried out on the front-axle assembly of the R 15 and R 17, involving *job-enlargement and enrichment*. The range of operations was increased at the head of the line by adding preparatory tasks, and increased lower down the line by adding retouching at the end and the anchoring of the axle unit on the painting line. The lessons learnt from the initial experiment made it easier to get this one under way. Training time was shortened and efficiency increased. The workers were volunteers; prior classroom training was carried out by the foreman; workers with previous experience were used to set up the new line; and the introduction was phased over a number of days. This second experiment went further into job-enlargement and enrichment. It was introduced more carefully, namely, by means of introducing the foreman into the preparation and training of the unskilled workers. It resulted in an indirect labour productivity-increase of between 5% to 7% and *increase in qualification and pay* for the unskilled workers. The Head of the Group concludes: 'The preparation of the operatives and the foremen enabled us to start without any major difficulty. The wage-rise doubtless made things easier.'

It seems important to us to underline the *inseparable* nature of the psycho-sociological advantages and the economic advantages which the workers expected. In spite of the workers' willingness, both the first experiment (the one involving the R 5) and the Rhône-Poulenc-Textile experiment at Besançon were held up by the fact that management was late in linking[55] economic advantages to the other advantages, although in other respects both sides strongly suspected that there would be an effect on productivity. We believe therefore that to go ahead and analyse a social sub-system within a socio-technical system, without making explicit reference to economic expectations, is to proceed naïvely. This naïvety can sometimes be seen in certain psycho-sociologists and sometimes in their critics. To want, in the name of a kind of psycho-social purity, to judge the impact of an experiment into raising the value of work without knowing the effect this has on economic motivation seems of necessity to limit the scope of the analysis. It is *perfectly logical* that the worker should *associate* the idea of increasing the value of work, of increasing his skills, of enriching the various functions, with the idea of an *increase in pay*. At a given wage it is easy to understand that unattractive working conditions disgust certain workers. However, the improvement of these conditions on their own is not likely to satisfy the worker's needs. Herzberg's idea, which has been called simplistic, of the different nature of negative and positive factors seems right to us, if the needs are considered as a whole and if economic motivation is therefore given its rightful place again. Certain psycho-sociologists have too often questioned this motivation in the name of a sort of modesty which we think is out of place. It has to be admitted, however, that in the chronological unfolding of change, management, even though it is not stupid and knows that the question will be raised, cannot easily give an *a priori* undertaking to guarantee higher wages. After having examined the economic file which we mentioned in the introduction, one can see, working from *measured results*, what will be the basis for sharing the value of the over-all increase in productivity in a given economic environment. The enrichment of human work in enterprises is not a panacea, a solution to all the social problems put forward by trade unions. The employer who is looking to these solutions to avoid wage demands or a power-struggle will probably be very disappointed, for *improving* the social climate *does not mean spiking the guns* of the traditional demands.

This digression must not lead us into forgetting the third Renault experiment, work in modules on the R 5 axle-units. The philosophy behind this results from the semi-autonomous groups.

In June 1973 the axle-unit assembly line was really abolished and replaced by two modules of eight people working at fixed posts in rotation. Each worker carried out ¼ of the assembly of left-hand or right-hand axle-unit. The production objective in terms of quantity and quality had been fixed and the group organized itself as it wished. The results proved to be very positive. There were rises in physical productivity which the personnel estimated at 20% (15% in direct labour and 5% in indirect labour), an increase in quality (and moreover a drop in manufacturing cost when retouching was included . . .). Investment is said to have been lower than for the line per real[56] equal volume of production, but the cost of dismantling the existing equipment has to be added. It is probable that the cost of this equipment in a new specially planned production unit would be lower. The differential economic evaluation of the module is therefore very positive. This experiment benefited from the lessons learnt in the first two, as far as both the solutions chosen and the implementation tactics were concerned. The foremen were associated with the preparation, they trained 'their' workers and their role was to give technical advice within the module at the request of the workers. It should be noted, however, that sceptical advisers in the hierarchy thought that the personnel was above all trying to obtain a higher qualification (and thereby a higher wage), after which they would return to the fragmented work they preferred. This behaviour was not observed though. In all the recorded experiments there has never been a collective about-turn[57] after a successful introduction. In addition this pessimistic view is the opposite extreme to the naïve view which we mentioned above, and it is the result more of a cynical view of what happens.

Other experiments are running at Renault or are at the project stage. At

Choisy-le-Roi at the standard-exchange engine plant there are two projects, one in the method department (4 intermediate lines) and the other in the factory itself (fixed posts with 3 workers − two on assembly, one on grinding and job-rotation). The second method has been retained because there was a higher level of productivity during the experiment. There are two comments to be made here. In the chronic staff-versus-line conflict the line won by dint of the bold realism of the project, which gave more scope to the workers' wishes, their capacity for autonomy and development. This workshop, which employs from 350 to 400 workers,[58] will soon be organized entirely on a work-group system. A project for an assembly plant at Douai, originally organized along traditional lines, has been modified in favour of an organization involving enlarged tasks and with the objective of adding auto-control and retouching, in spite of an additional investment in the region of 15%.[59]

Finally, the experiment carried out in the press shop at Le Mans is an exemplary one in different respects. It was due first of all to observations by the head of department who had had the chance to examine the Philips (Eindhoven) experiment into the reorganization of work in a press shop. This is a fine example of what the propagation of successful experiments can achieve. This experiment was equally exemplary because of the way it was put into motion and because of the respective attitudes of management and personnel. In June 1972 the personnel had asked for the promotion of certain unskilled workers to grade 9 (instead of grade 8). Some time later a semi-skilled category was created. Management replied that this was possible for 200 press operatives at Le Mans on condition that within four months the tool setters were replaced by a reorganization of the unskilled workers' jobs. Here we find both enrichment and economic motivation mixed at this preparatory stage. In July 1972 a work-group was appointed to prepare the content and setting-up of the experiment. It consisted of the head of department, the workshop head, the foreman, and the technicians. It is interesting to note that at the end of July 'the personnel expressed their concern at not seeing the procedure begin'. A date was fixed for September, and kept to.

This experiment is also exemplary because of the lessons learnt about the role of the supervisors, *the importance of training*, because of the initial motivation which was *economic* in nature, and because of the enormity of the consequences which resulted from the development of the experiment. The supervisory grades re-established the *sense of their own worth* in their own eyes and in the eyes of the workers because they were associated with the study-phase of the project and because they took charge of training. The result was likewise exemplary; a whole category of unskilled workers benefited from an increased qualification and a *revised wage.*

(c) The over-all evaluation of working conditions

The Department for job-restructuring together with the Technical Department (Methods) worked out a pragmatic method for the over-all evaluation of working

Table 2.4

Levels	A Physical strain	A' Hygiene Harmful effects	B Autonomy (time)	C Relationships	D Cycle length	E Job content
5	Very arduous or dangerous improvement priority	Arduous or dangerous in long term To be improved	1m	Isolated work	0.5m	Nil
4			5m	Relations possible but difficult	2m	
3	Acceptable To be improved if possible	Troublesome No danger	15m	Relations easy or necessary	5m	Average
2	Satisfactory	Low	30m	Responsibility and autonomy limited to group	10m	
1	Very satisfactory	None		Responsibility and autonomy extend beyond group		High
Criteria						

conditions. This method has the twofold objective of identifying the jobs which pose the most problems and of following up the evolution of these jobs after improvements have been introduced.[60] The basic concept is socio-technical in inspiration. It links predominantly physiological job-evaluation criteria: (A) physical strain, (A′) hygiene and harmful effects: psycho-sociological criteria: (B) autonomy, (C) relationships, (D) length of cycle, (E) job content. A five-point scale is given to these five levels corresponding overall to five degrees of satisfaction: (5) arduous task, priority for improvement; (4) arduous task, to be improved; (3) acceptable task, to be improved if possible; (2) satisfactory task; (1) very satisfactory task.

This evaluation grill (Table 2.4) enables us to draw up an analytical evaluation chart of the working conditions (Table 2.5) of a line. The line sequences are in the vertical axis; the horizontal axis contains the six criteria as well as the detailed bases which lead to the results grouped under each criterion. To analyse the situation of the whole complement of manufacturing unit, a histogram can be made from the total of all the detailed evaluations weighted according to the complement and converted into a percentage so as to facilitate comparisons. For each criterion the model percentage represents the situation of the majority of workers concerned. When the criterion being considered is rated (4) or (5) and is given a high percentage this indicates which reforms should be given priority (e.g. Figure 2.10 is an extract from a histogram concerning the criterion of possibilities for inter-personnel activities at work for 120 workers on an assembly line).

Finally, the results can be synthetized into an over-all profile which enables

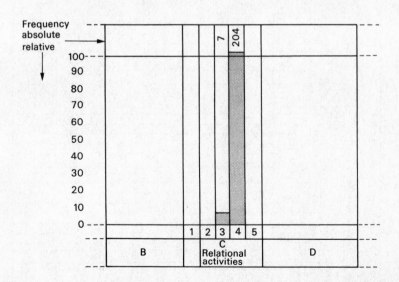

Fig. 2.10. Extract from histogram

Table 2.5

Column groups are: PHYSICAL EFFORT (POSTURE, WORK, HANDLING, A), HYGIENE (HARMFUL, A'), JOB STRUCTURE (Autonomy B, Relations C, Time of cycle D, Job Content A R C / E), OBSERVATIONS.

No. / Sequence	compl.	P_B	Posture (A B P D)	% time	P_1	Work effort time	P_2	Handling C D N T	posts take / place	P_3	A (1–5)	hygiene	HARMFUL (temp/noise/vib/light/toxic/safety)	A' (1–5)	Autonomy B	Relations C	Time of cycle D	Job Content A R C	Job Content E	Observations
1 unhook body	2	De	1 ... 1	80 •	4	40–60: 2	2				5 •	3		3 •	5 •	4 •	2½m •	5 5 5	5 •	
2 place fittings	2	De	2 ... 1	40–60 •	3	10	4	3 3 1 / 1.40	DN / Dex	3	4 +	3	toxic 2; safety 2	4 •	5 •	4 •	2½m •	5 4 5	5 •	
3 hook notches	2	De	1 1 1	60–80 •	4	60–80: 3	3				5 •	3	noise ½; vibrations ½	3 •	5 •	5 •	2½m •	5 5 5	5 •	
4 re-thread	2	De	1 1 1	60–80 •	4	60–80: 3	3				5 •	3	noise ½; vibrations ½	4 •	5 •	5 •	2½m •	5 5 5	5 •	
5 place protection	2	De	1 1 1	60–80 •	4	40–60: 2	2	1 6 1 / 1.40	DP / DN	2	4 •	3		4 •	5 •	5 •	2½m •	5 5 5	5 •	
6 balancing	2	De 2	1		5	40–60: 2	2	2 1 / Tc	DP / DN	2		3		5 •	5 •	5 •	2½m •	5 4 5	5 •	
7 mount fittings	1	De	1 1 1		2	60–80: 2	3	2 3 1 / Tc	DN / DN	1	3 •	3	toxic 2; safety 2	4 •	5 •	5 •	10 •	5 5 5	5 •	outside line, dependent on line
8 placement	4	AG 2	1		5	60–80: 2	2				5 •	3	lighting ½	5 •	5 •	5 •	2½m •	5 4 5	5 •	
9 screen-washers	1	De 2	1		5	40–60: 2	2				5 •	3		5 •	5 •	5 •	2½m •	5 5 5	5 •	
10 dashboard fitting	3	AG	1 1 1		5	60–80: 2	3				5 •	3	lighting ½	5 •	5 •	5 •	2½m •	4 4 5	4 •	
11 heating box	4	AG	1 1 1		5	60–80: 2	3				5 •	3		4 •	5 •	5 •	2½m •	4 4 5	4 •	
12 wing outflow	2	De 1	1 1 1		5	40–60: 2	2				5 •	3		5 •	5 •	5 •	2½m •	5 5 5	5 •	

us to evaluate several concurrent projects in order to be able to choose the best. It should also enable us to follow the evolution after the improvements have been introduced (in Figure 2.11 the results shown correspond to two situations for the same car-seating assembly: traditional organization in one factory and a task-enlargement organization in the other).

The interest in this method results, of course, not only from its operational nature but also from the attempt to quantify qualitative aspects of industrial and social life. A validation study is in progress with a view to verifying the degree of correlation between the level of physical strain (criterion A) and the direct measure of evaluation of cardiac cost.[61] From the operational point of view the method enables us to evaluate not only the therapeutic aspect introduced by the restructuring in the existing organization but also, by means of a prior evaluation of the industrial projects, the preventative capacity of a new organizational form which is to be set up.

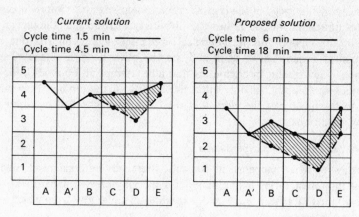

Fig. 2.11

ii. The Crédit Lyonnais Projects[62]

(a) The circumstances

Banking can perhaps be summarily divided into two: a commercial activity, which brings the bank's employees into contact with the customers and which is thought of as noble work; a production or abstract administrative activity, which involves no contact with the outside world.

It is in this production activity (involving 10 000 Crédit Lyonnais employees out of a total of 45 000) that the problems of recruitment can be observed particularly well. In certain American banks the labour shortage and the 40%–80% turnover of young people has made it necessary to redefine tasks. At the Crédit Lyonnais it seems that there was no strike action or noticeable social pressure before the experiments began. It was the turnover rate amongst young personnel, 20% in the production activity, which indicated new difficulties, since on the whole personnel stability is high (less than 4% turnover). We find here as well, however, an index which is comparable to what can be observed in the majority of enterprises before they undertake experiments into task restructuring. There is an increased intake of female workers (currently 70% of the employees are women and 53% of them are under 25 years of age). Finally, from February to April 1974, a long strike, which broke out in the production departments of several banks, and especially in the Crédit Lyonnais, upset French banking for several months. It is remarkable how, at the moment the strike broke out, the unions asserted their support for a continuation of experiments into restructuring, which were in progress or at the project stage. Here again we see our thesis confirmed. New forms of job-design do not spike the guns of more traditional claims and, given this, the unions' attitude to any experiments is favourable.

It must be made clear that at the Crédit Lyonnais the last ten years have seen an increase in the speed of the centralization of administrative jobs concomitant with 'the brutal arrival, or rather the disorderly intrusion, of the use of computers in the bank'. This technological implantation has, on the one hand, impoverished administrative work and, on the other hand, necessitated such a high rate of investment in computers that any attempt at job-modification has been blocked. Happily, in one sense, the quality of the product is so directly linked to the quality of the work that the bank was compelled to improve the working conditions.

(b) Two job-enrichment experiments

In contrast to what happened at Renault, there was no organic acknowledgement of job-restructuring in the shape of a specially created department. There are approximately fifteen projects or experiments under way from which an empirical method has arisen.

An initial job-enrichment and communication-restructuring experiment is to be carried out in the new production centre at Tours-Saint-Avertin. Semi-autonomous groups made up of about ten people will each have a particular geographical sector to look after. Those in charge of the agencies and of the production group will know one another so as to have more personal contact, and the group will handle *all* the specialized operations relating to a particular group of agencies. Each operator will thus have a greater variety of tasks to perform during the day, and the group will work, as it were, in unison with a group of agencies (same rhythm, more personal relationships).

This experiment gives rise to three initially expensive constraints; the triple necessity to:

adapt the computer programme to the newly-defined geographical units (classification order of the agency codes),

create buffer stocks between the administrative departments (preparation), which work on a geographical basis, and the computer departments (processing) which work on a product basis, set up a more extensive training programme to enable each employee to deal with all the products right from the start – drafts, cheques, customer accounts, name file, . . .

There are two implications for the future: the recruitment level will have to be raised and the system of remuneration re-evaluated since the globalization of tasks makes the work more complex. Here we find economic, technical, and psycho-sociological factors intimately linked.

We are looking for three effects from a drop in the number of mistakes: an increase in quality, an increase in physical productivity (in a less organized and more discrete way), a greater flexibility in personal career patterns because of the disappearance of the duality between the commercial sector and production work, as it becomes possible to alternate between the two sectors.

It should be noted, however, that in this initial experiment the technical element (the computer) has not been greatly affected. It has been more a question of adapting to it than changing it.

In the second experiment, which began on 1st July 1974 at the cheque processing centre, technology was incorporated into each of the semi-autonomous groups. At that time the work was very sectionalized and was carried out by a line of 200 employees. Cheque processing was carried out according to the schedule shown in Table 2.6.

During the procedure there is therefore a coming and going between administrative tasks, in the full sense, and computer tasks. Each belongs to two distinct

Table 2.6

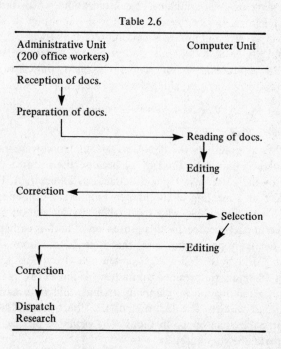

units. The work is repetitive, monotonous, and specialized in the extreme. There is a cumbersome hierarchical structure − 1 head of department, 3 or 4 assistant managers, 6 graded section heads, 24 graded group heads.[63] This division and the work in groups is necessary for the achievement of optimum use of the highly productive equipment. On the basis of the preceding job-enrichment experiments, the creation of cheque-handling modules was envisaged (e.g. the 'goodwill' in certain large administrative departments, which were set up according to socio-technical methods and which have replaced line work, and the experiments into the use of simple computer equipment in the Accounting Centres and the Production Centre at Rillieux which have helped to demystify computerization).[64]

The module of 50 people is made up of work-groups of 10. Each employee takes over a batch of cheques as it arrives and handles it through all stages: preparation, sorting, modification, accounting, research . . .

The autonomy here is at individual rather than group level. Each employee carries out all the tasks, including that of using the computer. He works at his own pace and always deals with the same agencies or colleagues. What is the nature of the group? The group is a spatial division, the place where the 10 employees work together. It is also a community, since they all have access to a computer, which each person uses on a self-service basis. There are several aspects to enrichment here: the integral nature of the task carried out by the employee, task alternation within a limited space of time, use of equipment which has a powerful public image: the computer. We can add some environmental improvements − geographical decentralization, which brings work and home closer together, flexible working hours, the abolition of shift work, an improvement in the size and internal disposition of the offices.

Management's aim is to extend the successful experiments progressively throughout the production sector, namely in the Lyon-Rillieux, Melun and Roubaix administrative centres, along the same lines as in Tours.

iii. *The BSN-Gervais-Danone Projects*[65]

(*a*) *The circumstances*

There are various reasons why the BSN-Gervais-Danone projects and experiments can be considered as models. First of all because the impetus came from the highest level of the hierarchy, from the Managing Director, A. Riboud, on 22 October 1972[66] at a meeting of the French Employers' Confederation (CNPF) in Marseille. There are people who have taken his declaration as being 'social publicity'. The impact created by this profession of faith is perhaps greater than we imagine. Let us hope, in any case, that it leads to action. The goodwill is given concrete form by the additional presence at Group Management level of the Personnel Director. He presided over a team of line heads: the head of social relations, managerial manpower-planning, training and information, structural development, and studies. The function of the director of studies is primarily to implement policy and apply methods. The planning of new forms of job-design is his particular responsibility.

This is a model firm because of its structural details. It is a federation of 15 companies, usually wholly-owned subsidiaries, whose objectives are determined in conjunction with the group's Managing Director and his staff. Labour costs represent between 40% and 65% of total turnover. Techniques used impose heavy procedural or financial constraints. There is a wide diversity of products and of management styles. The company is widespread geographically, both at home and abroad. Growth has been exceptionally rapid — 10 000 people were employed in 1966, 71 000 in 1974, 40 000 of whom were in France, for a turn-over of 9000 million francs.

The diversity of the social context is, likewise, a model one, depending on the regions. The rate of immigrant and female labour is low and all the French trade unions are represented, with the exception of the CFT.[67]

(b) The planning of new forms of job-design

We find BSN a model company because in spite of its social and economic diversity, the diversity of its products and sectors, in spite of its federal structure, it tends to unify the status of its personnel (managers and non-managers), it aims to improve working conditions overall, even if concrete results are not yet numerous.

This structural–global approach seems to us to be fundamental for the future of organizational innovation. In the face of economic planning, an experiment in *social planning* is being carried out at BSN. This bears witness both to a deter-mination to carry through change and to a sense of realism about the procedure to be adopted, i.e. to use the same weapons as are used in economic planning and to link the latter to social planning. Contrary to what can be observed in most other enterprises, the improvement in working conditions here is part of a veritable over-all policy which is the wish of a homogeneous management team. This situation ought to facilitate the realization of socio-organizational objec-tives. The plan should be drawn up *with* and *by*[68] the personnel but, in spite of this approach, the introduction of change is slow and laborious, notwithstanding the experiment begun in Rheims in 1972.

The director of studies was responsible for the experimental method which was worked out. We think, however, that the simple setting-up of the mechanism for a management–supervisor–worker dialogue and encouraging people to discuss concrete problems identified during various meetings (up to 437 problems were identified and grouped under headings, e.g. machine-siting, nuisances, relations with the planning office) are the way to facilitate the irreversibility of the movement which has begun, and to develop the beneficial effects of this plurality of suggestions.

The procedure can be shown as in Fig. 2.12. The analysis of the priority areas is a socio-technical one.[69]

Grids which use Herzberg's factors and Davis's criteria pell-mell have been constructed at BSN. Unfortunately it is not possible to reproduce them. By presenting them in matrix form we can observe the impact of the socio-technical

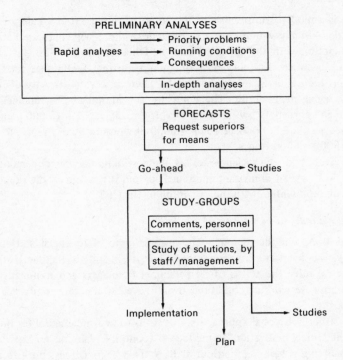

Fig. 2.12

approach on each of the other aspects of the analysis, and this enables us to demonstrate clearly the causal relationships of the factors and their effects. It should be noted in passing how difficult it is in this kind of analysis to convert the feelings of the personnel into expectations, the former being easier to identify than the latter.

The pre-eminence given to the interested parties' judgements should also be noted. After approximately one year of preliminary analyses, and when the study-groups had been set up, people did not hesitate to abandon the problems which had been defined at the preliminary level if they were not raised by the personnel. A certain continuity can be achieved, however, by making the same group-leaders take part in the study-groups as those who had carried out the preliminary analysis. (These leaders are managers who devote the whole of their time to training and organization. In each establishment there is this type of section, consisting of at least two managers.)

It is interesting to observe that:

there is close integration of organization, training, and information,

the adhesion shown by the personnel, their delegate, and the trade unions, increases as the concrete problems which arise locally are identified more closely,

this attitude on the part of the unions has a symmetrical effect on management and on the intermediate hierarchy,

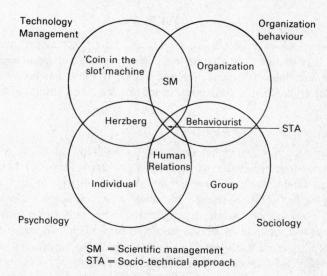

SM = Scientific management
STA = Socio-technical approach

Fig. 2.13

a veritable consultation explosion has been detonated which has had cumulative effects,

one has to start from what exists if one's aim is to get workers to express themselves.

On the debit side of the experiment we have to include a feature which is observed in the great majority of cases, namely the critical attitude of managers and supervisors. They appear to have been deliberately put on one side during the first phase of the experiment so as to enable a more spontaneous expression of ideas to take place. Because of this there is a feeling of great frustration. In spite of its favourable evolution, the trade-union attitude has not yet reached a point beyond which trade-unionists could completely shed their hostile reserve and co-operate actively.

D. The Methods of Experimentation

In the field of new forms of job-design we usually talk of experiments because the personnel affected, with rare exceptions, remain largely in a minority. It is, however, necessary to distinguish between the laboratory experiments so to speak, which are very clearly defined and are cut off from the rest of the enterprise, and the project experiments which are more definitive in nature and generally irreversible.

After an analysis of the content of the experiments a classification of the experiments in the broad sense can be made according to three criteria: the size of area of application; the study and implantation procedure; the 'democratic' character, i.e. the degree of participation by interested parties in the preliminary study and/or the implementation.

i. *The Field*

The majority of experiments are on a small scale, circumspect, and defined within a very limited area. Others, which take place less often, proceed from a more resolute desire for innovation and appear to show that people are ready and willing to accept the consequences and the secondary effects of the experiments.

(*a*) *The definition of the experiments*

The definition may be spatial (a factory, workshop, team) or by category (assembly workers exclusively, or production workers in the bank). In both cases there is an attempt to gain the maximum degree of liberty for carrying out or not carrying out the experiment. One refers to experiments 'under a bell-jar' (Philips),[70] one tries to isolate the experimental laboratory (Renault: standard exchange), even in spite of the evidence one pretends not to attach too much importance to the experiment in order to avoid the behavioural distortions which would falsify the results (the Hawthorne effect).[71]

These experiments have the advantage that they can be measured by means of a comparison between the experimental group and the traditionally organized control group. Synchronic comparisons are thereby made possible, but the validity of the comparison is weakened by the fact that the experimental group, thanks to its constitution (young volunteers) and/or the Hawthorne effect, is not strictly comparable to the control group. Inversely the control group, if it is in the know, can make an about-turn and begin to behave in an unaccustomed way, thereby falsifying the comparison.

The defined experiment of course does have the advantage that it facilitates the initial implementation which is always more costly, more hesitant, more cumbersome than those which follow (cf. above Ciapem-Thompson-Brandt, Renault). It also leaves a large proportion of the workers free not to '*undergo*' reorganization. This is not a negligible factor in view of the degree of inertia and anxiety which every attempt at reorganization has to cope with. Reaction and adaptation time is also extended.

The economic constraint must also not be neglected. It is difficult to be able to have simultaneous access to the finance necessary for the study, for the implementation, and for the new investments to which innovation leads. This is why innovation needs to be planned.

(*b*) *Experiments of a global nature*

These experiments are run in an entirely different way: from the start there exists a proven desire to experiment, with a view to a *relatively* rapid extension of the experiment. They result from a kind of wager where the stake is an escape from a harmful evolution of the industrial climate and an improvement of the enterprise's position in the competitive context, on both the product and the labour markets. It results from a long-term view of the enterprise and an evolutive concept of management.

The area into which the experiment is introduced may sometimes be just as limited as in the defined experiments, yet there exists from the start a prejudice in favour of innovation.

The project may relate to an entire establishment (the Fromageries Bel plant at Lons-le-Saunier, the Volvo factory at Kalmar), or to an entire company (BSN), or, in a less drastic way, to one or more production units (Renault, Crédit Lyonnais). There are other very rare but more ambitious projects (Norway's industrial democratization).

Several indicators enable us to identify the global experiments: the complexity in the planning arrangements which incorporate not only the restructuring of the work but also training, improvement of communications throughout the organization chart, reclassification, new forms of payment.

The essential difference with the other experiments seems to us to arise from the expectation of results and from the fact that they imply a consensus, especially on the part of the hierarchy, and well-informed supervisory grades and workers.

ii. *The Implantation Procedure*

Although the majority of enterprises have followed the classic line from the summit to the base of the hierarchy (up–bottom) a certain number have tried to develop experiments from the base and make them rise to the summit (bottom–up). Others have adopted a hybrid technique which combines the two procedures.

(a) *The up–bottom or descending procedure*

The decision to study and then introduce innovation is nearly always centralized, with the exception of a few 'free-lancers' who carry out social projects 'in their own little corner' (e.g. J.-L. Donnadieu at Boussois before 1966).

What is being questioned here is above all the procedure for working out the decision. When management sets up a separate study-project on its own authority, when it keeps the initiative at every stage to carry on or to stop, when it implements the project via the hierarchy, we speak of an up–bottom procedure. The advantage of this way of working lies in the time saved, the information rumours which can be avoided, the secrecy of the project (sometimes a necessary condition for its success), the adaptation of the project to the existing or anticipated human and technical resources.

There are several inconveniences to this way of working:

Communications: the project follows the classic path and risks coming across the usual stumbling-blocks which arise from inevitable interpersonnel opposition within the hierarchy, including supervisory grades and workers. This is a major inconvenience for the quality of the project.

Identification: by following the hierarchical path one runs the risk that few problems will come to the surface, because at each level of the hierarchy there will be a reflex action to the questioning of authority which will run counter to the search for and uncovering of such problems. To trust the hierarchy to spotlight difficulties which it is thought to have identified itself, implies a belief in its capacity for self-criticism.

Quality of the solutions: whenever operatives have been in a position to voice their opinions a rush of useful, serious, and practicable solutions (cf. DBA)[72] have come to light. Imagination requires a very precise area in which it can be applied and, sometimes, the opposite of the aptitude for abstraction.

This is, however, the path which most of the existing projects have followed. It should be noted that in certain cases (Fromageries Bel) it is a very fertile way, when the size of the unit to be organized (a few hundred workers) and the attitude of the hierarchy make possible the kind of concerted effort which tends to make the search 'descend' to the lower levels. In such cases it is a very practicable solution, which has the additional merit of placating sensitivity within the hierarchy.

(b) The bottom–up or ascending procedure

It should be remembered that it is a question of the procedure for working out an innovatory project and not a question of decision-making procedure.

The bottom–up procedure begins with an initiative taken at the summit (management) and communicated directly to the base (the workers) so that the operatives themselves are made to discover the problems, to make suggestions and then to transmit them to management, who studies both the solutions and the ways to implement them.[73]

The purest example of this procedure is the case of the engineers in the Shell (Dutch) laboratories (van Beinum) where for almost a year the role of the external consultants was restricted to running operatives' meetings and then to getting the *group itself* to write a *diagnostic* report.

This procedure has the virtue of being highly educative and an excellent way to learn about responsibility. It is, however, rather difficult to apply outside a laboratory experiment, given the cost in terms of men, money, and time that it implies.

The other advantages are the ones that appeared as disadvantages in the inverse procedure. The psycho-sociological inconveniences of this system arise from the bypassing of the supervisory grades.

The implementation of a bottom–up communication system seems to us to be both desirable and possible as long as the hierarchy is given a precise and sizeable role. It remains, however, a long-term prospect, one which will only come about in a more advanced phase of organizational innovation development than any we can see for the present.

(c) The looping or up–bottom–up–bottom hybrid procedure

This is a compromise between the two preceding procedures and one which aims at economy in terms of time.

A pre-diagnosis is made at the summit in a variety of ways so as to identify the problems, classify them in order of urgency, plan for the necessary means, and select a project that can be carried out in the short term.

Thereafter meetings at the base level are held, with and without supervisors (depending on local worker–supervisor relationships). The supervisory and middle-management grades are then involved so as to test the validity of the pre-diagnosis and, if need be, to modify it. In this way the solutions are envisaged *with* rather than *by* the workers. This procedure is difficult to instigate because of the risks of blockage which exist. If it were not for these it would probably be the optimum technique, incorporating the maximum of advantages for the minimum of inconveniences.

BSN is working on it, but it is as yet too early to say what the results are.

iii. *The Degree of Democratic Participation*[74]

In certain respects the debate about procedures is of little importance if we can obtain maximum participation from all interested parties in the working-out of projects. Those interested are: the workers, personnel representatives, supervisors, middle managers, management.

(a) *Participation by workers and their representatives (delegates, trade-union members)*

Worker participation[75] is always achieved in the 'bottom–up' and hybrid procedures and sometimes in the 'up–bottom' procedure.

The non-participation of workers in analysing and working out a project arises from the difficulty of getting them to express their opinions in confidence. The emphasis has to be put on a system which encourages participation. It should be noted that in the experiments in which participation is possible (Shell, BSN, OBA . . .) relations between management and unions are the best possible and that in other firms it appears to be difficult to arrive at this degree of collaboration without upsetting management–works' committee–trade-union relationships. This explains why in France initially an attempt is made to obtain the individual participation of volunteers. In theory and for the same reasons (to liberate spontaneous expression) the foreman and the personnel representative are excluded as such. Once the initial meetings have borne fruit (inventory of problems, of suggestions) the firms try to integrate personnel representatives, trade unionists, and supervisors into the procedure. On the one hand this is to make sure that the study is not cut short because of opposition from these groups, and, on the other hand, it is to enable the supervisor and personnel representatives (union delegates included) to be associated with the project in such a way that the project is compatible with the workers' interests which the representatives defend.

In the style of relationships which exist in France between employers and unions,[76] the trade unions' position is circumspect, because their bargaining position must not be weakened. In other countries the trade-union attitude is less ambiguous, particularly in the Scandinavian countries, but also in Great Britain, the Netherlands, and even in Italy.[77] This does not, however, avoid the difficulties.[78]

In addition to the explanations to be found in the traditionally polemical relationships which exist in France, we believe that there is also a specific explanation for the trade-union reservation, namely the way reorganization projects are presented. There is a deplorable clumsiness on the part of management (demand for productivity increase without any increase in wages and/or qualifications; e.g. the Renault factory at Le Mans, Rhône-Poulenc-Textile at Besançon).

On various occasions unions have been opposed to a worker's spontaneous expression in a study-group. They have used such simplistic and absurd arguments as those which involve saying that the director 'does not have the right to make workers speak when there is no trade-union representative present' . . . When management does not attach too much importance to this kind of reaction, and when it tries hard to elicit the workers' spontaneous and constructive comments, it generally arrives at positive results, in spite of the difficulties. It should be made clear that the more concrete and technical the questions raised are, the easier it is to gain participation. In one sense this is encouraging, but in another sense it limits the area of participation to a concept of the immediate work-place, very close to that of Dubreuil. At the present stage of industrial relations in France it is felt to be the wrong moment to make workers participate in studies or projects which imply broader reorganization, intra-hierarchical communication, etc. This is not the opinion of the psycho-sociologists of the Tavistock Institute who, because they are working in countries which, from this point of view, are very different, sometimes display a tendency to minimize this very real difficult which arises from socio-cultural differences.

Worker-participation in different studies limited to their own area of influence constitutes an immense step forward, not only from the point of view of the atmosphere, but also because of the quality of the solutions proposed. This is in itself a kind of job-enrichment, to say nothing of the greater adhesion which is obtained during the running of projects when the people concerned have participated in the working-out stage.

The active non-participation of the workers is not always due to the workers themselves or to their delegates. It is often the result of opposition from the hierarchy,[79] notably from the supervisors.

(b) Supervisor participation

Liaison between supervisors and workers is generally the sensitive nerve for inter-personnel relationships in the hierarchy. Renault's Le Mans experiment became very tense because of the personality of the foreman. The supervisory grades has to be changed progressively before their image was altered. There is a demographic factor to be added to this explanation, namely, the age difference between the supervisory grades and the workers in a large number of cases.[80]

If we are to promote free expression and the uncovering of problems, it is logical for the supervisory grades to be kept away from the initial meetings. At the Royaumont Seminar a senior manager from a large metallurgical company reported on the case of a 10-day strike in a grinding shop which brought the whole of the factory to a standstill. The cause was dermatitis as a result of drops of machine oil which splashed the operatives. It took Mr C., who is not a technical man at all, and who was in charge of organizing new ways of working, eight days to find a solution (housing on the machine), whereas the supervisors had never found one because of their indifference to everything concerning working conditions. The right training of supervisors should remedy this state of things easily.

Another participant at the Royaumont Seminar, an industrialist in pharmaceuticals, expressed the view that once the foremen's eyes have been opened to the problem, as revealed in a specific case, they can be trusted to understand and tackle such problems. The training of supervisors is insufficiently cultural in content. They have been 'badly brought up' in that they have been trained professionally but have had no general complementary training. Mr V. gave an example from his company where the supervisors are well trained progressively and where the repercussions of this on the operatives brought about unexpected results, namely 270 interesting ideas listed in 6 months.

After having been kept away from the initial meetings, the supervisory grades are then integrated in the bottom–up procedure with a view to looking for reorganization solutions and projects at their level. The practice of worker and supervisor participation is generally prolonged beyond the introductory phase in the change and tends to become institutionalized. This promotes change in the role of the foreman, who now has to receive the right training which aims at increasing his technical competence but which also, and most importantly, aims to teach him his role as a group leader. This is indispensable when semi-autonomous groups are constituted because the foreman then loses the majority of his current prerogatives and it is a matter of redefining his new function very precisely.

When, as the result of an up–bottom procedure, a project has been carried out, the supervisory grades are generally given an instructor's task and are put in charge of the setting-up of a project.

(c) Middle-management participation[81]

As with supervisory grades, middle management is, if anything, hostile to a restructuring of manual work. There are numerous reasons which explain the behaviour of middle management: a lack of interest in problems of working conditions, a certain rigid way of thinking which is the result of blind faith in scientific management, a concept of subordinate workers as operatives, lack of training in problems of human relations, a faith in technicality and the machine. We should add also a certain sensitiveness which has resulted from the current interest in manual work and workers. Middle managers have a less and less privileged position in the enterprise and, in France, their professional associations have done everything possible to strengthen this feeling.

The drastic changes in planning techniques and in the information circuit, which new forms of job-design imply, make the task of middle management more arduous. These new difficulties are not compensated for by the role of the manager in the new concept of the organization, although this role may in some ways have been given a new value. Is it because current experiments have not been concerned to redefine the manager's role, is it because managers are in a way jealous of the power that they have lost? Middle management always poses a problem and a place has to be found not only in the new organization but also in the strategy of change. But is the cause of the malaise not precisely at this point, i.e. the sceptical or resolutely opposed attitude of middle management, and is it not at the same time the cause of middle management's exclusion from any study and project procedure? We believe, however, that a global approach has the merit of posing difficulties at all levels simultaneously so that, even if it is true that change is thereby retarded, it does at least propagate a more positive attitude within the hierarchy as a result of the suspicions which have to be avoided during the planning of change. In certain medium-sized enterprises (a few hundred workers) where a restructuring has taken place, managers have been very closely associated with the study and have become the force for change.[82]

There are possibilities of job-enrichment for managers when the training of supervisors becomes part of their role.

Finally, managers ought to become the recipients of a sizeable share of the power which is delegated.[83]

2. THE FACTORS TO BE TAKEN INTO ACCOUNT IN ORGANIZATIONAL INNOVATION

Analysis of the above experiments brings out the various factors which must be taken into account when new forms of job-design are introduced. First and foremost innovation comes up against individuals, with their working habits and their socio-cultural differences. We can classify people into two general categories, those who in a given job put up with traditional organization and those who reject it.

The difficulty is increased when social groups are taken into account, either on the national scale, at union level, or within the enterprise. One of the powerful groups is the hierarchy.

Technology constitutes a formidable obstacle, to such a point that certain authors, who are otherwise quite confident about the future of new forms of work, are still of the belief that this factor is one of the major obstacles in the path of change.

It is generally admitted that the obstacles in the path of change which are due to mental, social, or even technical factors can be lessened by means of an appropriate effort to improve the education of workers at all levels. This effort must include training in and development of communication.

For organizational innovation to be viable it has to take into account the economic effectiveness imperative. Yet in this area there exists a deeply rooted belief in the exclusivity of economic performance within scientific management, and this puts a powerful brake on the introduction of new forms of job-design.

Finally, innovation in certain respects upsets structures, one of the most deeply stable of these being, by definition, the legal one. As a result, the success of the spatial propagation of efficient innovation has to be accompanied by a certain legal evolution and by a certain degree of economic and financial encouragement from the state.

A. The Mental Factor: the Psychological and Cultural Heterogeneity of Men at Work

There exists a dual reaction to the current organizational system. Alongside workers who reject or who fight against scientific management there are others who very easily get used to fragmented work,[84] as long as they receive compensation in the form of higher wages or a reduction in working hours. This implicit surrender, this veritable absence of feeling for one's work, generally arises from the absence of any overt individual project or from the existence of too limited a project. It is above all conditioned by economic factors, and sometimes collective demands are more economic than socio-cultural in nature. Thousands of years of history prove that man is capable of adapting to debilitating working conditions just as long as he is convinced that work is, by nature, unrewarding, and for as long as he transfers his desire for self-fulfilment to activities outside his work. Man's cultural development ought, however, to enable him to reject this frequently denounced dichotomy. The attitude of young workers corroborates this view of things. Correct observation of men at work shows, incidentally, that it is not the work itself which motivates the worker, but it is the *sense* of the work.

The rigid way of thinking indicated here manifests itself not only at the level of people's *judgement of what exists* but also at the level of the *projected change*. Later on we shall discuss the reticence which, crystallized at union level, surrounds the introduction of new forms of job-design and the ambiguity of the expected results. For the moment we shall confine ourselves to the inertia which all change comes up against. Change can introduce powerful frustrations because of the way in which individual work-techniques, responsibilities, and personal implication in one's work are called into question. An increase in the scope of a task implies increased memorization, a different arrangement of ideas, greater personal organization at work. Autonomous groups require a kind of flexibility in inter-personal relationships which large numbers of workers have never been used to as a result of their long experience of work which has been routine, individualized, and ordered, checked and sanctioned by others.

It is noticeable that immigrants, women, and, in general, older workers are less willing to work under other systems. One does, however, find that within these same categories there are the same promotion expectations and so one could reasonably expect these expectations to encourage some form of evolution.

Young people, on the other hand, because of their over-qualification[85] and because of the freedom which they enjoy over and against the existing systems, be they educational, political, even society itself, take a great deal of notice of the content of their jobs. The fact that young people are potentially in favour of enriched forms of job-design enables us to have a prospective age-pyramid which is increasingly made up of workers in favour of the setting-up of such forms. If we add to this the fact that the malleability observed in the majority of women may well help to promote the introduction of new forms of organization, and that the impact of recruiting difficulties leads to a higher rate of efficiency, where the present number of workers is concerned, we can predict a healthy future for new forms of job-design.

Finally it is noticeable that workers are conditioned by the existing system, by the organization which they experience, and that when they are placed in new *concrete* situations they generally adapt well to the new conditions. New organization is itself becoming more efficient as can be seen from the increase in workers' ability to grow accustomed to such forms. At Renault's Le Mans plant it took two months for workers to get used to the new system during the initial experiments (it took six months at l'Île Seguin, doubtless because of the high proportion of immigrants who experienced more difficulty). In both cases this was reduced in later experiments to one month only.

B. The Social Factor

The organization of workers, or of certain categories of workers, adds to individual features certain collective factors which promote or discourage human job-enrichment in enterprises.

i. The Trade-Union Attitude in France and Abroad

Delamotte[86] has analysed the diversity of trade-union attitudes. At union initiative the humanization of work has been the object of collective bargaining in certain industries in Italy. The Norwegian and Swedish unions have strongly encouraged management's and work specialists' efforts and have co-operated to institute 'industrial democracy', i.e. worker participation in job-management. Other trade-union organizations have, on the other hand, manifested their clear opposition. This is the case in France.

The objections of certain trade unions are due to various causes. First of all they are due to the way in which the changes have been introduced, i.e. without the unions being informed, let alone consulted. Then they are due to the fact that the changes create or ignore other problems, such as pay-scales which are inappropriate to the new forms of organization. Finally, most importantly, they are due to the fact that unions contest the merits of any job-restructuring policy which appears as an alternative to traditional union demands. Unions have always preferred compensation (wages, working hours, retirement age, fight against harmful working conditions) to the enrichment of job-content, as though the latter excludes the former.

Inasmuch as they have been clearly expressed at all, the respective positions of the CGT and the CFDT in France on this differ considerably. The CGT recommends its members to be sceptical about new forms of job-design as being more refined modes of worker exploitation. The union does not, however, denigrate them because of their aim but because they take place within capitalist society. The CFDT's attitude is more favourable towards new forms of job-design because semi-autonomous groups promote the learning of management at work-group level. Far from rejecting the experiments, the union would like to try and learn from them.

Trade-union attitudes in France are, however, not fixed. Consequently neither the CGT nor the CFDT has signed the national employer–union agreement on working conditions.[87]

In certain respects too much emphasis is often placed on the difference in attitude between French and foreign unions.[88] Although it is true that the union attitude in other countries is more, or fairly, positive, one should not underestimate the difficulties which exist in all countries and which are in the nature of things. Scandinavian unions, namely, are becoming less co-operative (Nobo . . .).[89]

The trade unions are factors which have to be taken into account, from both the theoretical and the pragmatic point of view (employer and state). They are, though, not only a source of difficulty; trade-union participation in major decisions with economic and social consequences is natural. In so far as they represent workers' interests, the unions are in any case a possible judge of the effects of these decisions.

It is sometimes difficult to include the unions in the social policy of the enterprise when existing relationships are not 'good', but it seems to us that it is necessary at any stage of the procedure and that it should take place as near as possible to the beginning of the setting-up of new forms of job-design. It is encouraging to note[90] that although certain enterprises may have totally ignored the unions in their experiments, others, on the contrary, have informed or even invited them to join in working out the content of a project or in setting up control procedures for experiments.

To be honest, organizational change does not pose any new specific problem where relations between unions and enterprises are concerned. Where relationships are good it is simply much easier to involve the unions. It has to be noted, however, that a certain reserve on the part of the unions can be explained by the ambiguity to which we have been calling attention since the beginning of our study; and which we believe results from the fact that the position of the psycho-sociologists in the debate has not been clear. They have not tried to integrate motivation and economic factors. Whenever new forms of organization have been accompanied or even extended by an improvement in economic working conditions (increase in salary and/or reduction in hours), union involvement has been easier. If, in addition, the new forms mean greater involvement, and therefore an increase in the amount of work, it is perfectly legitimate that the unions, as the traditional defenders of the wage/work relationship, should expect precise pledges from management, especially concerning salary level and the solutions envisaged for absorbing the physical increase in productivity (increase in production? redundancies? reduction in hours?).

ii. *The Behaviour of the Hierarchy*

The intermediate levels of the hierarchy between management and workers are often against any change. In addition to the mental and social factors which have already been explored, this behaviour can be explained by the specific characteristics of the man in the hierarchy (small or large) who wields the power.[91] We are well placed to know what disturbance takes place in university circles as the result of the (often not really fruitful) search for new ways of teaching and therefore new structures, new models of staff–student relationships. When one knows how difficult it is to find a new stable equilibrium, it is easy for us to appreciate the considerable problems which the introduction of new forms of job-design pose for the hierarchy.

In the present state of new job-design experiments and projects the supervisory grades are in a particularly delicate position. The creation of semi-autonomous groups or modules is often the death blow for the supervisory grades, whose role was, anyway, often in debate. An attempt is being made to find a solution to this situation by giving back to supervisors their real technical power, the power which had been lost with the proliferation of line grades. At Renault there exists a specially constituted group to study the realignment of supervisory grades.

There are, however, two considerations which allow us to be optimistic about the future. These are in addition to the strictly positive, if slightly cynical, point of view, which consists in saying that the hierarchy will of course have to carry out the orders.

The first consideration is that power – like money – generates itself at all levels and that it is wrong in these areas to reason in terms of a zero-sum game. It is possible to imagine that supervisors and managers, once they have been relieved of their former and often very crushing power and have been given new power, once they have been reassured by the improved *social viability* of the work-life system, will go along with the new projects. There are certain prior considerations to this in that firms have to accept the idea of developing internal communication. Some have done so already, albeit timidly.[92] They have introduced dialogue structures which are linked to decision-making procedures. Firms have to admit that task restructuring implies an over-all revision of their structures, since a margin for initiative is created at each level of human activity. The idea has to be accepted that semi-autonomous groups create more solid links within the whole hierarchy.

The second consideration is the convergence, albeit paradoxical, between the economic interests of workers, managers, and employers.[93] It is reassuring to see that the unions are preoccupied with productivity (cf. above) and that middle managers and management are often opposed to new forms of organization because they are afraid of a fall in productivity. This not only consolidates our economist standpoint already indicated, but it also enables us to predict that, if the current experiments are conclusive from the point of view of economic performance, the hierarchy's agreement will be easy to obtain because of the *economic viability* of the new organization.

C. The Technological Factor: Determination or Indetermination

One of the most important conclusions from the experiments which have been conducted is that, although technology may, within the framework of scientific management, lead to job-impoverishment, it is nevertheless possible to adapt a type of organization other than scientific management, one involving job-enrichment, to today's technology.

The Rhône-Poulenc-Textile experiment is an example of the creation of semi-autonomous groups concomitant with the implantation of new fibres in traditional weaving shops, all with no apparent initial cost differential. The Renault, Thompson-Brandt, and Volvo experiments show that it is possible to adapt existing technology to semi-autonomous groups at relatively low initial supplementary cost. The Crédit Lyonnais example demonstrates that for the price of readapting computer programs it has been possible to bring about a considerable enrichment in administrative work. It has likewise been possible to demystify the computer, which had created considerable anxiety amongst the staff, first and foremost amongst the managers. In this case it was the questioning of computer technology which set off a rejection process and which, in turn, led to the integration of that same technology.

We could give a host of examples to show that, although technological constraint exists, it is, contrary to the widespread myth, by no means totally rigid. Technology does not determine one single form of job-design. On the contrary, the imperatives born of research into new forms of job-design can lead to fruitful technological research, which in turn will bring about solutions compatible with more human types of organization.

It is also possible to outline a sequential development process based on the *dialectic relationship between technology and job-design.* Each impresses on the other a diachronic movement of successive research since the relationship between technology and job-design is biunivocal.

It is, however, important to make clear that in a given situation certain technologies constitute serious obstacles to the improvement of intrinsic and extrinsic working conditions, either because of the high cost involved in the reduction of harmful aspects or for technological reasons. Although technology is more malleable before than after the investment,[94] it is still possible to adapt progressively following the rhythm of the renewal of investments. Finally, it is not a question of accepting or rejecting efficient technology, it is a question of looking for forms of job-design which are compatible with both technology and the humanization of work.

D. The Educational Factor: Participation by Interested Parties in Finding a Solution, and Continuing Education[95]

It would appear that the effort required to have different levels of the hierarchy and the workers themselves participate in the search for new solutions constitutes an area in which it is difficult to measure the short-term efficiency or profitability.

Psycho-sociologists are right to stress the question of individuals' taking charge of their own problems. Occasionally they have laid too much stress on the virtues of a veritable pedagogic system born of an auto-diagnostic procedure (cf. Van Beinum on the Dutch Shell company), because such a system can be very costly and, anyway, it is difficult to apply in all cases. In effect the contradiction between the short-term interest and long-term effects of an action frequently prevents one from undertaking very costly initial investment (viz. loss of production) with a view to setting up a participative learning procedure.

On the other hand it is much easier to set up communications structures which ensure constant feed-back and which are a *sine qua non* for generating innovation in the modern enterprise.[96]

Continuing education is not only a matter of allocating financial and more or less classical teaching resources to the raising of the worker's professional or cultural level.[97] In a more informal concept nowadays, continuing education encompasses learning and the setting-up of professional, cultural, and social procedures, which aim at enriching individual aptitude within a network of richer and more efficient inter-personnel relations.[98]

The report of the French National Plan emphasizes the necessity to work out training schemes which are adapted to the new doctrine.[99] This bears out our view of the global aspect of the reorganization of work. Finally it is necessary to insist on the harmonizing of expectations born of training with the definition of new roles within the enterprise.

E. The Economic Factor and the Power of the Myth of Specialization

One of the mainsprings of our civilization is emulation — emulation of the consumer, of the producer, of the cultivated personality. Cultural and economic development are inextricably linked; the one feeds off the other and vice versa. Elsewhere we have had occasion to say that, from a macro-economic point of view, the leisure civilization is by no means opposed to consumer civilization, each lives off production, which is, in itself, the fruit of the human mind and work.

We have seen that unions, middle managers, management, and governments cannot dissociate the aim to increase, or at least maintain, the acquired standard of living from the search for more human forms of work. We have to take this natural conservation reflex very much into account, both from a desire to be logical and from a desire to be realistic.

The challenge of post-industrial society is to develop production alongside a more human form of organization. Experience shows that it is possible to reduce the number of hours worked without affecting production level. Without increasing monotony or repetition, and without impoverishing a man's work, it is possible to involve him to such an extent that his work gives him both psycho-sociological and economic advantages, even where these are traditionally opposed to each other. The problem for the economist is how to find the optimal point for these two advantages under a given constraint, which may be either the level of achieved production or a desirable rate of growth.

It is possible to work out a graph which shows the interdependence between economic and psycho-sociological advantage. Economic advantage can be calculated by an index made up of wage-level, social benefits (complementary welfare and security systems), or even net per capita income. The psycho-sociological index can be based on the Renault grid.

Let us plot some points of a curve which correspond to various modifications

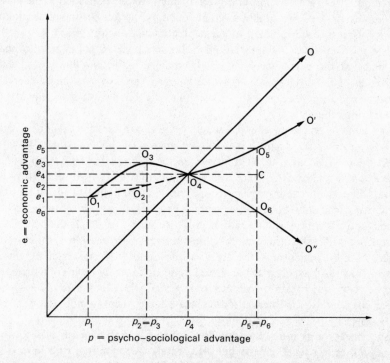

Fig. 2.14

introduced within a conventional form of Taylor organization O_1. Let O_4 be the optimum point, economic and psycho-sociological advantage being equal. The first question is to find out whether the curve passes via point O_2 or point O_3, which correspond to different levels of economic advantage, the advantage in terms of job-content being the same. If O_2 and O_3 correspond to two given organization projects, the choice of O_3 is logical because

$$\frac{e_3 - e_1}{p_3 - p_1} > \frac{e_2 - e_1}{p_2 - p_1}.$$

When the organization reaches O_4 it ought rationally to try and remain on the first bisector, which is where the geometric optimum points cross, or it ought more plausibly to oscillate around this upright. It is possible to envisage improving working conditions along O_1 to arrive at point O_5, which corresponds to an increased but proportionally lower economic advantage ($e_5 - e_4 < p_5 - p_4$). This appears to be the situation which could be reached if, on the macro-economic level, there was a decision to generalize the improvement in intrinsic and extrinsic working conditions beyond a fixed minimum level, and at no matter what cost (it could, for instance, be the result of a reduced growth-rate policy). On the other hand if the shape of the curve is such that from O_4 onwards the branch becomes O_4O'', the advantage level is attained along with a deterioration in terms of *absolute value* of the economic advantage (the classic extreme example of this situation can be found by the suppression of all production involving a certain amount of danger, certain unavoidable risks).

The problem in choosing a rational economic policy is, of course, to know the shape of the curve beyond O_4 and, perhaps, to fix two limits so that the oscillation of the differentiated growth patterns created by economic advantages at the next, is never too vigorous, so that the ones never show up too far 'behind' the others.

The analysis which we have just made of the weaknesses and the limits ought, however, to help us illustrate the interdependence of the aims sought in work.

At the level of the firm and, *a fortiori*, of the individual at his work place, the choice is not an easy one, except in a monopoly situation where the firm can recoup the cost of the improvement in order to avoid branch O''. In other situations firms will only agree to go beyond point O_4 to a point giving a psycho-sociological advantage as long as that point is either O or O'. If the point is O'', these firms will wait until legal obligation or fiscal encouragement, for example, leads to the introduction of the organizational innovation and enables them not to go below the y axis (e_4) of the critical point C, either by means of a reduction in cost or by some form of compensation which will affect prices. It may well be, of course, that the internal social climate forces them to innovate in spite of everything.

Specialization as introduced by Taylor has a capacity for survival not only amongst organizational experts but also amongst economists, who have often confused it with the problem of the division of labour. It has to be admitted that economic performance has increased hitherto and that industrial progress has coincided with the history of Taylorism. Let us also remember that scientific analysis of work has doubtless facilitated the substitution between the two factors of production, capital and labour. It is, however, time to demonstrate that specialist job-design, as the only system enabling us to achieve a certain level of economic performance, leads to impossible situations, especially when sociological factors are taken into account. Whatever results scientific management may have achieved in the past, nothing can prove that they can be inferred for the future.

The specialist process can be shown as in Fig. 2.15. Three paths (SO, SO′, SO″) correspond to the evolution of very advanced forms of Taylor organization. The most likely is the SO″ curve, which shows how, from a situation SO_1

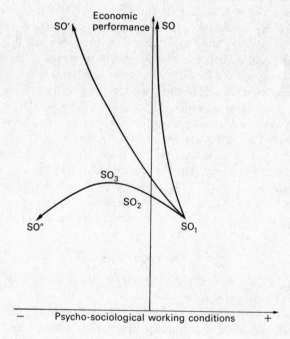

Fig. 2.15

where socio-psychological working conditions are poor, one moves on to situation SO_2 where they are zero, thence to SO_3 from when onwards poor psycho-sociological conditions have repercussions on economic performance.

This analysis calls for the following remarks:

it is founded on the notion of economic and psycho-sociological *advantages* *or conditions* and not on the intuitive notion of *satisfaction*, which is too imprecise, too subjective, and, moreover, too unstable.

the defined optimum is in theory micro-collective; it applies to a work-group or organization dependent on economic and social environmental conditions. The analysis could, given certain reservations, be generalized at the level of a macro-economic system.

the marginal neo-classical analysis in terms of wage–leisure substituion, or of the decrease in marginal utility, might well suggest a particular way of reasoning. It is, however, a way which does not appear pertinent in relation to that in which we approach the dialectic between the economic advantages and the extra-economic psycho-sociological advantages. It seems to us, therefore, that one should abstain from defining a marginal substitution rate between the two kinds of advantage (cf. below, p. 150, our criticism of the analysis in terms of supply and demand of working conditions).

Finally the question arises of the extension of new working conditions (in the broad sense of the term), especially when they are relatively expensive or not very productive. Direct State aid to enterprises which introduce far-reaching projects for working conditions or job-design poses no theoretical problem, since it is aimed at propagating and encouraging these projects and not at penalizing those enterprises which devote a certain amount of energy to these problems, energy which may well be to their short-term disadvantage in other areas of economic competition. The difficulty lies in determining the criteria with a view to making help available generally. This would place a considerable financial burden on the State and would perhaps not be very efficient, because it would be too scattered. The alternative would be to define a policy of giving aid to pilot enterprises in various leading sectors. Such a policy might well come up against the principle of equity. The French national agency for the improvement of working conditions (FNACT) has received such requests from enterprises, but it is still not known what kind of budget will be allocated or whether help will be given in the form of research grants or direct help based on results achieved.

F. The Legal Factor

Change makes it necessary to adjust the legal framework, either to facilitate change or even to make it possible.

French law used to be opposed to flexible hours, for working hours had to be the same for all personnel, or at least for all those in the same category. It is still true that periods of reference (for flexible hours) which exceed the week come up against the principle of the weekly definition of overtime, both in France and abroad.

Job-enrichment and, *a fortiori*, semi-autonomous groups imply a redefinition of jobs, rhythm, modes, and level of payment, which are such that the rigid framework imposed by collective agreements or company arrangements demand long and difficult negotiations. These act as brakes on experiments since it is not easy to make the existing statutes more supple without some form of bargaining currency. The French Parodi system of qualifications constitutes a strong force of inertia during discussions on collective agreements.

The problem does not exist only at worker level; the job-definitions of managers and supervisors are also called into question. It therefore becomes easier to understand BSN-Gervais-Danone's policy which aims at unifying the status of its managers in order to facilitate their mobility within the group.

The legal system is consequently obliged to take sides and legislate either with a view to breaking out of an inhibiting framework (the single daily time-table in France) or with a view to instituting structures which will promote progress in work and training (the July 1971 law on continuing education, the December 1973 law on working conditions, the creation of the national agency for the improvement of working conditions).[100]

On an international level the participation of the ILO or the OECD has been rather futile in terms of results, yet less rigid structures would well receive government aid in order to collect, diffuse, and generate information.[101]

NOTES

(1) The psycho-sociologists went into the enterprises at the request of management in order to resolve the disputes.
(2) '18 Aug. 1971, three unskilled immigrants blocked the pinions on three washing-machine production-lines' at Ciapem-Thompson-Brandt, Lyon. In 1972 a consultant was called in to set up a job-motivation scheme. Cf. article quoted in *L'Express-Rhône-Alpes*, Nov. 1973.
(3) Cf. employers' federation report, 'Le problème des OS', *CNPF*, Nov. 1971.
(4) Cf. 'Les ouvrières de Coframail (groupe Agache-Willot) obtiennent la suppression progressive du salaire au rendement', *Le Monde*, 11–12 Mar. 1973; cf. also Sudreau, Report cited, *Documentation française*, Feb. 1975.
(5) Cf. J.-L. Cavalié, *Le Bilan social*, Centre Interuniversitaire d'Éducation Permanente, Toulouse, 1974.
(6) Cf. Froidevaux, 'Étude sur les facteurs d'absentéisme et la façon dont ils sont perçus par l'encadrement d'une entreprise', unpublished doctoral thesis, University Lyon II, 1971, and his report on the OECD meeting of 17–19 Oct. 1973, 'L'absentéisme et la rotation du personnel' – Programme employeurs–travailleurs, OECD Paris, 15 May 1974.
(7) Cf. 'Les contrôles parallèles des congés de maladie suscitent des protestations', *Le Monde*, 28 June 1974. It is a question of checks carried out by the company based on agreements which guarantee full pay in case of sickness.
(8) Cf. above, OECD Report, p. 49.
(9) Cf., pp. 125 ff., our suggested method.
(10) Cf. B. Lebel, of the Institut Entreprise et Personnel, 'Deux exemples de situations', presented at the Royaumont seminar. It is a question of the second situation in the press-shop of a car-body factory. 'We discovered that a number of operatives preferred the short-cycle production-line . . . because on a line with a relatively low level of production, the work had been enlarged and not enriched. . . . Instead of welding one item every few seconds the workers were welding a whole series every 20 minutes.'
(11) Cf. *Bulletin de l'IRAS*, Dec. 1973; *L'Express-Rhône-Alpes*, Nov. 1973.
(12) Cf. in *Professions et entreprises*, May–June 1973, p. 25.
(13) Ibid.
(14) Ibid., p. 33.
(15) We would prefer to use the word *plurivalence* so as to avoid confusion with polyvalent

workers who could be employed at different jobs on the line, depending on staffing needs. (Cf. report by R. Robin, 'Deux approches pour de nouveaux modes de réorganisation, Kodak-Pathé'.)

(16) Cf. B. Lebel, op. cit.

(17) Cf. R. Robin, op. cit.

(18) W. J. Paul, 'Des expériences vécues d'enrichissement des fonctions', *Direction et gestion*, Sept.–Oct. 1972; cf. also W. J. Paul, K. B. Robertson, *Job Enrichment and Employee Motivation*, Gower Press, Epping, 1970.

(19) M. Liu, 'Réorganisation des emplois dans un atelier à automatisation incomplète', report presented at Royaumont, Mar. 1974.

(20) Cf. anonymous document presented at Royaumont, Mar. 1974, 'Expérience de nouvelles formes d'organisation du travail dans une entreprise de matériel électrique d'équipement industriel'.

(21) Cf. C. Prestat, 'Projet de communication sur une expérience de groupes semi-autonomes, Atelier Fil Textile', Royaumont, Mar. 1974.

(22) L. E. Davis, J. C. Taylor, *Design of Jobs*, Penguin Modern Management Readings, 1972.

(23) Cf. art. cit. n. 2 above.

(24) Likewise introduced on the traditional lines.

(25) This prudence can be explained by the fact that the social partners do not know what effect the results might have on the workers' traditional claims.

(26) Union attitude abroad seems to be more positive, more co-operative, more forceful. Cf. p. 98, however, our reservation based on recent trends.

(27) Cf. *Professions et entreprises*, May–June 1973, p. 29.

(28) Ibid., p. 34.

(29) Cf. J.-M. Clerc, 'Quelques aperçus sur un colloque', in *Bulletin*, no. 11 of the Institut International d'Études Sociales, Geneva.

(30) Cf. in *Professions et entreprises*, May–June 1973, 'Le cas des Ciments d'Origny-Desvroise', p. 27.

(31) Ibid., p. 31, 'les Charbonnages de France'.

(32) Ibid., p. 40, 'la SEB'.

(33) Cf. above, p. 29, 'reduction in number of hours worked'.

(34) Cf. ibid.

(35) Cf. *Bulletin intersocial*, no. 73, 5 Apr. 1974, pp. 15 f.

(36) Cf. *Personnel*, Nov.–Dec. 1971, p. 50.

(37) Cf. G. Rehn, 'Pour une plus grande flexibilité de la vie de travail', *L'Observateur*, OECD, no. 62, Feb. 1973, pp. 3 ff.

(38) Cf. O. Voronov, 'Le congé-éducation en URSS', *Revue internationale du travail*, Geneva, vol. 107, 6 June 1973, pp. 575 ff.; in France the 1971 law on Continuing Education.

(39) J. Barraux, 'Horaires de travail à la carte', *Entreprise*, 24 Sept. 1971, pp. 57 ff.

(40) E. B. Hoffman, 'The four-day week raises new problems', *Conference Board Record*, New York, vol. IX, no. 2, Feb. 1972, pp. 21 ff.

(41) Ibid., p. 26.

(42) J.-F. Baudraz, *L'Horaire variable de travail*, Vaudoise, Lausanne, 1971; B. Zumsteg, *L'Horaire dans l'entreprise, ses causes, ses problèmes, ses conséquences*, Delachaux and Niestlé, Neuchâtel, 1971.

(43) Cf. documents in *Entreprise et progrès*: 'Les expériences d'horaires dynamiques réalisées par les adhérents d'Entreprise et Progrès', Apr. 1973; 'L'amélioration des conditions de travail. Pour une approche experimental: les horaires personnalisés' (May 1973).

(44) Cf. J. de Chalendar, 'Vers un nouvel aménagement de l'année, *La Documentation française*, 1970.

(45) B. Zumsteg, op. cit.

(46) Comité pour l'étude et l'amènagement des horaires de travail et des temps de loisirs dans la région parisienne (17 Boulevard Morland, 75004 Paris).

(47) Cf. 'L'horaire variable ou libre', *La Documentation française*, 1972, pp. 76 ff. The CGC (Managers) seems to be the only union to have reservations rather than to be in

favour. J.-F. Baudraz, op. cit., points out that opposition from employers and unions is more tactical than final in nature (especially on the part of foreign unions, it would appear).

(48) Cf. *Le Monde*, 29 May 1973, p. 21, 'Horaires à la carte à la Caisse d'Assurance maladie des Côtes-du-Nord' (400 employees); *Le Monde*, 25 June 1974, p. 22, 'Décontracter la vie professionnelle' (Linvosges, a company employing 350 workers at Gérardmer, is the first in France to have applied flexi-time at production level).

(49) In article quoted, *Professions et entreprises*, May–June 1973, p. 38: IBM France (3,000 workers).

(50) Ibid., p. 31, Charbonnages de France.

(51) At the moment in France there is a great difference of opinion between management and unions concerning job-weighting. This is an amalgam of, on the one hand, skill and qualification and, on the other hand, working agreements. The workers strongly oppose the fact that the latter are taken into account.

(52) Cf. P. Viaud, 'L'évolution des modes de rémunération', document presented at Royaumont.

(53) There is plenty of published material on experiments abroad. Such information is often more general and less detailed, in certain respects, than our French sources. Cf. J.-M. Clerc, 'Quelques aperçus sur un colloque', *Bulletin de l'IIES*, Geneva, Jan. 1974, pp. 15 ff.; D. Arquie, D. Nebenhaus, J.-P. Noreck, 'Quelques expériences de nouvelle organisation des tâches en milieu industriel', CESA-HEC, Jouy-en-Josas; 'Compte rendu de mission. Nouvelles formes de travail et démocratie industrielle en Scandinvaie, 3–9 mars 1974', Institut Entreprise et Personnel, Paris, June 1974; J.-P. Norstedt, S. Aguren, 'Le rapport Saab-Scania. Une expérience de modification de l'organisation du travail et de ses méthodes', *Enseignement et gestion*, Nov. 1973; F. Novara, 'L'élargissement des tâches à la compagnie Olivetti', *Revue internationale du travail*, Oct. 1973; 'L'amélioration des conditions de travail chez Volvo', *Bulletin de l'IRAS*, 1974; J. Bedel, J.-M. Sylvestre, 'Huit schémas d'organisation du travail', *Formation continue*, no. 3, 1973, p. 43; 'Fiat lance un programme d'amélioration des conditions de travail', *Intersocial*, 1 June 1973, p. 9; G. de Faramond, 'En Suède, Volvo a inauguré sa première usine sans chaîne', *Le Monde*, 11 June 1974; 'Work in America', Institute for Educational Development; N. Foy, 'Industrial democracy at Norsk Hydro', *European Business*, Winter 1973, p. 30; J. F. Biggane, P. A. Stewart, 'Job enlargement: a case study', L. E. Davis, J. C. Taylor, *Design of Jobs*; H. Murray, art. cit.

(54) Documents for limited circulation: 'Trois expériences de restructuration de tâches à la Régie Renault (Usine du Mans)'; 'Différentes modalités d'organisation du travail' and 'L'évaluation globale des conditions de travail', Public Relations document, 27 June 1973; 'Conditions de travail: les expériences de la régie Renault', *Liaisons sociales*, 14 Aug. 1973; J.-P. Dumont, 'Amélioration des conditions de travail. Dans le domaine de l'élargissement des tâches, Renault va plus loin que FIAT', *Le Monde*, 10 July 1973, p. 13; 'Organisation du travail', section I, chapter I of report by Subcommittee D ('Prospective du travail') of the Commissariat Général du Plan, Feb., 1974.

(55) It is possible to account for such an attitude on the part of management in terms of their *a priori* ignorance of the nature and extent of the results, and the rigidity of the qualifications imposed. It does, however, appear important to us to stress the handicap which resulted because economic motivation was not taken into account. When a more general strategy of change is being defined, this element must have a bigger role.

(56) It is important to note that the theoretical capacity on the line is very much lower than that of a number of equivalent modules. The theoretical capacity is, however, never reached. One always has to think in terms of real capacity. (In the case in question: theoretical capacity of the line $9000 >$ its real capacity $= 6500$, for the 10 modules: theoretical capacity $=$ practical capacity $= 6500$.)

(57) With the exception of isolated individuals who are ill at ease in the experimental group and who sometimes ask not to participate in the experiment.

(58) In other words, half the total group of the new Volvo factory at Kalmar. The range

of operations is larger since the Swedish factory, unlike the Renault plant at Douai, does not include welding or pressing or mechanics. In January 1975 new operations were reorganized at Douai with enlarged tasks: painting, upholstery, and mechanics.

(59) Note that 10%–15% seems to be the spread of the supplementary cost of the investment (cf. Volvo at Kalmar which gave the figure of an extra 10m. kroner (i.e. 10%) for 700 workers, some £1200 per worker, for equipment with an average working life of 10 years).

(60) Cf. A. Laville, C. Teiger, A. Wisner, *Âge et contraintes de travail. Aspects physiques, psychologiques et sociaux*, NEB, Éditions scientifiques, Jouy-en-Josas, 1975.

(61) Cardiac cost = the difference in speed of heartbeat at work and at rest.

(62) Cf. Subcommittee D report, cit. n. 55 above; interview with D. Dautresme, Production Director of Crédit Lyonnais; D. Dautresme, 'Quelques réflexions sur la productivité dans la banque', *Bulletin du ministère des finances*, Nov. 1974; internal Crédit Lyonnais report, 'Centre de traitement modulaire des chèques', Crédit Lyonnais, Paris, 1974.

(63) These gradings in the bank correspond to the supervisory grades in industry. It should be noted that there are many graded and managerial posts at the Crédit Lyonnais (13 000 and 7000 respectively, for 25 000 clerks out of a total staff of 45 000).

(64) According to the author it really is a question of demystification and not only of demythologization.

(65) Cf. J.-L. Donnadieu in *Le Monde* article quoted above and his 'Carrefour sur les conditions de travail', *Professions et entreprises*; 'Expériences d'amélioration des conditions de travail à l'usine . . . chez BSN à Rheims, l'auto-organisation des ateliers se prépare activement', *La Croix*, 27 Sept. 1973; J.-L. Donnadieu, 'BSN: une prise de conscience d'aspirations nouvelles', *Professions et Entreprises*, May–June 1973, pp. 35 ff.; and J.-L. Donnadieu, G. Mital, oral exposés at Royaumont, 28 Mar. 1974.

(66) A. Riboud's speech, 'Croissance et qualité de la vie'.

(67) Confédération Française du Travail.

(68) Cf. J.-L. Donnadieu, 'Carrefour sur les conditions du travail', quoted above, n. 66.

(69) G. Mital at Royaumont.

It can be seen that our way of working is close to the socio-technical approach as illustrated in Fig. 2.12. The socio-technical approach (Fig. 2.13) occurs at the point of intersection of different large groups, one of which is the economic factor. The analysis partially incorporates scientific management and Herzberg's theory.

(70) Cf. Y. Delamotte, 'Recherches en vue d'une organisation plus humaine du travail industriel', *Formation continue*, no. 2, 1973, p. 6.

(71) For the Hawthorne effect cf. J.-D. Reynaud, op. cit. above, p. 68.

(72) At the DBA factory in Angers (new unit, one year old) only three ideas and problems out of 450 which emerged from a written questionnaire were rejected as being hare-brained.

(73) This is the form advocated by S. W. Gellerman in *Management by Motivation*, American Management Assoc., 1968, and 'L'onde de choc du job enrichment', *Le Management*, Apr. 1972.

(74) We define democracy as J.-D. Reynaud does: 'the more there are minorities with the right to participate in the decisions which affect them, the more democracy there is.'

(75) Here it is a question of participation in the formal sense and not, as J.-D. Reynaud suggests, of the simple constraint which means that the consumer, for example, 'participates' because his existence is taken into account.

(76) Cf. the declaration by H. Krasucki, Secretary of the CGT, in *Le Peuple*, no. 887, 'Job enrichment? WE WOULD NOT BE AGAINST IT, but it is an abstract, moral idea. In practice, whose enrichment are we on about? That's the real question!' The CFDT's position is summed up briefly by E. Maire, Secretary General, quoted by H. Douard in *Formation continue*, no. 2, 1973, p. 38, 'Partial solutions are envisaged as job-enlargement (i.e. doing several jobs on the production line instead of one) or as "job-enrichment" (i.e. participating more in working out and monitoring work). This is not without interest but it is only an attempt to correct the more exaggerated forms of Taylorism (fragmentation).'

(77) Cf. A. Fantoli at Royaumont: In Italy workers are quite willing to join in with

'collective management of the quality of work'.

(78) A. Cherns at Royaumont: 'one of the most teasing difficulties is involving Unions. . . .'

(79) It was, for instance, possible to use a written questionnaire in the DBA factory at Angers, but at Beauvais opposition from management meant that it was only possible to carry out interviews.

(80) At the Crédit Lyonnais, for example, the typical graded employee is 45 years old, while the clerk is only 20 years old.

(81) Cf. J.-D. Reynaud, op. cit., p. 85.

(82) Cf. P. Viaud at Royaumont, cf. also M. Beullac, editorial to Renault document quoted above.

(83) Interview with M. Ceyrac in *Project*, Oct. 1972: 'We want more decisions to be taken at the lowest level; that's delegation to management grades.' We still have to be clear about which management levels top management would be willing to delegate to. . . .

(84) It needs to be said that scientific management is intellectually a great comfort to job-designers, managers, and supervisory grades because of the aura of rationality which surrounds it. For this reason those who wish to introduce new organizational forms have first of all to go in for demythologization and demystification of the idea that scientific management leads to human productivity.

(85) It should be noted that we have to take the fact that young people at the Crédit Lyonnais have very little motivation to increase their professional qualifications as a means of rejecting administrative work in its practical form. The high failure rate in professional examinations corroborates this. Motivation ought to increase along with a fuller kind of work, one which implies polyvalent workers. In this way the structure explains, in part, the behaviour.

(86) Y. Delamotte, 'Recherches en vue d'une organisation plus humaine du travail industriel', quoted in *Bulletin de l'Institut international d'études sociales*, Geneva, Jan. 1974.

(87) Cf. below, p. 151.

(88) Cf. A. Cherns, above, n. 78.

(89) Cf. bibliography nn. 53 and 54, above.

(90) Cf. report of Commissariat Général du Plan quoted above.

(91) Cf. J.-D. Reynaud, op. cit., p. 78.

(92) Cf. report quoted above of Commissariat Général du Plan; cf. also J.-P. Bernard, 'Quel pouvoir pour les cadres?', *Responsables*, Paris, May 1974.

(93) Cf., however, P. de Backer's different thesis: 'Négociation et conflit dans l'entreprise. Quelques indications d'application de la psychologie des conflits', *Metra*, vol. 11, no. 1, Mar. 1972. The author spotlights the latent opposition of the hierarchy, the statutory opposition of individual roles and objectives, and condemns the 'so-called' great (common) objective shared by workers and bosses. He uses the Marxist analysis which attributes the cause of permanent class conflict to the method of investment.

(94) Cf. J. Régnier, 'Introduction des facteurs humains dans la conception des installations automatisées et de leur exploitation', *Metra*, Mar. 1972, p. 67; J.-D. Reynaud, P.-L. Rémy *et al.*, 'Rapport remis au Ministre du Travail sur la restructuration des tâches', May 1974, published by *La Documentation française* (cf. bibliography); P. Bois, 'L'aménagement des conditions du travail au stade de la conception des bâtiments industriels', report to French Minister of Employment, 1974.

(95) Cf. H. Savall, 'Formation et conditions de vie au travail', *Revue française de gestion*, Mar.–Apr. 1977.

(96) Cf. A.-J. Rigny, *Structure de l'entreprise et capacité d'innovation*, Éditions Hommes et Techniques, Puteaux, 1973; P. de Woot, *Pour une doctrine de l'entreprise*, Seuil, Paris, 1968, chap. 7, 'Créativité et participation'; cf. also 'Le problème des OS', CNPF document quoted below.

(97) Cf. articles in *Personnel*, Nov.–Dec. 1971; J. Bernasse, 'Les obstacles à la formation', 'L'éducation récurrente', J.-M. Raimond, 'Stratégie de la formation des adultes'. Cf. also in *Formation continue*, no. 3, 1973, 'Et ils n'étaient que huit . . . (un point de vue d'ouvriers sur la formation des ouvriers)'. Cf. in *Chronique sociale de France*, Jan.–Feb. 1974, special number devoted to Continuing Education; cf. R. Reichenbach,

'Le coût humain de la formation permanente', *Project*, Mar. 1972; *Project*, Feb. 1974, special number devoted to Continuing Education.

(98) Cf. three articles in *Éducation permanente*, Nov.–Dec. 1973: G. Schade, 'Les femmes et l'éducation récurrente'; CERFI, 'Formation de la force collective de travail'; M. Salmona, 'Formation économique et changement social, langage, et coûts mentaux'.

(99) Cf. M. Liu, 'Élaboration d'une pédagogie nouvelle pour la formation du personnel ouvrier', unpublished document; F. Lantier, 'L'analyse des systèmes socio-techniques, moyen de connaissance et d'action pour les formateurs', unpublished document presented at Royaumont, Mar. 1974; O. Ortsman, 'Une expérience très ponctuelle de formation d'ingénieurs à la démarche socio-technique', FNEGE, Paris, Mar. 1974, unpublished.

(100) Cf. also below, p. 155, 'Legal Aspect'.

(101) Cf. the creation of the international committee on the Quality of Working Life.

3

THE STRATEGY OF CHANGE

There is always a certain wisdom in undertaking more than that which is merely rational.   François Perroux[1]

Change in industrial life is necessary because of the attitudes of job-refusal and their tendency to increase. It is necessary to plan today so as to be able to carry out change in the future. We have to forecast and create the means and conditions which are necessary for this to be done successfully.

Before starting out on a process of change it is necessary to undertake an economic evaluation, and for this we have to revise existing models and measuring instruments.

Finally, in the context of a decentralized market economy, we have to create and cultivate the forces which will propagate the desired change.

1. THE NEED FOR CHANGE

The need for change can be determined at two different levels: at the global level and at the level of the firm or the production unit.

A. The Irreversibility of the Global Process of Aptitude Enrichment[2]

The current situation which, for the majority of workers, can be described as one of an overqualification in terms of skills for an underqualification in terms of work, cannot logically continue in a free society which is aspiring after stability.

A doubly new situation has been gradually created by compulsory education, in-service training, professional and technical training. These factors have either been institutionalized as a result of legal or financial measures or been developed spontaneously by the media.

Various communication media diffuse a deodorized image of life and thereby develop intellectual or professional expectations, aspirations, and ambitions. There is a well-developed sense of emulation. People involved in education bear witness to the fact that young people have a tremendous intellectual appetite.

Skills develop as a corollary. It is the result of the twofold combination of training facilities and the need to learn. This development of skills will reach levels which we refuse to define in advance.

The term explosive development has sometimes been used in connection with population, economics, and science. There is an enormous store of possibilities as a result of accumulated knowledge. We have no real idea of the development potential of human skill. Judging from recent economic and scientific history, there is no reason to believe that there is any limit, for even the most optimistic forecast has been exceeded. The arrival on the labour market of armies of young people who are better and better qualified is an indication now of what the situation could be like in a few decades, or even in a few years. This is one of the results of a national educational system which is hardly a hundred years old.

We are now seeing an acceleration in this process. There has been a progression, albeit too slight at times, in expenditure on national education. The law on continuing education has made it obligatory for all firms to invest in training. These represent the powerful seeds which will lead to a rapid increase in the growth of qualification, even if training is sometimes considered too general or not sufficiently operational. This is a point where there is still a need for clarification.

This is not the place to enter into a debate about the efficiency of this training from a purely productivist perspective. Let us say simply that the development of general qualifications corresponds to a development of the capacity to adapt to new situations. Mobility, be it professional or spatial, is regarded as progressive, and even if it were true that training is too general, the fact still remains that, on the one hand, it corresponds to a need in such a way that one cannot imagine a reversal of the situation, and on the other hand, this evolution shows up again and even more clearly the duality between skill and real work or, to use the economist's language, between supply and demand for work. There is often a reflex reaction which is sometimes, but not always, legitimate, and which consists in thinking that the system of training does not prepare people well for a qualitative balance between supply and demand for work. Is this not, however, to make the implicit hypothesis that one of the systems – current job-design in production units – is good and that the other – the education and training system – is bad? Is it not to assert that it is the latter which should adapt itself to the former? Is it not to push to the extreme the *de facto* pre-eminence of the market in our economic and industrial organization?

As a result the job market should become more complex and the balance between job supply and demand more difficult, more costly.[3] The economist will have to conduct new research into the job market and include psycho-sociological factors and other criteria than pay for job-assessment.

It is still true that all considerations converge towards the conclusion that in the *natural* evolution[4] of our society there is a tendency towards an increase in skills on the general, national, and global level. These skills are elastic and are confronted with a relatively rigid structure, viz. job-offers based on an organizational system which is seventy-five years old already.

B. Societal Development Within Micro-Organizations

It is reasonable to believe that progress implies better harmonization between life at work and life outside work. The general calculations which lead people to say that monthly working hours represent only a fraction of total time[5] are too clumsy. They do not show that working time represents two-thirds of waking time.[6] Is it not legitimate to try to improve the conditions of this working life which represents two-thirds of our conscious existence? Is it not conceivable that the great majority of workers will one day exert pressure to have these working conditions improved?

Is it absurd to believe that, as basic incompressible needs are by and large satisfied, men will notice more acutely the things that are wrong with their working life? Is it absurd to believe that they will look for a more balanced form of progress for this life, which provides them with both income and non-economic advantages (or disadvantages)?

Can authority be preserved in the same oppressive form over workers whose professional skills and whose prerogatives as citizens and as consumers are increasing?

Without a doubt there is a growing need to improve communication at the level of the small, formal and/or informal group with which each worker is in daily contact. It is an important condition for the dignity of labour. There can be no discrimination in this respect as the cases of poor communication which have been investigated all show. The question is a general one; everyone perceives the need to improve relations within their group life: the top or middle manager, the research or manufacturing engineer, the supervisor, foreman, or charge-hand, the office-worker, the worker, the secondary-school teacher, the primary-school teacher. In this respect the work group, which is merely one amongst many other groups in our daily lives, is in a privileged position, only because of the length of time spent in it and because of the constraints it imposes (economic necessity).

If we admit that a change in working conditions is unavoidable, we have to envisage a strategy of disturbance amongst the healthier and more positive elements of the existing system. It seems to us that planning the new forms of job-design is the most appropriate way of doing this.

2. THE NECESSITY FOR CHANGE TO BE PLANNED

First and foremost, planning, in our area of concern, needs to be looked at as a means to reduce uncertainties. History can be written in two ways. The simplest, safest, and most frequent way consists in looking at the evolution which has come about; this is the history of the victors. The other way can teach us a lot but is less attractive, more discreet, and most difficult to pin-point. It is the history of abortive events and developments; it is a kind of history of the vanquished. A good way to prepare the ground for the future history of the victors is first of all to *want* a certain evolution. The post-war economy, as shown by the French national, economic, and industrial plan, shows us what this 'wanting' of events can be. We give all the more importance to the planning of organizational change because it is a question of *supple and decentralized planning* which does not imply enormous prior decisions at national level, but which operates, more prosaically, at production unit level or at company group level.

A. The Planning of Organizational Change; A Corrollary to Economic and Technical Planning

When it comes to planning at the micro-economic level there is only one approach at the moment, viz. the economic and technical approach. It ought to be replaced by a socio-technical approach, one which incorporates social data.[7]

Planning nowadays is carried out by a projection of economic and technical data which are compiled from within the firm or collected from the economic environment. It aims at forecasting the means, primarily the material and financial means, necessary for achieving production objectives and, in addition, the human means. The additional objective of improving intrinsic and extrinsic working conditions implies a reallocation of resources, a new technical choice. Such is the corollary of the socio-technical approach viewed from a time perspective. In other words, the inclusion of change within one's objectives calls into question all technical and economic planning. It falsifies the economic forecasts and imposes a supplementary financial constraint.

The quality of economic and technical planning depends on the extent to which the organizational innovation to be incorporated is taken into account. Not to take it into account is to deprive oneself of the search for the financial material and human means that will enable the social and organizational objectives to be carried out; it means risking declaring null and void the projects decided on; it means failing to improve working conditions and, therefore, weakening the firm's competitiveness on the product, finance, and labour markets. When one is aware of all the possibilities offered by new factories conceived along socio-technical lines,[8] when one is faced with the cost of the technical constraint if an attempt is made to introduce organizational change after the event, it is easy to see that the *choice* of the organization-equipment ambisystem should take place *beforehand and jointly*.

The planning of change has to be carried out in a way that enables one to improve projects, whilst at the same time not losing sight of one's aim to encourage a form of human development which is compatible with economic and technical constraints.

B. The Dangers of the Non-Planning of Human Development

Having tried to demonstrate by deductive reasoning how the planning of change can improve the quality of economic planning at the micro-organizational level, let us now, in order to complete the demonstration, try to spotlight the negative aspect of the non-planification of change. We shall begin from empirical observation and use inductive reasoning.

The history of experiments into human job-enrichment is not one of successes only.[9] It is a difficult history to write but it is said to be full of lessons for us. Careful observation shows that limited experiments do not usually lead to an extension of their effects. This is true in the case of both successful and unsuccessful experiments. It is likewise true for experiments carried out in all secrecy 'in the laboratory' as well as for more large-scale experiments with more lasting results. Experiments do not combat reticence on the part of the hierarchy and supervisory grades, neither do they gain the necessary solid backing from the board, or create much interest amongst workers' representatives. The history of these obstacles is a rich one, both when they are caused by psychological factors[10] and when they are caused by other factors.

One-off experiments are historically valuable as laboratory experiments in that they open up new horizons. They have benefited from the degree of secrecy necessary for the avoidance of great ideological debates and for the running of them. They have frequently demonstrated the possibilities of new forms of job-design. In that they have avoided the enormous difficulties mentioned above, could we not say that they have taken a step backwards in order to make a great leap forwards? It is staggering to see that experiments giving economically unambiguous results have not been extended. It would have been reasonable to assume that successes would have created valid precedents. It is significant that the way these experiments were conceived goes against any extension of the results, for they are seen as being very much one-off experiments carried out in artificially favourable conditions. People want to know how long the positive effects will last and how much is due to the Hawthorne effect, so much so that they question the viability of the results and thereby considerably reduce the exemplary nature of such experiments.

It is always the case that one or two experiments, even when they are enlarged on a modest scale, do not constitute or replace an authentic company policy, one which resolutely aims, if not at solutions, then at least at a search for concrete short- or medium-term reform of working conditions.

At Renault a change-planning strategy has been set up in the form of the 'industrial committee' in order to maintain the impetus given by the board. Instead of giving the factories directives, the procedure consists of supplying them with a prediagnosis in order to identify the sectors where the conditions for job-restructuring are favourable. A balance sheet of all the existing experiments in all the Renault factories is drawn up and they are asked to work out further projects in collaboration with the job-restructuring department. In this way decentralized change-planning is making headway.

Certain authors are sceptical about how long all these experiments will last. There is perhaps a hope that the new forms of organization will take as long to dislodge scientific management as the latter took to establish itself.

At a variety of levels – enterprise, sectoral, and national – management, trade unions, and employers' associations can all add their own effort to the effort being made in enterprises where experiments are being carried out. The effectiveness of people's awareness is one way of replying to the question which has been raised.

Change is the assertion of the principle of strategic effectiveness; we have to add it to the cautious, hair-splitting empiricism of free-lance, limited experiments. Everything in a political, economic, and social system is planned and programmed; to leave change to the mercy of chance is equivalent to not asserting the need for change forcefully.

C. The Content of the Planning of Change

Donnadieu[11] has suggested a planning method which takes its inspiration from the socio-technical approach.

The planning of social and organizational change is in essence *decentralized*, in that it aims at forecasting objectives and means at two levels within the organization chart. Hitherto the workers have been the prime area because they are the ones with the greatest needs in this respect.

It is essential to have some form of spatial limitation so that ideas emerge from as close as possible to the place where they will be applied. For this reason local, annual programmes based on specific local problems have to be set up within each firm or workshop by the workers concerned. The firm is the spatial framework in which studies will be carried out at two levels, at shop-floor and at office level.

As far as the workers are concerned, the objective is threefold:

to invite workers to voice the daily problems they meet with at their jobs. This leads to a shop-by-shop situation analysis,

to help workers to study and work out solutions to the problems,

to apply the adopted solutions with the agreement of all interested parties. This is programmed in such a way as to take into account technical, economic, and social constraints.

Before doing this, managers and supervisors will have been involved in:

making an inventory of their specific problems and drawing up a programme of action necessary to solve them.

carrying out prior analysis of workers' problems, drawing up and costing hypotheses and priority programmes

preparing the people in charge of the programme which is to be carried out to take on their role of group leader with a view to launching the study phase with and by the workers.

Useful technical effects in respect of the quality of the solutions result from involving all interested parties, as long as any problems posed by the representative nature of participants can be avoided. There is, in addition, a considerable psycho-sociological impact, since there is a reduction in the uncertainty and risk factors brought about by all change, especially social, cultural, and structural change. Such involvement has the great advantage of letting everyone play a part, even at the study stage. It represents the setting-up of a real and highly decentralized learning process. As such it ought to avoid any distortion in behaviour patterns caused by uncertainty about the future.

Like all planning, the planning of change will have to move through three stages. The definition of company policy in this area will have to be made *public* so that there is a precise frame of reference for everyone. There must be an explicitly detailed policy content. Company policy can, for example, be defined by two major features, such as economic development and social and human progress. This second feature must be made clear by saying, for example, that it is a question of encouraging solidarity, responsibility, and personalization. Each of these elements will, in turn, have to be made clear by concrete measures. Solidarity can be reinforced by means of the creation of work-groups, by measures to help weaker members of the company, by doing away with payment by results . . . Responsibility can be encouraged by job-enrichment, maximum decentralization of decision-making, the creation of semi-autonomous teams . . . Personalization can consist of improving inter-personal relationships and increasing the quantity and quality of information.

The choice of an appropriate strategy will determine the means to be adopted and the way they are to be used. The author makes two hypotheses: an aim-low hypothesis based on a modest interpretation of results, where caution rules; an aim-high hypothesis, which calls for a general mobilization of all forces. We believe that the aim-low hypothesis contradicts the very idea of planning. It is an alternative not a plan.[12] We have to point out that, during the phase of strategic choice, one has to make clear the programme to be adopted with regard to the various categories of social partners. Such a procedure would allow one to take local usable factors into account so that change could be introduced more rapidly, e.g. friendly relations with local unions. The change strategy must also allow for tangible and unequivocal results to be made public. This will make it easier for people at all levels of the hierarchy to accept the idea and be willing to take an active part.

Finally, a plan of campaign will have to be drawn up in such a way that it includes a calendar of decisions and events, arranged in order of priority. Time-limits and control-points will have to be fixed. A five-year plan can be sub-divided into annual stages and the cost integrated into the budget forecasting of different accounting periods. Control-points provide information feed-back and enable the plan to be brought up to date annually.

It seems to us that the structuralization of social change at the level of economic planning is a fundamental necessity. To plan is not only to acknowledge change, it is to initiate it and equip oneself with the means to carry it out. It means that one has to assert publicly to all interested parties one's *willingness to change* the stage of things. 'The objective is to arrive at a bivalent management system in which economic logic and that of the market-place are continually confronted with the perspective of social change. . . . The planning of change should be seen less as management's search for new forms of job-design and more as the search for a system which will allow the work-force to discover for itself new organizational solutions. The working-out of the plan will be more meaningful than its content.'[13]

If there exists a plan then it profits from being made explicit. Certain large nationalized companies prefer, however, to remain discreet, others can do nothing at all about working out a plan, given the hostile attitude of the board. They are restricted to the 'aim-low hypothesis' and to laboratory experiments. Certain large private companies have been true to the French tradition and have chosen a strategy of secrecy.

In addition to providing the impetus to this planning, the personnel staff's role is to promote the idea of a veritable social accounting system and to strive to set it up in order to facilitate planning. This is done by adopting a quantified approach to the social and organizational problems. By speaking the *language* of the technician, the finance specialist, and the economist, the personnel director will be able to communicate much better with the other members of the company's general staff and even with the middle levels of the hierarchy.

3. THE NEED TO EVALUATE CHANGE ECONOMICALLY[14]

No change in the type of job-design will be more than a one-off experiment unless an economic forecast is first made of the new organization, and unless the mechanism for some readjustment is introduced. There is a need to comment on the position adopted by certain psychologists who believe that events such as social conflict at enterprise level will impose change with complete disregard for any economic calculation. The point of departure for such a belief is an observation of particular cases, more often than not of situations and experiments in very large prosperous companies. It is based on an implicit hypothesis and on a macro-economic view of the interdependent factors. The implicit hypothesis is that the company has room for manœuvre at its disposal thanks to the considerable size of its profit margins. It can therefore support increased costs without increased productivity. On the other hand, if such companies exist, the precariousness of their privileged situation is comparable to that of industrialized economies on the eve of monetary crises and of crises of energy and raw materials. Finally, if the economic calculation led to negative results in the strictly economic sense, the general introduction of new ways of working would imply a generalized price readjustment and would put a brake on growth. This is a possibility not to be dismissed, but one should at least be aware of it and discuss it as an option to be chosen in the full knowledge of the facts.

We believe that *the economic calculation of change has to be made explicit*, even though it is only one element of the debate. Our thesis is founded on empirical observation and aims at making out an economic case for change.

This being so, it is nevertheless true that, in certain companies, expensive decisions, which are imposed by the evolution of certain industrial disputes, are taken with no consideration being given to *immediate* economic effects or constraints. It has to be noted, however, that this is possible where the environmental structures of the companies observed are *plastic*, and that any attempt to generalize would, in any case, be incompatible with the over-all equilibrium of the company. In addition it must be mentioned that the quasi-permanent inflationary economic situation, which has been with us for several decades, encourages decisions to be taken, apparently, without regard to the constraints of productivity. The idea is that the propagation of inflation facilitates the re-establishing of a balance in the long term.

The first criticism to which we lay ourselves open is that of the accuracy of the costs as identified by classical accounting methods. We know, in fact, that certain elements which encourage change cannot be explained by classical accounting methods. It is a question of identifying the weaknesses and insufficiencies of current accounting practice and suggesting a few *simple* cost-analysis methods. There is an increase in the number of complicated manpower accounting models which are not only questionable but also difficult to apply.[15] Cost accounting has not been sufficiently widespread and has not been applied correctly because of the supplementary data-processing constraint involved when compared with traditional accounting. It is also a very imperfect functional instrument: for example, at the Crédit Lyonnais[16] and the ORTF.[17]

By suggesting a simple measuring instrument one increases the likelihood that it will be applied.

Our methodological contribution, however, cannot entirely satisfy the definition of what the really complete economic cost is supposed to be. The fact that the full cost can only be measured within the complexity of the entire economic system makes the identification of this cost an illusion. We shall limit ourselves to outlining a practical method which aims at integrating only a number of significant variables which can be taken as performance indices. Our method, which is not perfect, will only allow us to calculate accurately certain external effects.

A. The Weaknesses of General and Cost Accounting[18]

i. *General Accounting*

One of the general principles of accounting is the working-out of the financial result of successive trading periods while taking great care to apportion those costs to be included in the current period and those which are not. There are two ways of going about this time allocation.

During the accounting period the charge accounts (management accounts) are debited with expenditure of a repetitive nature and of limited duration (the expenses themselves). Expenses of a productive nature which extend beyond the trading year are debited to capital expenditure accounts (balance sheet) because at the end of the accounting period they have a transfer value. It should, however, be noted that certain non-transferable expenses, the effects of which extend beyond the year in question, are nevertheless included in the balance sheet. This is the case with initial expenses, which are, however, regarded as being a non-realizable element. It can be seen therefore that this distinction has not benefited certain other expenses, viz. those belonging to human resources.

At the end of the accounting period an attempt is made to identify the expenses initiated during the accounting period in question but which are to be included in the following accounting period, i.e. purchases and stock manufacturing costs. Transfers are made between accounts, assets and liabilities are calculated and an inventory of materials, stocks, half-finished products, and unfinished goods is drawn up.

Accounting has two techniques at its disposal to enable the distinct nature of expenses and assets to be identified. It should be possible to use them with a view to producing a balance sheet and a trading account which are far more accurate.

Costs involved in recruiting, training, familiarizing with new work rhythms, maintaining and improving of acquired skills, all extend beyond a single accounting period. On the other hand, laying-off costs can be included in the current accounting period since it is a question of an outgoing with no hope of any corresponding future income.

By including these costs in the current accounting year, one is in fact falsifying one's picture of the over-all result of that trading period. Such a mistake is not too serious for a group of companies or for a large company. It is much more serious for small or medium-sized companies whose recruiting and training costs are closely linked to the economic situation and to the firm's growth.

If, as a result of a lasting increase in the size of a firm's order books during a period P_i, there has been a sizeable recruitment followed by training and familiarization, the costs of manpower investment $MI(p_i)$ will be overestimated comparison with production $P(p_i)$ whereas during the following accounting period the inverse will take place:

$$\frac{P(p_i)}{MI(p_i)} < \frac{P(p_{i+1})}{MI(p_{i+1})}$$

everything else being equal.

The over-all production cost for the period p_i is overestimated while that of the following period p_{i+1} is underestimated, at the same time that production increases as a result of the investments made during the preceding accounting period. Both the numerator and the denominator in

$$\frac{P(p_{i+1})}{MI(p_{i+1})}$$

are wrong because $P(p_{i+1}) = f(Pp_i, MIp_i)$.

A fraction of the profit from the accounting period p_i is carried over to accounting period p_{i+1}. This can be a financial advantage which facilitates self-financing. It would, however, be possible to achieve the same result by using an accounting system which would enable a company to keep any gain from investment in manpower resources in reserve.

A possible inconvenience of a more accurate accounting system would be of a fiscal nature. In France the period during which a sizeable investment is made (p_i) is taxed at a relatively lower rate than would have been the case during a period involving a smaller investment. In France the period of reference for effective payment of the major part of the tax bill is the preceding year, with the result that productivity increase due to MIp_i, which does not come about until p_{i+1}, enables a company to find the money necessary to pay the relatively high p_i tax bill. During the changeover period there would follow, however, an advance against tax. This could be solved by using a technique which is already applied to allowances for depreciation or other costs which cannot be deducted from tax. Manpower investment could, at least for the time being, be deductible from the fiscal result of the current accounting year. At the moment the French finance laws identify the costs which we propose to consider as investments as fiscal charges, so that under the current legislation our suggestion could quite easily fit into established fiscal practice.

The dissociation of the fiscal result from the real accounting result is very common. It is in fact the general rule. The case where the real account result corresponds to the fiscal result implies a series of coincidences. According to our proposal, costs of recruiting and training would be considered as capital expenditure and not as overheads when working out the accounting result, but they would continue to be considered as overheads and not as capital expenditure for determining the fiscal result.

ii. *Cost Accounting*

Whether or not it is incorporated into the accounting system itself, cost accounting is very closely tied in with general accounting practice. The practice of incorporating supplementary elements into the costs and of excluding unincorporated elements,[19] however, gives cost accounting a measure of autonomy which we sometimes do not make sufficient use of.

The aim of cost accounting is to explain the elements of any cost. Current systems, though, have difficulty doing this, the main reasons being intermittent stock control, non-allowance for waste, rejects, loss and other forms of wastage.

The following data can be expressed schematically in two different trading accounts:

Purchases : 100
Material consumed : 95
Material wastage : 5
Sales : 200
Rejects : 10
Opening stock : 50
Closing stock : 60

Classical trading account				Advocated trading account			
Opening stock	50	Closing stock	60	Opening stock	50	Closing stock	60
Purchases	100	Sales	200	Material consumed	95	Gross sales	210
Gross profit	110			Material wastage	5		
				Production rejects	10		
	260		260	Gross profit	110		
					270		270

In exactly the same way the ratio $\dfrac{\text{turnover}}{\text{personnel costs}}$ hides the labour wastage due to lack of interest, absenteeism, under-production. Yet methods of expressing these gaps in accounting terms offer possibilities which could well be put to good use.

It is, however, a very complex and very costly thing to run an exhaustive cost-accounting system well. At the Crédit Lyonnais, for example, they have given up a full cost-accounting system because the prohibitive cost bore no relationship to the actual usefulness of the system. Instead they have arrived at a system of indicators based on a partial cost-accounting system. This is more manageable and, moreover, more usable.[20] We have to remember that all cognitive or control systems bring with them additional management costs. Care has to be taken to suggest information systems that are viable in terms of both practical operation and of cost.

Cost accounting has doubtless been used *relatively* little because of its frequently amorphous nature. Accounting only has any real sense if objectives and observable control points are fixed in advance. It is the aim of management accounting to satisfy this demand.

We have to make sure that cost accounting is as functional as possible. It has to avoid exhaustive and general explanations and confine itself to strictly defined limits which can be varied in time, depending on the explicit objectives of management. We have to arrive at a true *accounting by objectives*.

Of all known methods of cost accounting the one which can best be applied to our problem of making an economic calculation of change is one which includes rational allocation of fixed costs and the method of pre-established costs with variance analysis.

B. Suggestion for New Methods of Human Resource Accounting

Our proposal is based on the rejection of an exhaustive evaluation of human capital and only collects certain financial data which are significant in terms of manpower resources. For the moment we only intend to suggest *simple* solutions which show that it would be easy to apply them, starting from *existing* information. Our methodology is pragmatic. We want to show that change can be measured *easily and cheaply*.

i. *The Criticism of Attempts at Accounting in Terms of Human Capital and the Balance Sheet*[21]

At the University of Michigan, Ann Arbor, in 1965, a team was set up around the sociologist R. Likert, which consisted of L. Brummet, a professor of accounting, and E. Flamholtz and W. C. Pyle. An experiment was conducted in the Barry Corporation, a firm employing 2000 workers. Since 1969 they have published a classical balance sheet and trading account as well as the same documents taking human resources into account (cf. Table 3.1).

It is not this first method which we intend to criticize, since it only takes account in the balance sheet of the costs generated when taking on and keeping personnel. These are included as an expenditure depreciation covering several accounting periods.

(a) *Attempts to evaluate human capital*[22]

The attempts which we oppose are more recent. B. Lev and A. Schwartz[23] try to make an intrinsic evaluation of human capital by actualizing each worker's future salary evaluated in comparison with the wages paid within the same enterprise to workers with the same degree of qualification, but whose age is different. The capital value is expressed in terms of cost and not in terms of productivity. Lev and Schwartz suggest the formula:

$$V_\zeta^* = \sum_{t=\zeta}^{T} \frac{I^*(t)}{(1+r)^{t-\zeta}}$$

where V_ζ^* represents the capital value of someone aged ζ, $I^*(t)$ represents the person's estimated earnings each successive period up to retirement, r represents the chosen rate of actualization, T represents the age of retirement.

This formula can be corrected by taking into account the probability $P(t)$ of dying before age t:

$$E(V_\zeta^*) = \sum_{t=\zeta}^{T} P_\zeta(t+1) \sum_{i=\zeta}^{t} \frac{I^*i}{(1+r)^{t-\zeta}}.$$

The method suggested by Hekimian and Jones aims only at determining the value of manpower which is scarce. Although the 'reserve price' system by means of which a figure is put on this manpower shocks one from a theoretical point

Table 3.1
Balance Sheet as at 31/12/71 (in dollars) after distribution of dividends

	Human resources taken into account	Conventional financial calculation only
ASSETS		
Fixed assets	4 634 458	4 634 458
Net investments in human resources	1 561 264	
trading results	12 810 346	12 810 346
other assets	209 419	209 419
	19 215 487	17 654 223
LIABILITIES		
Capital	9 403 395	9 403 395
Human resource capital	780 632	
long-term liabilities	5 190 252	5 190 252
deferred income taxes based upon full tax deductions for human resource costs	780 632	
short-term liabilities	3 060 576	3 060 576
	19 215 487	17 654 223

Profit and Loss Account 1971 (in dollars)

	Human resources taken into account	Conventional financial calculation only
Turnover	34 123 202	34 123 202
Cost of sales	21 918 942	21 918 942
Gross profit	12 204 260	12 204 260
Commercial and administrative costs	9 417 933	9 417 933
Profit before tax and deductions	2 786 327	2 786 327
Sundry deductions	383 174	383 174
Profit before tax	2 403 153	2 403 153
Human resources (net)	137 700	
Adjusted pre-tax profit	2 540 853	2 403 153
Federal taxes	1 197 850	1 129 000
Profit	1 197 850	1 129 000

Source: *Le Management*, décembre 1973.

of view, it is in fact a system which is implicitly used not only in enterprises but also in professional sport.

A more global method is the one suggested by Giles and Robinson.[24] It consists of determining by subtraction an initial human capital value equal to the over-all transfer value of the enterprise, less the value of the physical assets and comparing this with a second value calculated on share-capitalization (a method inspired by stock-exchange capitalization). This method is more remarkable for its pragmatic than for its scientific nature.

(b) A criticism of the search for the evaluation of human capital

The concept of human capital merits an intrinsic semantic criticism. As for the methods suggested, they can be criticized likewise from the accounting point of view.

The semantic criticism. The term human capital calls for several different comments:

Legally: capital is that which is the object of ownership, it is a part of a person's patrimony and something over which he exercises certain rights. The amount of work at the disposal of the enterprise is low and subject to strong conditions. Even when looked at from a positive point of view it is not possible to draw such an analogy.

Ethically: the notion of capital arises from a materialist concept of man, as seen by the instrumental concept of the worker which we have already had occasion to criticize. Man cannot be a unit of capital either from the ethical normative point of view or from the historical positivist point of view (the recent evolution identified above demonstrates this).

Pragmatically: man's potential is conditional. The whole of a man's life makes capital out of his experience and his know-how but his economic value is the result of a multitude of variables, many of which belong to and which fluctuate with the evolution of the system. A man's productivity depends very largely on his role in society, in the enterprise, and in his environment.[25]

Metrical: for reasons of time (evolution and instability of the value and meaning of the accounting unit in the long term) and for spatial reasons (anthropological and cultural difference) there cannot be an objective unit of measure of human capital.

For these reasons we therefore use the expression *human resources* and not human capital.

The accounting criticism. Even if we leave aside the question of whom the human capital on the balance sheet belongs to, we can still criticize the accounting aspect of human capital from a more operational point of view.

The total evaluation of the human capital of an enterprise would add but little in so far as the latter relies on the accounting system. Any attempt to try and calculate a human-capital average productivity ratio merely asserts that the basis of this calculation is arguable or without foundation. One wonders what use it would be, for one is caught in a vicious circle: productivity ⇒ human capital ⇒ productivity. In effect human capital is a function of its own productivity brought up to date, yet productivity is a partial function of human capital, which is tantamount to saying that the only non-relative link between productivity and capital is the length of time and the rate of actualization, i.e. two risky and/or arbitrary elements . . . On the other hand it is tantamount to ignoring that productivity depends on a large number of other variables such as investment, incorporation of technical progress, and organizational innovation.

The only useful models are the marginalist models, even if they are subject to the same ethical criticisms as the global models.[26] The variation in human capital and its relationship to its effects (to productivity amongst other things) can have a certain meaning and be of interest in defining a personnel policy. Opportunity costs can also serve as indicators when two alternative decisions are being studied. But let it be stated again that it is a (frequent) mistake to want to deduce the total evaluation of human capital by means of methods which have been conceived to compare alternative choices. The mistake arises because the marginalist theory is applied in far too general a way.

ii. *A Meaningful and Useful Accounting System: Collection of the Financial and Real Flow Concerned with Human Resources*

Even though it may be a vain task, we should not give up the search for a way of calculating human resources. In the same way that the assets on a balance sheet only show the real costs for the period of a *part* of the company's patrimony and in the same way that the liabilities do not show up all the company's financial obligations, our aim is not to perfect something which cannot be perfected, viz. the evaluation of the company's financial and/or human resources.

We shall take up a strictly accounting position, i.e. one based on past cost. We shall, however, add effective non-monetary costs to effective monetary costs.[27]

(a) *The differential view of the economic calculation of organizational change*

We are trying to evaluate the economic effect on the *enterprise* of change which is due to the introduction of new forms of job-design.

E_r is a collection of elements of the real total cost in a current Taylor-type organization, and E_r' is all the elements of the total real cost within a new organization. Current accounting systems enable us to evaluate a sub-group of E_r, $\mathcal{E}_r$, and a sub-group of E_r', $\mathcal{E}_r'$, both composed of the *identified* cost elements. The first line to take could well be to elicit all the elements in E_r and E_r' which do not appear either in $\mathcal{E}_r$ or in $\mathcal{E}_r'$. This is a difficult thing to try and there is no guarantee of success.

We can adopt a second approach which consists of saying that the evolution of the similar elements of E and of E' may be represented by the measurable variance $(\mathcal{E}_r' - \mathcal{E}_r)$. We implicitly reason this way every time we attribute to the variation of one sum a viability which is greater than the viability of the representativity of this sum. It is generally considered to be more exact to say that the per capita income in France has risen by 4.5% in one year, than to say that it is 17 000 francs. It is important to make this clear beforehand for the sake of the credibility of our methodological proposals.

We shall therefore attempt to identify the meaningful variations of the organizational system and we shall attribute them, for lack of anything better, to the change which has taken place.

(b) The method of rational allocation

Rational allocation is a method of allocating fixed or structural costs associated with homogeneous departments and which aims at correcting the effect of variations in the level of activity of the departments on the average cost of their unit of measurement.[28] The correction consists in keeping the average cost of the unit of measure at the level it would reach for the typical productivity of the department. One takes the level of normal activity (N) and uses it as a reference to link, on the one hand, the sum of the fixed costs (F) to be included in the production costs with, on the other hand, the real level of activity (n).

In accounting terms the following appears:

$$(a) \qquad n < N$$

93	Cost of production	$F \times \dfrac{n}{N}$	
976	Variance due to rational allocation	$F\left(1 - \dfrac{n}{N}\right)$	
906	Reflected expenses and shared costs		F

$$(b) \qquad n > N$$

93	Cost of production	$F \times \dfrac{n}{N}$	
906	Reflected expenses and shared costs		F
976	Variance due to rational allocation		$F\left(\dfrac{n}{N} - 1\right)$

Let us take $F = 30\,000$; $n_1 = 0.9$; $N = 1$ and $n_2 = 1.15$. For example, if the real financial cost $= 30\,000\,F$ and the output for March has been 10% below normal output (and not below maximum potential output), and for April output is 15% above, the accounts show the two situations quite clearly:

93 — Cost of Production					976 — Variance due to rational allocation			
March	90	27 000			March	3000	April	4500
April	115	34 500			(minus)	1500	(plus)	
	205	61 500					balance	1500

906 — Reflected expenses and shared costs

	March	30 000
	April	30 000
		60 000

Interpretation. In this simple case the costs recorded in the normal accounting system are fixed (fixed wages and constant intermediate consumption, for example) whatever the level of production. This is normally calculated at 100 items per month, the production cost being constant: 27 000/90 = 300 in March, 34 500/115 = 300 in April. The invariability of 'direct' unit costs is logical since the sales prices do not fluctuate in the immediate short-term along with work rhythms or events which affect production. Fluctuation in output is shown by the 'variance due to rational allocation' heading which gives the output positives and negatives. A simple reading of this heading will enable one at the end of the accounting period to evaluate the financial gap between the cost of normal output and real output. One of the principal complaints against this method is the subjectivity attached to the notion of the *normal* output level. In the paragraph below we shall see that this objection disappears of its own accord in the way we suggest applying the method.

We should like briefly to defend the principle of rational allocation. This method is tantamount to saying that fixed charges must only be included on a pro-rata basis with real output in comparison with a reference level which was previously judged to be normal. This ex-ante fixing of a norm shows quite clearly the operational object of the method, a method which is not content to go in for a historical cost analysis but which adds a *normative* criterion and thereby enables one to separate the gaps, study the causes, and take action so as to reduce them or rectify the norm, as the case may be.

Let us take the case of a workshop involving fixed costs of 1000 francs per month (e.g. rent) for a normal production output of 1000 items per month. The cost calculated includes 1 franc per item, by virtue of this, and hence it is possible to give estimates, to fix a unit sales price, and take advance orders. Let us suppose that because of a strike, or for some other reason, there is an output of 400 items in a particular month. It is impossible to rectify the estimated cost and the unit sales price. One cannot disregard the orders taken at the previously agreed price on the pretext that output only reached a total of 400, the fixed-cost price now being 1000/400 = 2.50 francs per item. The only sensible conclusion is to debit the missing 600 francs to an account which contains the cost of the strike for the workshop in question and to try and recuperate this sum by means of increased productivity over the following months.

(c) The adaptation of the method to the control of change

Let us take two cost-centre workshops, A and B, with the same number of workers and the same type of production. As with normal experimental procedure there is an experimental and a control group. If it proves impossible to have homogeneous experimental and control groups simultaneously,[29] there is another hypothesis which can be used; in this case A is the traditional pre-innovation workshop and B the same workshop after the introduction of the organizational change. This is, however, a less valid comparison than in the previous case of two parallel groups.

The *normal* level of activity (N) will be that of workshop A and the level of activity (n) of B will correspond to the real level of the method of simple rational allocation. The value differences will therefore be measured as f(B) — f(A).

We shall use four significant variables of the incidence of change: absenteeism, turnover, rejects, physical productivity.[30]

The cost of differential absenteeism between B and A will be charged to the 'variance due to differential absenteeism' account.

Let us take: 10 000 francs = fixed monthly charges of each of the two workshops, A and B,

8% (= 100) = average rate of absenteeism for A during the preceding periods

7% (= 101.01) = real rate of absenteeism for A during the monitored period

4% (= 104.17) = observed rate of absenteeism for B during the same period.

B's and A's production costs will be recorded under the following entries:

93	Production cost for B	10 417	
906	Reflected expenses and shared costs		10 000
9761	Variance due to differential absenteeism (B)		417
93	Production cost for A	10 101	
906	Reflected expenses and shared costs		10 000
9761	Variance due to differential absenteeism (A)		101

Absenteeism can be measured in hours lost in comparison with the normal working hours of all the personnel in the groups. It can very easily be measured by using an individual card-index or the timer-clock recording tape.

The comparison between the two variance accounts can be formulated by transferring the entries of the two variance accounts resulting from the differential absenteeism of A and B to a general account of variance due to organizational innovation.

9761	Variance due to differential absenteeism (A)	101	
9761	Variance due to differential absenteeism (B)	417	
97	Variance due to innovation (A)		101
97	Variance due to innovation (B)		417

The turnover can be measured directly by using the register of personnel taken on and personnel leaving. It is possible to ascertain the cost for each successive period. The previous cost of period p_i can be used as the basis for calculating period p_{i+1}.

In the same month three operatives from group A and one worker from group B left the company. The replacement cost as calculated from the accounting data of the preceding period is 4000 francs per worker.

9762	Cost of turnover (A)	12 000	
9762	Cost of turnover (B)	4000	
906			
or			
972	Costs and reflected depreciation expenses or Incorporated supplementary elements[a]		16 000

[a]If the accounting system does not record human resource fluctuations according to the method which we suggest above.

When transferred to a recapitulative account:

97	Variance due to innovation (A)	12 000	
97	Variance due to innovation (B)	4000	
9762	Cost of turnover (A)		12 000
9762	Cost of turnover (B)		4000

Rejects can be calculated by working from quality-control and production records. The cost for the given manufacturing stage can be worked out on the basis of the past cost worked out for the preceding period. It can be given a different completion weighting according to the stage reached.

A's rejects comprise 12 completely finished but 100% unusable items (unit cost = 15 F) and 2 completely finished but 50% usable items (unit cost = 7.50 F). B's rejects comprise 3 completely finished but 100% unusable items (unit cost = 15 F) and 2 partially finished but 100% unusable items (unit cost = 8.50 F).

9763	Cost of rejects for A	195	
9763	Cost of rejects for B	62	
972	Incorporated auxiliary elements		257

It is the 'Incorporated auxiliary elements' account which is credited because these amounts do not correspond to effective monetary expenditure. Together with the account which records unincorporated charges, this account enables us to re-establish the balance between cost accounting and general accounting so that the result of the latter RG is equal to the result of the former RC plus or minus the incorporation differences ($\pm$ ID) and plus auxiliary elements (AE):

$$RG = RC \pm ID + AE.$$

We can read off the organizational charge 'balance'[31] of the first three variables by making a comparison between the 'Variance due to organizational innovation' accounts for A and B.

97. Variance due to innovation (A)				97. Variance due to innovation (B)			
turnover	12 000	absenteeism	101	turnover	4000	absenteeism	417
rejects	195			rejects	62		
debit				debit			
balance	12 094			balance	3645		

The productivity level is determined in non-accounting terms and will be incorporated in a non-accounting balance sheet.

Table 3.2
Balance Sheet by Value of the Effects of Organizational Change
(beginning of March 1974)

Variables	A. (traditional organization)		B. (new organization)		B − A	
	−	+	−	+	−	+
absenteeism		101		417		316
turnover	12 000		4000			8000
rejects	195		62			133
productivity		150	450		600	
Totals	12 195	251	4512	417	600	8449
balance	11 944 $= (e_1)$		4095 $= (e_2)$		+ 7849 $= (e_{2n})$	

If there is no control group involved in the experiment, A represents B prior to reorganization. In this case there is only one set of entries which leads to the 'balance sheet' and in which A represents the average of the calculated variables over the three, six, or twelve final months of the previous organization.

If groups A and B, either synchronically or diachronically, are not numerically the same, the final totals can be weighted by applying coefficients which take into account, for example, the total wage bill for each group. This will enable us to obtain a variance $(e)'$ related to the measurement unit which can be either the worker, if groups A and B involve similar qualifications, or the wage $(e)''$ or a (composite) abstract index, if they do not.

Let us suppose that there are 20 workers in group A whose total wage bill comes to 40 000 F, and that in group B there are 20 workers whose total wage bill comes to 41 000 F. It is possible to make the following calculation:

$$(e_1)' = \frac{-11\,944}{40\,000} = -0.2986,$$

which means that lost production for every 1 F paid in wages is 0.2986 F and that

$$(e_2)' = \frac{-4095}{41\,000} = -0.099\,878$$

so that $(e_{2/1})' = (e_2)' - (e_1)' = +0.198\,722.$

This means that for 1 F paid in wages under the new system one escapes a loss of 0.198722 F, i.e. nearly 20% of lost production.

One final correction enables us to make the comparisons homogeneous. It is important, however, to calculate a variance relative to the number of workers, since this variance is a better way of representing the prospects of a wage increase for the individual worker in relation to the positive group earnings.

$$(e_1)'' \text{ becomes } \frac{-11\,944}{20} = -597.20$$

$$(e_2)'' \text{ becomes } \frac{-4095}{20} = -204.75$$

$$\text{and } (e_{2/1})'' = (e_2)'' - (e_1)'' = +392.45$$

Table 3.3
Balance Sheet by Value of the Effects of Organizational Change
(end of March 1974)

Variables	A		B		B − A	
	−	+	−	+	−	+
balance	−11 944 $= (e_1)$		−4095 $=(e_2)$		+7849 $=(e_{2/1})$	
total wage bill for group	40 000		41 000			
average variance for 1 F paid in wages	−0.2986 $=(e_1)'$		−0.099878 $=(e_2)'$		+0.198722 $=(e_{2/1})'$	
size of group	20		20			
average variance per worker	−597.20 $=(e_1)''$		−204.75 $=(e_2)''$		+392.45 $=(e_{2/1})''$	

This sum represents the *maximum* wage variance which management could grant to those workers who are part of the new organizational system, compared with the others, as long as it could be shown that, on the one hand, the positive result achieved by B compared with A is a lasting result and that, on the other hand, other physical or monetary conditions remain unchanged.

Our only desire has been to show that it is possible to go beyond the stage of mere criticism or protestations of powerlessness where the measurability of the economic effects of change are concerned. It is possible to set up *uncomplicated* apparatus to measure the *localized* effects of new forms of job-design. It is possible to evaluate a sufficient number of economic variables to be able to arrive at a significant result.

If the balance sheet worked out in this way reveals that the variance $e_{2/1} = e_2 - e_1$, is not positive, there are several ways in which this can be interpreted. None of them, *a priori*, calls the efficiency of the change into question:

perhaps the number of *economic* variables is insufficient.

perhaps there exists a *synergy* between groups A and B so that it is no longer possible for A to be considered as fulfilling the usual conditions of a traditional organizational system (this has already been observed, cf. above). In this case two balance sheets can be drawn up, one of which compares B and A (contemporary groups) and the other B and a group A' (a fictional group having the same average performance as A before the change was introduced).

perhaps the negative balance at the local level can be compensated for by *subsidiary effects* of an economic nature at the *global* company level.

perhaps the experiment has yet to reach its *threshold of effectiveness*.

the negative balance may well represent an apparent additional *necessary* cost (e.g. conditions of hygiene, safety) which will have to be absorbed either by the profit margin or by a price increase. Even in this case, however, long-term positive effects on the firm's costs have to be taken into account (decrease in the number of accidents leading to a reduction of industrial accidents or to a slowing down of the rate of increase of such accidents)[32] and on the social costs for society as a whole.

It is possible to use more sophisticated allocation indices or calculation bases (personnel costs for calculating $(e)'$, or the number of workers for calculating $(e)''$) than the more simple demonstration ones we have suggested. In order to be able to do that, it is enough to take local job-design conditions, and the nature and quality of available information into account. The number of workers can be weighted by using coefficients of qualification.

By including in the analysis of the 'balance sheet' a time vector, comprising references which correspond to significant company or environmental events, one will, after a certain number of months, arrive at an interpretation of the effects of organizational innovation which is as broad and as unsubjective as it is possible to be.

iii. *Adaptations to the Accounting System with a View to Taking Account of Movements of Human Resources*

It is not a question of evaluating human resources but more simply of recording the expenditure flow in such a way that, on the one hand, outgoings which extend beyond the current accounting period are counted as investments, and that, on the other hand, any events which affect the movement of personnel are likewise recorded in the accounted costs.

Table 3.4

Period	Notable event	$e_{2/1}$	$(e_{2/1})'$	$(e_{2/1})''$	Observations
March 1974	2nd month of experiment for group B	+7849	+0.198722	+392.45	productivity increase for B (required rhythm attained)
April 1974	3rd month of experiment for group B	+9200	+0.1992	+397	
May 1974	Slowing down of manufacturing programme (economic environment)	+4500	+0.051	+ 86	
June 1974	4 weeks sick-leave on full pay for one of workers in group B	−512	−0.006	− 9	

(a) *Accounting for human resources – the three methods of allocating costs connected with human resources*

In order to be able to classify costs we are obliged to identify in the accounts the elements relating to recruitment, training, and upkeep of personnel. It is because of this that a fraction of the wages and salaries paid to workers and management (recorded in the 'personnel costs' account) is allocated to these three ends. Bills for fees from recruiting and training agencies (recorded in the 'Work, supplies, and external services' account) and a proportion of the personnel department's stationery and office goods are handled the same way.

The first method consists of identifying those costs which are part of the investment in human resources. It is done as the costs are incurred. It is easy to do this for the salaries of personnel who deal exclusively with recruiting and training (a rarity in small or medium-sized companies) or for fees and expenditure connected specifically with recruiting or training. There are other cases in which such costs are difficult to identify and allocate directly, and which therefore make this a difficult method to adopt. Such is the case both with the fraction of wages and salaries paid to supervisors and managers who are involved part-time in recruiting and training, and with the proportion of intermediate consumption of energy and office goods.

The other two methods have recourse to cost accounting in order to evaluate the investment expenditure.

One of the methods consists of creating a functional cost centre for personnel recruiting and training, starting from certain elements of the cost of the personnel department.

Recruiting and training can likewise be taken into account by incorporating a part of the costs incurred based either on a fixed scale (e.g. one-eighth of the foreman's wage) or on a variable scale by breaking down on to monthly cards the time spent by different categories of personnel (certain managers, certain supervisors, certain workers) on activities of which one would like to calculate the cost.

It is possible to calculate recruiting and training costs independent of the cost-accounting system, should such a system exist. They can also be incorporated as an auxiliary department if the company goes in for cost accounting by departments.

By using a card-index system, it is possible to calculate the training 'production', i.e. number of workers recruited, number of workers trained, by homogeneous category.

It is necessary to create a certain number of homogeneous categories which do not necessarily correspond to the qualification scale but which are determined on such criteria as the recruitment network, type of training, labour shortage, difficulty and probable cost of recruitment . . . Direct costs will be allocated directly to each category. As for indirect costs, they can be allocated on a time pro rata basis, according to information recorded on individual cards filled in by recruiting and training staff (Table 3.5).

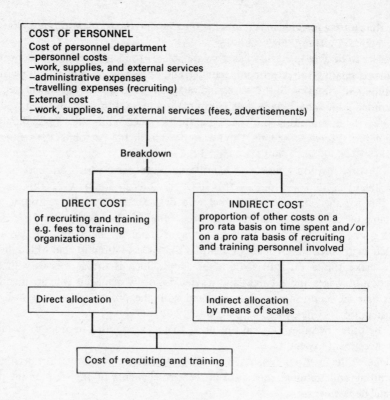

Fig. 3.1

Table 3.5

Mr K . . . . recruiting department					June 1974	cost per hour
Categories	Coefficient	To be recruited	Applicants	Appointments made	Time spent	Allocated cost
A		4	43	4	100	
B						
C		10	12	8	28	
.						
.						
F		10	20		47	
			75		=175 hrs	

When the cost of recruiting and training is calculated by category of personnel, it can be assumed that when a person leaves the company the non-amortized remainder of the cost is a cost chargeable entirely to the current accounting period. The net investment for the period will be equal to: Investment

in Human Resources = cost of recruiting and training − regularization of turnover cost − paying off the recruiting cost for the period.

The cost of training and recruiting for the month of June is 47 000 F. Three
workers and one manager left during the month (unit cost of the recruiting and
training = 3500 F and 22 000 F respectively). The investment in human
resources to be amortized on 30 June is 252 000 F (monthly amortization =
2.5%).

30.06

207	Investment in human resources	47 000	
79	Unincorporated costs relating to human resources		47 000
	Total cost of recruiting and training		
79	Unincorporated costs relating to human resources	32 500	
207	Investment in human resources		32 500
	Disinvestment for the period due to persons leaving		
681	Allowance for depreciation	6300	
2078	Amortization of the investment in human resources		6300

Balance Sheet

Gross investment	+14500	
Depreciation	− 6300	

Trading Account

Share in amortization	6300	Cost	14 500

The third method consists of taking the same results and drawing up a non-
accounting balance sheet of investment made in human resources. This information is not incorporated in either the balance sheet or the trading account.

(b) Time adjustments made in the human resource investments

Amortization of human resource investments must comply with the traditional
criteria, viz. that the length of time taken must coincide by and large with the
life-expectation of the object in question and that the amounts to be amortized
must be dated so that only non-amortized sums are amortized. In this respect it
is interesting to keep a monthly index-card for each category of personnel which
records the amount invested in recruiting and training (Table 3.6).

The first method consists of taking account only of the investments and
amortizing them, e.g. straight-line method. Amortization for the month of June
1974 will comprise a certain number of terms a_i for personnel in category A
(40 = 1/2.5%, when the system has been working for some time), a certain

Table 3.6

Investment in human resources				June 1974
Categories	Amounts	Monthly rate of amortization	Amount	First and last dates of amortization
A	20 000	2.5%	500	30/6/74–30/9/77
B	10 000	3%	300	30/6/74–31/3/77
. . . .				
F	17 000	5%	850	30/6/74–31/1/76
	47 000	3.51%	1650	30/6/74–31/10/76

number of terms b_i for personnel in category B (here $34 = 33 + $ a remainder of $\frac{1}{3}$), and a certain number of terms f_i for personnel in category F(20).

The amortization of the investment in human resources at 30 June 1974 will be the sum of

$$a_1 + \ldots + (a_{\text{June 74}} = 500) + b_1 + \ldots + (b_{\text{June 74}} = 300) +$$

$$+ f_1 + \ldots + (f_{\text{June 74}} = 850).$$

This information can be read directly from the monthly investment cards.

When the system is too difficult to refine or too unmanageable, an average rate of amortization can be used (in this case 47 000 F to be amortized at 3.51% per month from 30/6/74 to 31/10/76) without the need to carry out a breakdown by category. The result is less good but also less costly.

The second method takes population movements into account: arrivals and departures of new personnel. It implies a fuller monthly card-index investment system (Table 3.7). In this table adjustable information has been underlined. It is updated in pencil by taking details from individual index-cards and including them on the monthly card, if and when a worker leaves the firm (Table 3.8).

Each worker has a recruitment date which enables us to go straight to the monthly card which records the investment made in human resources. This will indicate the number of outstanding payments according to each category. Let us suppose that a worker (F) recruited and trained in June 1974, leaves the company on 31 August 1974. The investment made in this worker will already have been amortized at the end of June, of July, and August. The loss made on the non-amortized investment will be equal to the sum of the outstanding monthly payments.

$$\sum_{i=\text{September 74}}^{i=\text{January 76}} f_i = 50 \times 17 = 850.$$

The method can be improved by keeping a personnel card-index system in such a way that each worker's individual card can be credited with the investment made for each worker (Table 3.8).

Whether these cards are filled in and kept by the accounts department or by the personnel department, they do not mean a great increase in work, because of the amount of information which has already been dealt with. Use of computers can make the whole operation much easier.

If worker N leaves the firm on 31 August 1974, the card enables us to see straight away that his recruiting cost has already been completely amortized and that of the cost of his complementary training (machine adjustment course No. 73/103 June 1974) there remains:

$$\sum_{i=\text{September 74}}^{i=\text{January 75}} (f_i)' = 15 \times 6 = 90.$$

Table 3.7

Investments in human resources

						June 1974			
Categories	Numbers concerned	Amounts	Cost per worker	Rate of amortization	Monthly amortization per worker	Number of workers	Total monthly amortization	Departures	First and last amortization
A	2	20 000	10 000	2.5%	250	2	500	0	6/74-9/77
B	5	10 000	2000	3%	60	3	180	2	6/74-3/77
.									
.									
F	17	17 000	1000	5%	50	16	800	1	6/74-1/76
Totals	24	47 000					1480		

Table 3.8

Name: N . . . .
Starting Date:

Investment in Recruiting and Training

Date	Nature	Total sum	Rate of Amortization	Monthly amount	Amortization Period	Observations
October 1972	R	800	5%	40	October 72 to May 74	
June 1973	T	300	5%	15	June 73 to January 75	Training to adjust machines Op. 73/103

As for the person who is taken on to replace N in September 1974, ᵢ
initial recruiting and training cost will be calculated on the monthly investmeᵢ
card and then transferred to his personal card. In September the firm will recor
the cost of N's replacement as an investment and will begin to amortize it fron
the end of September onwards.

This simple system enables us to calculate the financial effects of changes
in personnel. We take into account not only the losses incurred when a worker
leaves, costs which are based on costs generated in the past, but all current
costs, by calculating the replacement investment cost of human resources. The
cost of this calculation is directly proportional to the degree of precision, so that
each firm will have to find its own optimum cost-advantage point, depending on
its size and the existing administrative and/or computer system in existence. All
these methods can be applied to centralized or decentralized accounting centres.
It is perfectly possible for autonomous groups to manage their own cards based
on information received – indeed, this is desirable.

Each cost centre incorporates these elements, amortization and disinvestment
costs into its cost accounting. In the books, it will appear as an aggregate of all
the figures. There will therefore be, on the one hand, entries in the asset
accounts 'Investment in human resources', and 'Amortization of investment in
human resources', and, on the other hand, in the management account
'Unincorporated costs relating to human resources'. It is also possible to create a
new management account ('cost of personnel departure') so that the trading
account at the end of the accounting period will allow us to read off directly
the total amount of investment (credit) and the total amount of the disinvestment so as to avoid any confusion in their balancing out.

During the month of August 1974 seven people left the firm. The disinvestment costs, when evaluated as above, amount to 23 000 F. The related
amortization so far carried out amounts to 12 000 F. For the rest, amortization
and investment are calculated as normal for the month of August.

We must remember that this calculation can have no fixed effect. For this to
be achieved one has to reincorporate the total amount of the net investment for
the accounting period when working out the fiscal result: = Investment – disinvestment – depreciation.

Regularization for disinvestment

31/8/74

79	Unincorporated charges relating to human resources		
or			
69	*or* cost of departure	23 000	
2078	Amortization of investment in human resources	12 000	
207	Investments in human resources		35 000
	Departure of two technicians and five workers		
	Total investment 35 000, amortization already		
	made up to and including 31/8/74: 12 000		

Record of investment and amortization for month
31/8/74

681	Allowance for depreciation	5000	
2078	Amortization of investment in human resources		5000
207	Investment in human resources	9000	
79	Unincorporated charges relating to human resources		9000
	Cost of recruiting and initial training for month, according to monthly investment card		

(c) Cost accounting of change

In addition to applying the method which has already been suggested[33] it consists of bringing together on the one hand the results of the method inspired by rational allocation and, on the other hand, the accounting results.[34] These are centralized in accounts dealing with functional costs such as 'Cost of Absenteeism' and 'Cost of turnover'.

The cost to the firm of absenteeism will be evaluated by aggregating the 'Variances due to differential absenteeism'. In the same way the cost of turnover will be the sum of the 'Costs of personnel departure'. It will be seen that we have quite resolutely adopted the *real historic* costs point of view and that we have done so without taking account of loss in productivity. We have done this for two reasons. The first is a tactical reason; it does not seem to us to be healthy to embellish the balance sheet of change too much by trying to over-evaluate the effects of traditional organization on absenteeism and turnover. The second reason arises from the need for coherence with our analysis of *isoproductive* time.[35] It is in effect difficult to evaluate lost production, because of the *elasticity of production per unit of time*. A 4% loss in working hours within a semi-autonomous group can be more than made up by an increase in the workers' voluntary effort (*intensity* of work) to reach output objectives in spite of the absenteeism. Everything else being equal, it seems to us a waste of time to calculate lost production, hence we have only taken account of actual outgoings.

It would, however, be possible to take lost productivity into account as a *complementary* index, by calculating the cost of absenteeism in terms of output. This would take into account production lost because of absenteeism, but corrected by applying a coefficient lower than one. It would enable us to allow for the hypothesis which says that lost time is (or can be) less productive.

Cost of absenteeism in terms of output = average hourly physical productivity $\times$ margin on variable cost $\times$ (number of hours absent $\times$ corrective coefficient $Cc < 1$).

It is possible to fix a maximum absenteeism objective[36] by taking the average annual rate and measuring the periodic differences in order to identify the absences and to try and reduce them. These differences can be evaluated in lost hours, a neutral but not very significant way, or evaluated in terms of fixed costs, or, lastly, in terms of output.

It is possible to work in the same way with other variables and act on them if there is a well-developed decentralized information system. Consistently high turnover in one workshop can lead to investigations which reveal the reasons for leaving and provide preventive measures, which are valid for this shop as well as being applicable in other cases.

It is also possible to calculate the cost in terms of replacement cost, in order to accentuate the negative aspect of turnover, at least in the short term. This means replacing the non-amortized recruiting cost by the cost of replacement. Because of the evaluation of the average cost of recruiting and training, this means 'over-evaluating' the loss due to a person's leaving (implicitly deemed productive). This cost can be useful complementary information, for the loss of a worker from category F (cf. above) recruited at least 20 months beforehand would go 'unnoticed' from the accounting point of view, since the cost of recruiting and initial training would have been entirely amortized. This is a case where it would be a question of making sure that the head of the workshop or the group knew the cost of replacement, so as to make sure that the necessary effort is made to integrate the worker better in his work place and reduce the turnover.

The flexibility which cost accounting gives in its own right makes it superfluous for us to suggest solutions.

We shall suggest therefore evaluation calculated in terms of past costs, and for certain variables, we shall suggest non-accounting evaluations in terms of replacement costs or in terms of output.

C. Innovation – The Economic Calculation[37]

The various ways we have suggested of evaluating the economic effects created when new forms of job-design are introduced are not exhaustive. For the most part they take into account those variables and their localized effects which it is easy to identify.

There are, however, numerous *indirect* effects (cf. above). It ought to be possible to determine all the elements of the total economic cost of E_r and not those of the known sub-section $\mathcal{E}_r$. This is what Davis does.[38]

Certain of these elements are internal to the firm; others affect it indirectly through the economic environment. There are others which have no repercussions on the firm but which affect economic activity in general.

Any *static* economic calculation is in any case not enough. Our suggestions for adjusting the human resource investment have the merit of establishing a bridge between the differing trading periods which are likely to profit from the *supposed* effects of those investments. The task still remains, however, to measure how long these effects will last in the long and the short term. Will the positive effects currently observed be maintained? Our study has no ambitions in that direction. We have, in effect, to come back to the psycho-sociological concept of change if we are to find a justification for what we assert to be the need to set up new forms of job-design. We have to stop using economic reasons *for* explaining the willingness or the desire to change. Change will come about for non-economic reasons, for the economic structures are sufficiently 'flexible to allow change to take place in the short and in the long term. Keynes has already said that we shall all be dead in the long term.

If the result of the balance sheet of change in terms of value is not a positive one, we can make up the difference by logging the advantages and disadvantages which have not been evaluated.

There are four possible hypotheses:

the balance is lasting and *positive*, at least in the short term. There is no major economic obstacle in the way of change.

the balance is *negative*, at least in the short term. It is necessary to set the differential cost of the new organization against the probable updated costs involved in the tension and disputes inherent in the status quo (traditional inhibiting organization).

if the cost is offset, change is *justified* from a micro-economic point of view.[39]

if the cost is not offset, change can still be justified for reasons of *external savings*. By adjusting the costing and relative price system a new equilibrium can be achieved. The Government will have to intervene in the market with subsidies and/or, for want of anything better, legal obligations so as to unify working conditions.

the differential cost cannot even be offset by external savings. The Government, enterprises, and unions can impose change by *adjusting relative prices*, either for ethical reasons or for political expedience.

At the end of this chapter devoted to the economic calculation of change, let us once again go over what we have been doing.

Any analysis of the economic effects connected with the introduction of new forms of job-design runs up against two difficulties:

current accounting practice makes it impossible to identify all the input.

there is no simple instrument for measuring the net output from change. Non-financial elements have still to find their place in this output, yet these are still elements which it is difficult to quantify and it is a lasting problem to know how much weight to give them, with a view to incorporating them into the total economic calculation (in Davis's sense). Only by developing the social indicators will it be possible to include these new performance criteria progressively (cf. chap. 2–ii) within, or in liaison with, the economic calculation.

Our present contribution has been limited to methodological suggestions made with a view to improving the calculation of a particular input and with a view to constructing a *simple* evaluation model of the economic effects of change.

This is not an exhaustive study and it does not include, for example, the differential cost of physical investment, or specific equipment necessary for improving both extrinsic and intrinsic working conditions (implicit in job-enrichment and the creation of semi-autonomous groups). Although we have raised this important question (cf. Chap. 2), we have not really incorporated it into our way of calculating because the evolution of the differential cost of equipment does not pose any accounting difficulty. Besides, in the observed experiments, the methods departments always begin by evaluating the cost of new equipment necessary for the reorganization of work.

In the same way we have done no more than touch on the need to take *non-financial output* into account (cf. p. 147). The current state of research into this area means it is not possible to incorporate financial and non-financial results into the economic calculation. It is only possible to set them against each other. We do not have a strong contribution to make in this area.

Finally, we have not determined all the elements of the economic balance sheet of change. We have concentrated on the so-called auxiliary elements (those which the recruiting system does not identify as cost elements). We should like, however, to point out that when making a differential economic calculation, one would have to incorporate elements such as training levies. For a firm which does not spend the whole[40] of its statutory training levy on training its own personnel and which consequently has to pay the difference to the Government, the training cost required by the introduction of a plan for improving working conditions can quite easily be allocated to the proportion of the levy previously paid directly to the tax authorities. This would bring with it a sizeable reduction in the cost of organizational innovation and improve the result of the economic calculation.

4. THE PROPAGATION OF CHANGE

In order to evaluate the probabilities involved in carrying through change, it is necessary to determine which paths can be taken by the extension of new forms of job-design (intrinsic conditions) and of extrinsic conditions. There are many paths, some of which are outside the enterprise (markets, social and professional organization), and some of which are inside (behaviour of workers, consultants, and those in charge of training). Nevertheless no combination of any of these will be enough unless the Government of the day, through its official bodies, acknowledges and attempts to extend the irreversible nature of change.

A. External Propagation of Change through the Market-Place

Any change in working conditions can be analysed either as an innovation which the market of goods and services can extend, or as a condition which workers 'impose' on the job market.

i. *The Market of Goods and Services*

(a) *Organizational innovation*

Certain aspects of new forms of job-design or working conditions correspond to an analysis in terms of truly productive innovation, others to complementary by-products of the quality of the products.

When the result is positive, new forms of job-design are a productive innovation in the same way that the invention or production of new effective equipment is productive. It is in the interest of companies to extend such organizational changes so as to maintain and even improve their competitive position on the product market.

In the same way certain new forms of job-design (notably semi-autonomous groups) bring with them a high degree of flexibility when it comes to adapting products rapidly to the needs of the market and to diversifying (e.g. Olivetti's adding machines; the possibility at Ciapem for one work-group to produce different models). Under the same conditions of productivity and over-all economic cost, these new forms are a *plus*[41] under existing working conditions. From this point of view such an innovation is productive and the product market can 'impose' the propagation thereof.

Managers are very responsive to the argument about the management flexibility which new organizational forms will encourage: greater ability to adapt products to markets; flexibility of planning and launching, supply and manufacture; greater internal mobility of production personnel because of their polyvalence.

Finally the *plus* can be carried over to the product itself. Suggestions have been made for a quality label called 'working conditions' which would enable people to identify products which come from firms which have something to show in this field.[42] The plus becomes a consumer product which the customer can take into consideration when choosing, and which he can weigh up when he works out the cost/quality ratio of the product.

(b) *Factors which encourage and impede propagation*

'Innovation is no longer a matter of choice' is the way Rigny[43] sums up the situation in which enterprises find themselves today. They have to adapt to the economic environment or face a social death penalty: 'the enterprise has to innovate to grow, and grow to survive'. This is the way the systems school (Von Bertallanfy, Katz and Kahn) spotlight the irreversibility, the entropy, and the absence of choice. They complete and go beyond Schumpeter's entrepreneur theory where innovation was a kind of state of grace reserved for an élite and where the only sanction was the difference in profit.

It is easy to guess the factors which impede the propagation of change: anxiety about the internal evolution and consequences of the new organization in terms of division of power, uncertainty as far as the calculated results are concerned, and the possibility of being able to bear the financial costs of the change and its consequences in the short term. In spite of this we can say that the law of natural expansion,[44] to which innovation is subject in our social system, will be victorious over the factors that impede progress.

ii. *The Job Market*

We have already seen how in a large number of enterprises certain indicators, such as the difficulty of recruiting young people, have sparked off research into new forms of organization and have led directly to experiments being carried out.

(a) *Supply and demand of working conditions*

On the job market there exists a system of supply and demand. Without the bonus payments demanded for poor working conditions there would be no labour supply. There is likewise a problem for certain jobs which do not satisfy a minimum number of conditions required by the worker. . . .

The neo-classical analyses[45] in terms of supply and demand of labour tend to explain these facts. Job conditions are an economic good which is supplied by employers and demanded by workers. Becker's notion of 'full income' takes both monetary and 'psychic income' into account. The worker can obtain a larger amount of the former by giving up part of the latter. On the job market the worker will maximize his 'full income' by an optimum combination of wages and working conditions. Owen's model is an attempt to supply an explanation for the choice between income and leisure.

(b) *The insufficiency or non-pertinence of the analysis in terms of supply and demand of working conditions*

These analyses are interesting and incorporate a certain number of the ideas we have put forward during our study. There is, however, one hereditary default which the neo-classical models do have and which our essentially *dynamic* point of view does not. They are based on an implicit postulate of *static* analysis in terms of a *zero* sum *choice*. Tchobanian sums up Owen and Wolfelsperger's idea in the following terms: 'Since the improvement of working conditions is part of the indirect cost of the work factor, it is necessary to see the supply of working conditions by the enterprises in terms of a possible substitution between wages and the expenditure undertaken with a view to this improvement.'[46]

Such an analysis in terms of substitution is eminently static. As for regarding a flow of expenditure leading to lasting effects as an indirect cost, our accounting analysis made from Likert's and Davis's ideas is enough to prove the absence of any foundation to this. From this point of view we subscribe to Gélinier's analysis[47] in terms of the 'profitability'[48] of social investment both from a micro-economic (enterprise) and a macro-economic (harmful social effects) point of view.

In spite of these defaults the analysis of working conditions in terms of supply and demand (worker's point of view) takes very careful account of the situation which has been created, or which can develop on the job market, when companies offer jobs where the intrinsic and/or extrinsic conditions are bad, or felt to be bad. In Chapters 1.1 and 2.1 we underlined the fact that enterprises are becoming more and more aware of the difficulties of recruiting and training young people. These difficulties are largely explained by the above considerations. It ought to urge them on to make a qualitative improvement of the supply of working conditions, not from a static point of view of the substitution of salary for working conditions, but from the dynamic point of view which we are defending, based on the socio-technical approach.

B. External Propagation through Social Organization

Under this heading we shall be looking at the part played by professional organizations and the strength of public opinion.

i. *Professional Organizations*

For a long time now trade unions have been involved in claims dealing with extrinsic working conditions. They have obtained results which recent legislation will continue to develop. In this area the unions are a force for the propagation of change. While trade unions abroad are also involved in intrinsic working conditions, in France they are more reticent, both for historical reasons (relations with employers) and because of the ambiguity of the employers' attitude when new forms of organization are tried out experimentally. We have already shown that from our point of view any dissociation of economic motives from psychological motivation to work, both by theoreticians and by practitioners (consultants, management, hierarchy), is a tactical *mistake* which can only serve to consolidate trade-union mistrust. Once this obstacle has been removed we believe that unions in France will become the same *efficient force* for the propagation of change that they are abroad.

Nevertheless the evolution of the labour market comes up against reticence where non-economic motivation is concerned. The French trade unions cannot at the moment see beyond the quantitative/qualitative advantage relationship (wage, working hours/working conditions). Certain unskilled workers involved in shift work see such a financial advantage in their working conditions that they are not willing to support trade-union claims for any improvement. As a result the unions are understandably cautious and pragmatic; they do not want to fight their own members. In addition, for ideological reasons, they do not wish to become part of an economic process which they basically disapprove of. In spite of widespread knowledge about the positive results we have been discussing, it has not been possible for the qualitative aspect of work to make headway.

In March 1975 the FO, CFTC, and the CGC gave their approval to the CNPF's proposed agreement on working conditions. The CGT and the CFDT, however, refused to sign because they felt the proposals were too vague. We feel that considerable progress can be seen in the fact that people are not only looking at job-enlargement and changes in working hours but that there is also serious, albeit cautious, talk of setting up semi-autonomous work groups and giving them a good measure of autonomy. This is being done in spite of the risks of a certain redistribution of power which is involved. There is talk of limiting shift work and output-linked pay schemes. There is talk of changing the role of the supervisory grades. Unions ought to be able to turn the many declarations of positive intentions to their own account when it comes to reaching agreements in various sectors of the economy. In spite of the length of time involved in putting such measures through (up to two years in some cases), it seems to us that such a contractual policy is infinitely more realistic and hence more effective than mere Government legislation.

In other countries, employers' organizations are playing a very important role, for example, the Swedish SAB. These organizations are beginning to assume the same degree of importance in France. The CNPF is still rather timid but other, more homogeneous organizations, are more advanced — the Centre des Jeunes Dirigeants d'Entreprise, the association called Entreprise et Progrès, GERIS, ANDCP, the Institut Entreprise et Personnel. On an international level the OECD and the EEC have held conferences.[49]

ii. *Public Opinion*

In any democracy information about working conditions, and particularly public exposure of the most intolerable working conditions, is part of the arsenal which public authorities have at their disposal for increasing people's awareness and acceptance of a programme of change. Information on the energy crisis and growing concern for ecological issues are important means for implementing national policy in these areas. In the same way information about certain working conditions can contribute to the creation of public awareness.[50] This will, in turn, press for change and even, in certain cases, for example, costly safety precautions in blast-furnaces, create a collective acceptance of the possible extra expense caused by such change.

In spite of the reticence indicated there is, nevertheless, evidence of progress. The number of international conferences and meetings, the evolution of trade-union attitudes, and the proliferation and development of experiments are all indicative of the extent to which the idea of organizational change has been diffused.

C. Internal Propagation of Change

The techniques of change and the development of organizations are more a question of state of mind than of total investment made. This is the opinion of an industrialist confronted with training problems and with promoting management education.[51] In other words, the propagation of change depends more on the will to carry it through than on the financial means employed. This is all the more so within the enterprise.

It must be stressed that one of the reasons for communication problems between different social cultural groups within the firm is *language*. It is frequently a source of misunderstanding and hence of potential blockages. It is essential to be precise about the *semantic* content of the information available prior to negotiations and decisions; thus a frequently heard expression such as 'diabolical pace' is open to misinterpretation by the hierarchy because the workers actually manage to finish their work an hour early. When added to varying individual ability, the different perception of events which language provokes is a source of misunderstanding and of conflict.

i. *Management and Consultants*

In the majority of cases studied it is the will of a single individual or, more often, of a single group at the top of the hierarchy which is the determining factor, at least where a project has progressed beyond the experimental stage. The desire for change is the most clearly evident in the choice of the people called in. By calling in a particular, well-known, multi-national company as a consultant, one is opting for a particular solution. This is the inverse of the socio-technical approach which aims at working out an original solution.

On the other hand the fact that a halt is called to the extension of successful experiments shows that the division of the hierarchy into conservationists and innovators is the reason for the delay in many cases.

It is therefore of the greatest importance to encourage the idea of the necessity of change. Information about successful examples, imitation of examples from abroad, and comparison between experiments can all be effective, since the initiative always come from management or the hierarchy. When change is introduced at this level, the economic study of change and diffusion of results can make a decisive contribution and allay any fears about the results due to change.

ii. *Educators*

Because of the importance which is attached to training problems involving man and methods in the supervisory and management grades (cf. above), full-time or part-time educators from inside or outside the enterprise, or training bodies, all of whom have been won over to new methods of job-design, can be powerful forces for change.

It should be noted that the differences in status of the various members of management and the technostructure engender differences in the conception of training (ends and means) as a result of the varying nature of the constraints imposed on the hierarchy. These constraints are transferred to the educators and can possibly lead to some distortion in the training of workers.

The importance of the role of educators is underlined in the reports[52] on the contribution made by training to the improvement in working conditions. At the suggestion of the two working parties appointed to advise on initial and continuing education, the Secretary of State for Manual Workers has given the ANACT the task of organizing an important experimental course on the training of educators. Some experimental work has been organized by certain companies (e.g. PUK and BSN) and training bodies (e.g. CESI-Est) with a view to running courses for managers which will bring together the economic constraints, the social dimension of investment, and improvement in living conditions at work.

iii. *Workers*

Successful experiments into new working conditions ought to incite workers to ask for further experiments to bet set up and carried out, either with or without their unions. It should be noted that in France trade-unionism is an important but minority fact and is a movement which is undergoing considerable upheaval. The unions are not concerned with asking for an improvement in intrinsic working conditions. Unskilled workers and operatives in general are, however, potentially interested. They will be all the more interested once they know that viable solutions exist and have been successfully implemented in certain companies. In this way the people who are directly concerned can influence the unions' position. If the unions do not adapt there is a risk that they will thereby exclude themselves from the real management–worker dialogue on job-design, whatever the provisions of the 1973 law on working conditions may be.

The immediate duality or opposition between wage-rises and costly improvements in working conditions provokes internal tension amongst the workers and unions because of the different order of priorities.

Certain events can precipitate the increase in speed of the propagation of change. In this way an 'exemplary' dispute – such as that at Lip, the French watch-making company, in 1973 – can amplify the diffusion of information about working conditions. This was how the Renault (Le Mans) dispute in 1971, which started out as a wage-claim, was interpreted by the outside world as being a dispute about working conditions. It is now considered to be the event which helped to encourage claims based on working conditions. In this way our didactic and (of necessity) dichotomous representation of the various forms or sources of propagation must not allow one to forget dialectic interrelations, e.g. between workers' actions (strikes) and public opinion.

D. The Specific Role of Public Bodies

The role of public bodies is to prevent distortions in the way markets function, particularly the labour market.

Public bodies can have a catalytic role in this area, within the general framework of Government economic intervention. In this respect governments' desire for a change in working conditions should not be evaluated merely according to the volume of legislation, but also, and especially, according to the effort put into encouragement. Government effectiveness will be measured in this, as in all areas, by the amount of money allocated to the encouragement of change. It is the initial effort which is decisive, because the natural forces for propagation only become operative once a certain level of concrete results has been reached.

i. *The Legal Aspect*

Statutory legislation is particularly applicable, it would seem, to extrinsic conditions. It aims at unifying working conditions, banning the continuation of unacceptable situations, and, moreover, at guaranteeing indirectly the equality of competing conditions. It should also enable us to make sure that study groups and participatory decision-making processes are set up.

The December 1973 law was introduced with this objective in view. It still needs to be worked on and made more precise in nature.[53]

The report of the Sudreau Committee[54] pays particular attention to the problems raised in this book, although the object of the committee's proposals is not directly linked to job-design. The report includes a certain number of ideas which we have defended, e.g. 'denunciation of productivity' (pp. 16 and 36), 'questioning the organizational principles of the enterprise' (pp. 17 and 37), the need to facilitate the dialogue within the enterprise in spite of 'the difficulty of inter-personal and hierarchical relationships' (pp. 25, 38, 41, and 42 ff.), the need to increase motivation and individual promotion prospects (p. 45). The possibilities for Government action are frequently mentioned (pp. 28 f., 40). Although there are those in some unions who will be disappointed by the note of prudence sounded by a number of proposals, it seems that any legislative step taken to improve current conditions within the enterprise will be appreciated by a sizeable proportion of the workers. From this point of view, company reforms made by law should create a favourable framework for the development of successful experiments into life at work.

ii. *The Economic, Financial, and Fiscal Aspect*

The role of ANACT is to study means of encouragement or, possibly, of dissuasion, although its scope depends largely on the funds available.[55]

The great advantage of a law such as the Continuing Education law of 1971 is that it has created the financial means necessary for guaranteeing the effectiveness and viability of the Continuing Education system.

It must be admitted, however, that it is difficult always to accept the added financial burden imposed, especially in the present economic situation. In this respect it is to be hoped that Continuing Education will have the effect on working conditions which we have foreseen.

5. A METHOD FOR A SOCIO-ECONOMIC DIAGNOSIS OF THE ENTERPRISE[56]

The method for a diagnosis of the enterprise which is presented here should be considered primarily in a perspective of therapy and decision-making. It aims at linking the organ to its function: the enterprise being a complex body defined by its structures and by a system of behaviours; its two main functions being to achieve economic performance (production and distribution of goods and services, and distribution of resources) and to achieve social performance (by providing, so to speak, proper and decent working conditions).

Compared to the methods based on a financial analysis, the socio-economic diagnosis has deeper roots and should be inserted right in the enterprise activity, as it tends to provide an *explanation* which indicates both practical and *operational* processes. It is the result of our research since 1973, and also the work of a new research group into Working Conditions called ISEOR.[57]

Our socio-economic approach – an approach which integrates sociological and economic implications – consists in establishing a relationship between the *sociological* variables as defined in organizational theory, the sociology of work, and social psychology, and the *economic* variables, more specifically the financial ones. Thus it is a true *cross-disciplinary* approach that should not be confused with any common definition of the socio-economic sciences that simply tends to reinsert economic sciences among the numerous social sciences.

This approach strives to sublimate the two main currents of thought: that of Behaviourism and that of Structuralism, though, at some point, both have contributed to the improvement of the social, economic, and management sciences (and sometimes to an unavoidable deviation). To sublimate, here, means to *synthesize and to go beyond*, in Hegel's sense of the word, as opposed to the 'monist' or so-called 'pure' theories (i.e. the monodisciplinary and unmethodological ones) which continually demonstrate their fundamental inadequacy when applied to facts. Thus to synthesize and to go beyond means to adopt an *eclectic* attitude when considering those two major currents of behaviourism and structuralism. These are the components that are really significant for the researcher and for the practitioner eager to understand before acting.[58]

Among the structures which characterize an organization the working conditions contain some fundamental items for the understanding of efficiency in the enterprise and the organization. Working conditions[59] include industrial relations, human relations between man and his physical working environment, the nature of the work, his social working environment, the internal relations between the different functions in the enterprise and the different components of personal management (i.e. employment, training, salary).

These structures appear to be comparatively permanent (= parametric variables) and determine to a certain extent the 'actor's' behaviour, i.e. they impose restraining conditions, logical orientations, and *probabilities* of behaviour . . .

Those who favour the structuralist approach put forward the well-known argument: as long as structures remain unchanged, nothing will change. But who should undertake to change the structures? Could it be one single decision-maker who, by himself, would be totally free to choose from amongst different possibilities or should it be *a complex system of 'trade-off'*[60] or dialectical decision? If it is a complex decision-making system, as it probably is, then we must find out the data and motivation underlying the *strategic activity* of the components of this system, their possible antagonism, their conflict, and their potential co-operative forces.[61] If we call 'change agent' an individual or a group who aims at changing the structures, or rather at contributing to their changing, then the 'active contribution to the changing of the structures' is a behaviour. Acting agents have different potential energy. Those who have the biggest potential energy for change (= active units, as Perroux says) have a strong capacity for changing their environment. Thus there are, in the enterprise (and out of it as well) some individuals or groups who are, actually or potentially, change agents. Their behaviour tends deliberately towards the changing of structures (which in our case, means the improvement of working conditions).

If we accept that the combination (energy-stimuli allocation (individual or group interests, visionary schemes, search for a better social status)) is a necessary and sufficient condition for the following relationship: Variation of Behaviour → Variation of Structures (= distortions of these structures according to their individual plasticity), and this is an acceptable idea for a behaviourist, then we should admit at the same time that there exists also and *a priori* another relationship: Variation of Structures → Variation of Behaviour.

This dual and diachronic relationship can be seen by means of an empiric, even pragmatic, observation. To some extent, it is the chronobiology[62] (= vital pulsations) of all organization, more precisely of enterprises which have proved to be comparatively unstable systems over the last twenty years or more. If we accept the allocation of structures and behaviour patterns that are presumed to be permanent during the observed period (short term) as being the company's resources, then we can admit that there is a relationship between structures, behaviours, and economic efficiency in the organization.

Although it fits into a general pattern of a *non-defined* strategy or of social politics, our socio-economic approach is fundamentally different: it differs from the theoretical elements that have been published so far by authors who are supposed to be 'socially motivated' and it differs also from the disappointing undertakings of French or foreign enterprises which have run long and unsatisfactory experiments within the framework of a social planning which was *disconnected* from economic reality and strategy. (From this point of view, those who implemented the socio-technical approach of the Tavistock Institute were quite promising but did not bring much as a whole, though their contribution to research and action proved stimulating.)

If, within this general approach, we admit that, at some point, the search for economic efficiency constitutes the dynamic principle underlying the dialectics of progress (after all, unions, enterprises, and the Government all wish to reduce unemployment and to increase production and profits), then we must demonstrate *scientifically*,[63] and not only according to a simple metaphysical scheme vaguely and abstractedly assessed, that:

a change of structure is desirable and possible (here, we mean the improvement of working conditions);

when this change occurs, it brings social efficiency and economic efficiency, or at least it *does not spoil* economic efficiency.

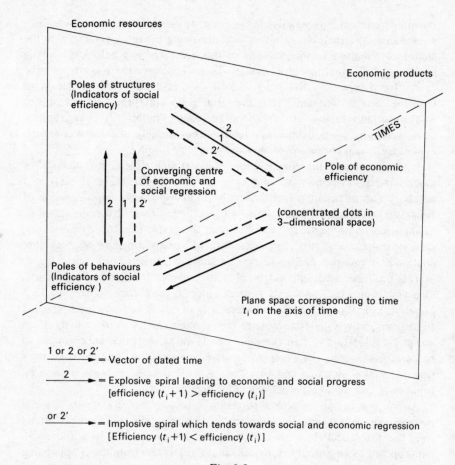

Fig. 3.2

A. Tracing Hidden Costs and Performance[64]

As a first approximation, hidden costs are items that do not show in the economic information system of the enterprise (balance sheet, trading accounts, cost accounting, operating budget).

Hidden costs are highly relevant for our socio-economic diagnosis as they can be clustered into so-called socio-economic variables which have a particular feature: they are indicators of structures and behaviours on one hand, and they can be evaluated in financial terms, on the other hand. Thus those hidden costs can be aggregated in the economic information system of the firm.

i. *Major Concepts*

One should keep in mind that all methods of computation are based on principles which constitute the standard of reference to the unit system to be considered.

Economic computation works this way too, but it should be clear that the fundamental principle of a socio-economic calculation implies necessarily the concept of *expected* operation (one could say 'normal', but this word now has a strong social connotation).

(a) Expected operation of the organization and dysfunction

Any organization — a company particularly — can be analysed (then evaluated) in terms of a comparison with a norm of operation that we shall call *expected operation*, a concept that ought to be defined now.

The expected operation should be the one that allows the company or the organization to fulfil its goals while taking into account its social constraints: those constraints are psychological, physiological, and sociological. They are either individual (work-load, self-fulfilment . . .) or collective (specialization, career organization, interplay of professional and union organizations) according to their possible coalition of interests and to the possible evolution of those interests.[65] The goals of the organization are fixed by the microsystem of power using autocratic or technocratic proceedings, and sometimes democratic ones (?).

Whatever the characteristics of the social group on the one hand and of the decision-making system on the other, there is always a problem for adjusting individual or small-group behaviour to a collective norm, particularly within the model of conflict/co-operation analysis.[66] It proves hazardous to give a definition and a precise meaning to a concept such as 'apparent consensus' when one tries to analyse thoroughly the sociogram of the different groups within the firm. Dysfunctions observed are deviations from the expected operation . . . Table 3.9, though very succinct, should help towards a better understanding of this particular problem.

In this perspective, because of the concept of 'expected operation', or negotiated standard operation, absenteeism appears to be a phenomenon whose

Table 3.9

Social goals / Economic goals	Non-priority	Priority
Non-priority	Consensus based on laxity Suicidal management	Utopian consensus (etymological sense) Politician strategies (trial of strength, negotiating powers, structural 'encroachments' of the different groups)*
Priority	Techno-economic management Traditionality strategy	Socio-economic management Contractual socio-economic strategy (in research)

*Structural 'encroachment', a concept created by F. Perroux, the capacity for an 'active unit' to change its environment for its own benefit.

elements are heterogeneous and capable of being analysed discriminately. Anyone who is absent from work for other than 'legitimate' reasons (family events, training, time allowed for union representation, injury, 'real' illness) deliberately uses a drawing right which is not legal and which contributes either to comparative counter-performances of the company (loss of production, disadvantages caused to others because of general delays . . .) or to an overload of work for workers who are present, or to a combination of both effects.

In order to be realistic, one should not underestimate the difficulties encountered in determining this norm. Indeed, some practices interfere with others: for instance, medical practice, practice of collective absence according to regulations or collective agreements. Such difficulties arise from the fact that the 'actors' have different interpretations of the rules, which anyway are ambiguous because they represent the outcome of trade-off negotiations and thus are constantly modified.

(b) Socio-economic variables as indicators of structure and indicators of behaviour

Initially (1974) we selected four indicators of dysfunction: absenteeism, turnover, product quality, and direct physical productivity. More recently we have to take a fifth indicator: industrial accidents, which hitherto had been included under absenteeism. We did so because we thought it was significant of the degree of safety at work.

These indicators of dysfunctions are both indicators of structure and indicators

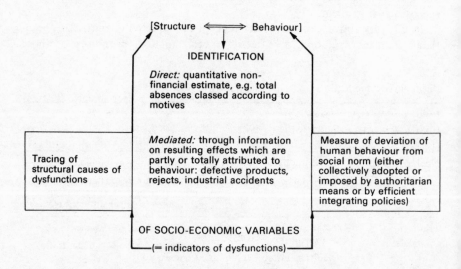

Fig. 3.3

of behaviour. In addition, in our socio-economic approach, we shall consider these indicators as socio-economic synthesis variables: as such, they disclose the social efficiency of the system (structure ⇔ behaviour) and can be measured in financial terms, owing to the relationship between indicators of dysfunctions and economic efficiency.[67]

Table 3.10 shows how the five selected variables of dysfunction are ambivalent on the structural level and on the behavioural one.

Table 3.10

Socio-economic variables (indicators of dysfunctions)	Structure	Behaviour
	Working conditions	Individual and collective behaviour
Absenteeism	Interest of the work Relationships with colleagues Working hours	Human causes: perception of the norm, need for a psychological regulation outside working life Feeling of equity
Industrial accidents (= safety)	Technical causes: equipment, information on and training to safety problems	Accidental human causes could be reduced by adapting information and training of personnel
Turnover	Ability of the company to keep personnel	Instability: avoidance or refusal of working conditions (limit: positive aspect of mobility due to turnover)
Product quality	Technical causes: organization of control, wage structure, definition of production goals, training and information	Human causes: attention, professional skill
Direct physical productivity	Complementary indicator of the four preceding ones (in order to control possible overlapping between indicators)	

(c) *Hidden costs linked with the company's operation*[68]

Hidden costs are those (either historical or opportunity costs) that are *not clearly stated.*

Input: 900 ⟶

┌─────────────────────────────┐
│ Black box masking   │
│ hidden costs   │
│   │
│ (Absenteeism, industrial   │
│ accident, turnover, product │
│ quality, variations of direct │
│ physical productivity)   │
└─────────────────────────────┘

Output: 1000 ⟶

Our method for diagnosis relies on stating the costs that are hidden by the ordinary economic information system of the company. It is made possible by measuring the additional amount of production that could be achieved if the different dysfunctions had either no value at all (absenteeism, work injury, quality of product), or a *'normal'* estimated value (turnover: standard duration, direct physical productivity: standard efficiency).

According to the information system theories, behaviour and decision-making are determined according to *explicit* data. But the traditional accounting system works like a black box which makes some of the main explanatory items that are essential to analyse the economic activity of the enterprise. These items are the costs derived from the combination: [Structure ⟺ Behaviour]. To perceive, imagine, and evaluate the different alternatives of possible decision-making, would it be sufficient for a manager or for one who makes everyday decisions (production engineers, heads of departments) to know only what is going into and coming out of the black box? We think it is not sufficient: as a matter of fact, *explicit* information is disclosed, discussed, assimilated. This leads to conscious or unconscious specific behaviour (behaviour and decision-making), i.e. behaviour that is different from what it would be if there was no information or if information were implicit. Everyone knows that absenteeism is bound to be costly, but if one knows for certain that the cost has been calculated in, for example, a wire-drawing mill,[69] where it represents up to 40% of the total wage bill, then all managers (economic, personnel, and even those in trade unions) will view things differently. This will give rise to three types of reaction:

more exploratory research will be undertaken by company managers to find out the structural or behavioural causes of absenteeism;

there will be a change of outlook. Managers will insist on checking absenteeism;

action will be taken. People begin to accept that non-repressive solutions may well be less expensive and more effective.

We shall see later that it is the same for strategic decision-making, particularly for choosing investments.

ii. *Measure of Hidden Costs*

(a) *General methodology: experimental clinical and action research for tracing the costs*

From 1973 to 1976, our studies were conducted individually; from 1976 onwards we conducted them collectively within the 'Working Conditions' Research Unit. This research is both conceptual and clinical. Owing to our specific methodology, it can be classified as experimental research (which, within the field of social sciences — management sciences in particular — is unfortunately not so common). The methodological process is as follows:

Conceptual analysis and creation → methodological models 'negotiated' with the observation field → testing of the method → application → results → comparison with working hypothesis → improvement of conceptual and methodological tools.

Our clinical studies were conducted thoroughly. Some of us spent three or four days a week in a company over nine to twelve months. This method of research has something in common with the so-called Action-Research method which, by providing a deep understanding of the social microsystem and its permanent evolution, becomes both a method and a source of scientific investigation. Even isolated experiments are of significance in management research. Consequently this experimental research has many implications for the actors because it goes together with an autotraining process and with practical studies which fulfil the need for managerial self-motivation and, at the same time, it meets the practical requirements of any decision-making. We mean the everyday decision-making which contributes to the fulfilment of objectives of social and economic efficiency.

(b) Principles of computation

We have defined three principles for calculating hidden costs: isoproductivity, productivity of management and indirect labour, rational allocation of overheads.

The isoproductivity of time spent at work confirms that the organization of production allows an average permanent production for the time unit, whatever is the time of the day, of the week, whatever are the physical individual differences. Ergonomic studies prove that such a principle is not accurate: productivity per time unit is variable (e.g. working hours). Nevertheless we had to comply to the norms of numerical calculus and stick to this principle. However we must point out that this method of calculation does not take into account the compensatory micro-regulations that develop on the working field itself. With some types of job-design, it may happen that people present at work have a higher level of direct physical productivity than the norm. This, however, is no real objection when using our complete model of socio-economic evaluation, i.e. including its fifth indicator: direct physical productivity, as this indicator allows one to measure these micro-regulations of activity and thus to modulate the principle of isoproductivity. Consequently we calculate the loss of production caused by absenteeism as if average productivity of people present at work could be transposed on to those who are absent (= necessary condition to aggregate times and costs).[70]

Working time of indirect and managerial labour is calculated as if there was no dysfunction at all, thus the whole length of time spent at work in the firm is considered as totally spent to achieve productive tasks (maintenance, management, training, information), and the non-achievement of those tasks is considered prejudicial to the firm. With this principle, working time spent by managerial people on regulating the firm's activity because of absenteeism, and time that supervisors spend on remedying the defective quality of products is evaluated and considered as elements of the costs of dysfunction: this leads to the hypothesis that the level of equipment and labour has been rationally determined according to an expected level of production and activity.

The third principle: rational allocation of structural costs is based on that hypothesis: one should keep in mind that this third principle relies on the idea that overhead costs (which are considered to be approximately permanent whatever the short-time fluctuations of activity) are implemented for a determined level of production (standard of activity). Consequently, if the actual level of activity is equal to or higher or lower than the standard level, the actual operations should either absorb overhead charges completely or allow a surplus of overactivity or a deficit of underactivity. In our method of diagnosis, for practical reasons, we shall regard absenteeism as the most important factor of underactivity. This means that we shall neutralize other factors of underproduction, such as counter-performance of marketing services coming either from a lack of efficiency of those services and/or from the over-all economic situation, errors of management or wrong decisions which lead to a comparative overequipment and consequently to comparatively excessive overhead charges. In fact, the cost of underactivity arising from absenteeism should really be allocated to four different causes: absence itself, ability of managerial people in charge of the regulation of activity when workers are missing, previous errors of management which hinder present management, the over-all economic situation and the marketing conditions. Since it is a statistical computation (the cost of absenteeism is evaluated during a given period of time in a shop or in a factory), it is possible to remedy the inconvenience of a multiple allocation by choosing a period of time when the order book and consequently the work-load are considered to be normal (= corresponding to the budget, for instance). Thus, we can consider that, in the very short term and for the considered period of time at least, the effects of inadequate decision-making which concern overheads and the know-how needed for regulation of activity are *structural data which the analyst must use.* Anyway, absenteeism *increases* the cost of errors in management, and for a given level of absenteeism, comparatively inefficient regulation increases the cost of absenteeism.

We have two more arguments in favour of the choice of our methodology: in the short term, absenteeism is the variable 'that can be controlled' according to a logic of the integration of labour. This logic of integration is asserted if one keeps in mind that, in the end, the real matter is a better observance of the social norm in the firm. Someone who does not come to work uses in fact a drawing right which is *sometimes* discretionary, and its use is prejudicial to the financial performance of any organization but it is also prejudicial to the working community (i.e. labour as a whole). It is an economic disadvantage but *also*, in some respects, a social and a moral one. Absent workers are responsible for a real underactivity (qualitative and quantitative) owing to their absence. If some other factors occur at the same time (decrease in orders, repair work, technical break) they will mask the effects of absenteeism, but they will not cancel them out. One can, however, only consider that the cost of real underactivity derived from absenteeism is easier to tolerate in certain circumstances and that consequently the cost of underactivity in those circumstances should be allocated differently.

Cost of underactivity = cost of underactivity due to absenteeism + cost of underactivity due to other causes (e.g. economic).

The principle of rational allocation can be used for a financial evaluation of some of the elements of the cost of several indicators of dysfunction: absenteeism, industrial accident, turnover, direct physical productivity. This element is particularly weighty for absenteeism, so that we will take this indicator of dysfunction to illustrate the application of this principle of calculus:

$$C_{ua} = f(A, R, K, ME) \tag{1}$$

C_{ua} = cost of underactivity.
A = absenteeism $\rightarrow$ level (a)
R = mode of regulation of activity when people are absent
K = level of structural charges (for simplification: amortization)
ME = marketing efficiency $\rightarrow$ level (me)
Cost of underactivity = cost of absenteeism + cost of marketing inefficiency

$$C_{ua} = f(a, R, K) + f'(me, K). \tag{2}$$

Hidden costs can be evaluated in terms of historical costs: C_h (real charges or loss of profit during the considered period of time, owing to some actual dysfunctions) or in terms of opportunity costs: C_{op}.

In the latter case, we should include opportunities to reduce charges or to increase the level of production which will be lost in the future because of the dysfunction. In other words we must evaluate the *deferred counterperformances*.

In this way, considering the other variables (over-all marketing situation, for instance), the opportunity cost of absenteeism can be higher than, equal to, or lower than the historical cost of underactivity, depending on the importance of time effects of absenteeism: loss in market shares, strategical decisions which are not taken because of the reluctance of the investor confronted with increasing absenteeism.

The postulate of our method for evaluating hidden costs (elements of underactivity) is based on the hypothesis (which should be carefully interpreted) that marketing inefficiency is nil. In order to comply with the calculus requirements, if we take as a starting-point Equation 2, we can write:

Historical cost of Absenteeism = Historical cost of underactivity
(when cost of marketing inefficiency = 0).

Then we have to interpret the case when the historical cost of marketing inefficiency is positive:

$f'(me, K)_h > 0 \Rightarrow f(a, R, K)_h < C_{ua_h}$

The cost of underactivity is allocated to two different causes instead of a single one.

$\Rightarrow$ or $f(a, R, K)_{op} < C_{ua_h}$

> In this case, absenteeism does not endanger the plausible objectives fixed according to the real order book.

or $f(a, R, K)_{op} > C_{ua_h}$

> In this case, we consider that absenteeism masks marketing inefficiency for a comparatively long period of time and thus tends to prove it to be normal in the minds of managers and decision-makers.

So far, in our experimental studies, we have evaluated historical hidden costs which provide us with some basic data. From these data, we can make a non-numerical analysis in order to compare approximately the opportunity costs and the calculated historical cost, even though the opportunity costs have not been numerically evaluated. In our next stage, we will incorporate an evaluation of the hidden costs in terms of opportunity costs and thus we will be able to 'probabilize' our model so as to bring *a real contribution to the socio-economic decision-making theory.*

(c) The main components of hidden costs

The elements that can be financially evaluated and that we have identified in our recent research[71] can be grouped into four basic elements: salaries, regulation time, non-production (= underactivity), and rejects. In order to make a dynamic economic computation we must incorporate the deferred effects which can be assimilated to some of the opportunity costs: risks and cumulative effects.

(d) Costs of regulation or of absorption of the dysfunctions and cost of prevention or correction

According to another classification, in the dual perspective of the application of the 'direct costing' method and the intervention that can be made on dysfunctions, we can group the different elements of the hidden costs components into two large categories. These can, in turn, be divided into two smaller categories: permanent elements and variable ones. The first category includes the cost of absorbing real dysfunctions. The second category includes the cost of the measures for correcting and preventing future dysfunctions. This classification is interesting in that we can analyse what could be the 'optimal' allocation (or rather, the allocation that would be desirable, according to the socio-economic criteria): distribution of costs between regulatory action that has immediate or very short-term positive effects, and correcting action which brings long-term results.

Table 3.11
Model for analysing socio-economic variables

Approaches	Components of hidden costs common to all five indicators	Detailed description of hidden costs (case of absenteeism)
STATIC COMPUTATION	Salaries	Money paid to person absent (in certain justified cases) Labour cost of quasi-permanent additional personnel Higher salaries given to substitute workers (either shifting of people already working in the firm or engaging temporary workers) Compensatory higher salaries for overtime
	Regulation time	Additional work for supervisors (finding the best mode of regulation, transmitting instructions) ⇒ change in the supervisor's role (other tasks not well assimilated ⇒ decrease in quality and/or productivity) Additional controls Increase in work force at some posts that have no permanent holder Additional work for polyvalents (who were allocated to other tasks) Over-frequent calls on maintenance services
	Non-production	Machines stopped because of lack of substitute workers Underproductivity of substitutes (even if they are polyvalent)
	Rejects	Cost of inattention and of unfamiliarity of substitute workers
DYNAMIC COMPUTATION	Observed Risks	Risk of inducing new absenteeism (cumulative effects of absenteeism coming from previous absenteeism: absence ⇒ regulation ⇒ unplanned shifting ⇒ dissatisfaction of the substitute worker ⇒ absence of the substitute worker) Machine stopped Industrial accidents more frequent with substitute workers Reduced reliability on the products or non-conformity to norms Upset time-tabling Disturbing of activity in other sectors of the firm Marketing prejudice: loss of existing market, loss of opportunities of increasing activity

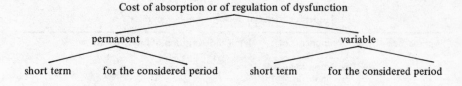

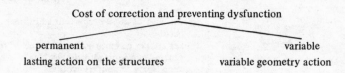

iii. *Outline of Models for Evaluating Hidden Costs and Numerical Results*

(a) Evaluation of costs linked to absenteeism and industrial accidents

In our model of analysis, the absenteeism indicator does not include absenteeism due to industrial accident. As a matter of fact, it has become evident that this sort of absenteeism does not have the same logic as absenteeism due to other causes. We could also dissociate absenteeism resulting from strikes, because strikes appear to be a phenomenon of *collective* regulation. We did not, however, do so because this dysfunction constitutes a particular problem within current conflict theory.

If we dissociate these two elements, our dysfunction indicator becomes more homogeneous and thus a true indicator of individual absence behaviour.

We have grouped all 11 motives for absence within three categories:

absenteeism that can be partly reduced if working conditions are improved (illness, absence for no reason, internal strikes, industrial accident, 'injuries');

absenteeism that is indicative of life within the firm (training, union representation);

absenteeism which, *a priori*, has nothing to do with working conditions (unpaid leave, family events).

Such a discriminative analysis proves to be necessary in order to separate absenteeism which is the result of *non directly* productive *activity* (absence for training, time for union representation) and absenteeism as a rejection of the social norm (it may sometimes have ambiguous reasons: illness or injury). Lastly, absence may constitute an indicator of social performance, a response of the organization to the 'normal' demands of life outside work (= ordinary life: family events, unpaid leave . . .). In this case, absence appears to be a mode of external regulation between working life and life outside work. The standard of reference to compute absenteeism is the number of hours of work expected from each member of the organization, excluding annual leave. This standard can change according to the evolution of legal or conventional rules.

We are most interested by the rate of absenteeism with the set of motives that we have grouped under the category of 'absenteeism that can be partly reduced' by improving working conditions. It is an important part of absenteeism (ranging from 70% to 85%, in the cases we observed).[72] The logical corrective action consists in tending to reduce the number of hours of absence in this category. A careful application of the value analysis should enable one to find a mode of regulation which takes into account the 'legitimate' phenomenon of absenteeism that cannot be reduced and that corresponds to an accepted concept of social welfare granted by implicit or explicit consensus.

There are a great many modes of regulation due to absence (110 different modes have been observed over a period of one month with 96 people and 469 absences grouped into 26 standard cases). The unit cost of regulation depending on the standard type of absence, for eight hours of work, ranges from 181 F (regulation by adding people to the working team) to 2886 F (numerous shifts combined with machines stopped, with intermediary cases: 330 F, for instance, for replacing the person absent by a polyvalent worker.[73] Those modes can, however, be grouped into three categories:

$M1$ = the person absent is not replaced, thus machines are stopped and consequently there is non-production at the considered post ($\Rightarrow$ underactivity);

$M2$ = the person absent is replaced by a temporary worker (from inside or outside the firm = transfer);

$M3$ = the person absent is replaced by another agent belonging to the same section which might induce numerous shifts (we have recorded up to 7 shifts) and at the last step of the regulation chain, a foreman or an 'indirect' worker takes the place of the normal worker.

The cost of absenteeism in the firm is a complex function which has four main variables:

The number of hours which fluctuate according to individual or collective behaviour;

The legal nature of absence: the monthly salary system has, for instance, lawfully increased the individual's right to absenteeism;

The structural nature of absence: if missing people are ones employed at some key posts, either in the workshops or in the departments, then the resulting effects of their absence are more important and the cost higher than for other jobs ($\Rightarrow$ heterogeneity of hours of absence);

The know-how concerning the mode of regulation: ability of the staff to compensate for absence so as to fulfil the goals of production.

Figure 3.4 shows the relationship between the two phenomena: absenteeism due to factors other than industrial accidents, and the degree of safety as indicated by industrial accidents.

The cost of industrial accidents is represented by the sub-set S_1 determined at $A(S_1)$. It is composed of two elements which can be cumulated: the cost of specific effects of industrial accidents and the cost of the effects of subsequent absenteeism.

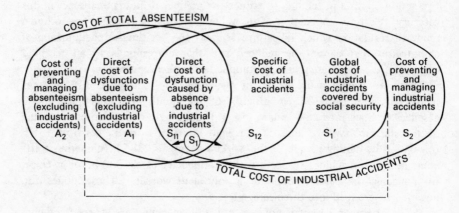

Fig. 3.4. Costs that can be integrated into the budget and the different sections'
accounts (= partial costs)

Specific effect of industrial accidents

Disturbance when the accident occurs: time for regulation, non-production,
rejects . . .

Deferred disturbances:

Increased perception of the risk of accident by other people working in
identical or 'similar' conditions, cost of survey;

Variance dysfunctions;

Cost of managing industrial accidents: internal survey, survey by factory
inspectorate (time spent for those surveys, particularly).

Effects of absenteeism

Direct effect: absence of the injured worker;

Indirect: Absenteeism induced amongst non-injured workers.

The cost of the effects of absenteeism has already been studied for the
absenteeism indicator, *stricto sensu.* In order to compute and integrate into the
firm's accounts the costs of the specific effects of industrial accidents, a classification of all types of industrial accidents into large categories is required,
and, moreover, a classification of the standards of costs that can be utilized in
the economic data system of the firm.

The data and the results concerning the two socio-economic variables can be
collected and represented as in the two matrices shown in Fig. 3.5.

Over-all absenteeism

Calculation of cost / Motives for absence	A_1	A_2	A_3 (industrial accidents)		A_n	A_i
Standard cost (determined through preliminary study)						
Frequency of the period						
Cost of the time period			$C(A_3)$			$\Sigma\, C(A_i)$
Cost of absenteeism excluding industrial accident			✕			$\Sigma\, C(A_1)$ $-C(A_3)$

Industrial accident

Calculation of cost / Categories of accident	$(IA)_1$	$(IA)_2$	$(IA)_3$	$(IA)_i$	$(IA)_n$	$\Sigma\,(IA)_i$
Standard of cost of specific effect determined through preliminary survey						
Frequency of the time period						
Cost of the time period						
Cost of the effect of absenteeism which can be allocated to the period						$C\Sigma\,(IA)_i$ $-C(A_3)$
Total cost						

Fig. 3.5

Some researchers have studied the cost of absenteeism in, amongst others, a shoe factory, domestic electrical appliances factory,[74] and a wire-drawing mill. So far, the most exhaustive study concerns the wire-drawing mill and shows that in 1977 absenteeism amounted to 19% of the production budget, i.e. to about 40% of the total salary bill. This is significant of the room for manœuvre that the actors involved in absenteeism can develop. Solutions for improving working conditions which involve an increase of correctly qualified jobs, for instance, appear to be inexpensive compared to the level of the hidden costs of dysfunctions which the firm has actually to undergo.

(b) The quality of products

Clinical research has proved that job-design or, more widely speaking, working conditions (WC) are a fundamental variable of the quality of products. One of the available indicators of this quality is the quantity of standard defects that should be defined through a marketing, organizational, and technical analysis. Then one can set up the following probable relation:

$$Q = f(WC \Leftrightarrow Behaviour).$$

One can assume that it is more credible and thus more efficient to 'work' on improving behaviour while working at the same time on improving the structure of working life. As a matter of fact, the firm which endeavours to improve the quality of working life should logically benefit in return of effort from the personnel and staff, to improve the quality (see the psycho-sociological theory of exchanges). In such a case, Q constitutes a very useful item for the socioeconomic diagnosis (evaluation of economic efficiency and social efficiency of the firm as the social group). The level of Q can *reveal* some dysfunctions [Structures $\Leftrightarrow$ Behaviour] that the firm cannot tolerate, considering the over-all situation (market requirements $\Leftrightarrow$ financial situation) or considering its development programme (for example, in the shoe factory that we used in our research, quality becomes an essential variable for marketing action, consequently for its economic performance, and, in the end, for its survival, considering the actual process of the new international specialization).

Q could be simply a numerical item, not a financial one. However, a financial evaluation of Q reveals that corrective action is necessary and also allows one to evaluate the financial amount (= financial stakes) available for the financing of such corrective action.

The procedure for evaluating the costs involved in maintaining the quality level consists in creating a measuring tool and in making periodic records:

The tools: Definition, through multiple interviews and direct observation in the workshops, of categories of relevant standard defects;
Evaluation of the unit cost (= standard cost) of each category, after a survey of accounting files;
A grid for recapitulating the costs for maintaining the quality level.

Periodic records: A monthly recording of the number of defects according to category;
Calculation of the total cost per month of maintaining the quality level.

The elements of the cost of quality can be grouped into five categories:

defects in semi-finished products, returned products, disqualified products, time spent on indirect intervention, over-all costs.

In 1977, in a shoe factory (about 350 employees), a partial evaluation revealed that the cost of maintaining the quality level was 5.3% of the standard production cost. This represents only historical costs since we could not evaluate the marketing prejudice (loss of clientele, loss of orders, loss of opportunity for increasing turnover). If we had evaluated those opportunity costs, we would probably have found something like 8% of the standard production cost.

(c) Costs linked to turnover

For the firm, the cost of turnover is that of the in-and-out movements of labour, evaluated in terms of historical costs. They might possibly be evaluated also in terms of replacement costs and opportunity costs.

In the traditional accounting systems, the cost of recruiting personnel, the cost of the adaptation to their posts and the cost of their training, are hidden because they are included in some items of over-all costs for the current period. However, those costs are undertaken during a precise period of the financial year, but their effects, in terms of productivity, will extend beyond this precise period.

Human resource accounting (HRA) consists in considering those charges as real investments to be amortized over a certain period of 'life' (PL), just like any material investment. This period of 'life', which is not the same for all personal qualifications (unskilled, semi-skilled or skilled workers, staff, middle or top executives), can be fixed more or less arbitrarily (as it is for ordinary investment charges which are arbitrarily paid back over three years) or it could be fixed according to the average duration of life of the considered category, as observed over the past years.

Roughly, the cost of turnover can be defined by evaluating the following items: the standard period of life 'spent' in the firm, and the investment in human resources which is composed of the cost of recruiting personnel and the cost of apprenticeship and training. These costs allow one to determine the standard period amortization of HRA.

With these factual data, one can determine the effective period of life spent in the firm. If there is a deviation (as is generally the case) between the standard period of life spent in the firm and the effective one, then it is possible to calculate the differential cost of turnover. It pinpoints the fact that leaving must be monitored. The costs do not, however, appear in traditional accounting systems.

The outcome of calculations that we have carried out in three factories belonging to three different sectors of the economy has shown that the cost of turnover can be very high. In 1974, in a large industrial machine factory, the differential cost of turnover was evaluated and amounted to about 8m F for recruiting 3000 unskilled workers.

Firms greatly underestimate the recruiting and training costs. Our detailed evaluation proves the trebling, even the quadrupling, of the costs found compared with rough evaluations: the cost of taking on unskilled workers amounts to about 4000 F per worker, i.e. 9000 F per job.[75]

With this numerical evaluation,[76] one of the main things we learn is that the importance of hidden costs is totally unexpected: 40% of the total salary bill in the case of absenteeism, 5.3% to 8% of the production budget in the case of product quality,[77] four to six times the salary for the cost of recruiting personnel. For the practitioner, it is an encouraging outcome, since in these vast hidden costs some resources can be found to finance partly or totally the correcting processes (e.g. changing the structures such as the improvement of working conditions).

(*d*) *Direct physical productivity* (yield)

There is no specific problem here since the traditional management organization systems take into account this indicator of economic performance.

However it is necessary to include it in our model for evaluation because of the presence of the combination: product quality/direct physical productivity. Indeed, if the indicator of quality increases while the indicator of physical productivity decreases (which is not always the case), then it is necessary to make a financial evaluation of the variations of both indicators in order to cumulate them.

B. Tools used for the Socio-Economic Diagnosis: Towards a New Management Analysis

i. *Principle of Inserting Hidden Costs in the New Cost-Accounting System*

(*a*) *Brief description of the model*

The unit of production (firm or company) is divided into several micro-spaces which are comparatively homogeneous as regards working conditions. Let us suppose that we keep the segmentation of the budget and cost accounting in homogeneous sections.

A, B, C, D, and E are those sections: a, s, t, q, p, are the so-called socio-economic variables, i.e. the significant dysfunctions for the intersection [Structures (WC) $\Leftrightarrow$ Behaviours] : i.e. absenteeism, safety, turnover, product quality, physical or direct productivity. The hidden costs of the firm are grouped into the financial matrix $[M(F)]$.

(*b*) *Relation between the matrix for hidden costs and the matrix for visible production costs*

Some elements of the hidden costs of a given period can be aggregated to visible costs of production (e.g. non-production, rejects), since if there was no reject at all, there would be either less waste of time and materials or more products to be invoiced.

1st method: minimal evaluation in terms of production cost;

Section 1 / Dysfunctions	A	B	C	D	E	Σ_i
Absenteeism	a_A	a_B	a_C	a_D	a_E	Σa_i
Security	s_A	s_B	s_C	s_D	s_E	Σs_i
Turnover	t_A					Σt_i
Product quality	q_A					Σq_i
Direct physical productivity	p_A					Σp_i
Aggregate of dysfunctions						Σ hidden costs

Fig. 3.6

2nd method: maximal evaluation in terms of selling prices.

Let us take the evaluation in terms of historical costs *stricto sensu* (1st method). These hidden costs have a 'status' of an auxiliary element in cost-accounting terminology. It is the same for non-production, which is evaluated in terms of added value or cost (= it adds nothing to covering structural costs).

As for evaluating the activity, we can consider:

	Costs	Products
(1)	'Visible' production costs	Sales figures really achieved
(2)	'Hidden' production costs	'Potential' counterpart
(3)	Real costs or total costs $(1 + 2)$	Standard sales figures or normal or expected ones = achieved + potential ('wasted')

Time spent on regulation is the most questionable element in the aggregation. In order to aggregate this time spent relevantly to the other visible or hidden costs, one must postulate that the regulation time of a dysfunction is in fact an additional cost as long as the dysfunction (according to the principle of iso-productivity, i.e. no micro-regulation of productivity) absorbs a time that could have been utilized for useful and profitable production either directly (time wasted by 'direct' labour) or indirectly (time wasted by 'indirect' labour or managerial staff).

The firm does not necessarily carry this cost (extra hours of work for managerial staff that are not paid by the firm). It seems, however, that actually there is a general tendency to regularize this 'abnormal' situation (either in day-to-day practice, or for the future: demands).

In these conditions, the costs of dysfunctions could have a real financial counterpart in terms of 'marketable' products.

ii. *Socio-Economic Control System: From the Control System of the Personnel Department to the Control System of the Operational Hierarchy*

During our elaborate and lengthy research in the firms themselves, we studied the relationships between the functional departments and the operational departments, and we were forced to the conclusion that the operational hierarchy had *necessarily* to be involved in diagnosing the situation and in the social policy of the firm. The personnel work in fact is very diffuse and is not carried out only by the functional personnel departments. Training, improvement of working conditions, and security at work are, amongst other things, processes in which both the personnel department and the operational staff department can co-operate in a particularly efficient way.

(a) Principles

Clearly, it appears that the social control system and the social balance sheet are quite insufficient, operationally speaking. Personnel people trace some data concerning the level of absenteeism, of turnover, the number of industrial accidents, and such data are practically always quantified, but they are *very seldom* (it is a euphemism) evaluated in financial terms.

Socio-economic integration: there is no integration in the *daily* economic calculation used in the operational hierarchy (balance sheet, cost accounting). Because of our rational way of thinking, this induces us to oppose economic performance to social performance: x tons that have been produced despite a particular level of absenteeism or, on the contrary, there has been a lack of production because there have been stoppages. The tracing, when it is quanitifed but not financially evaluated, appears to be inefficient.

Decentralization: aggregating the data of all absenteeism in the whole firm, by adding together all hours of absence for training, industrial accidents, illness, and strikes, gives a control system composed of a whole set of *aggregated items* which is not particularly operative. The process of aggregation reduces to a great extent the sensitiveness of barometers and indicators: the black-spots, i.e. critical situations which should be the first to catch the manager's attention, are diluted into a monotonous average muddle.

Thus it is essential that in all departments, sections, and workshops, the control system should reveal all elements clearly and, for this, personnel staff and the production engineers must collaborate on the very spot where information and· phenomena occur, and as close as possible to the decision and intervention centres (head of departments or head foremen).

(b) Instruments

These are information tools and consist in fixing standards associated to policy for reducing hidden costs, e.g. a programme for improving working conditions. They are tools such as *frequency grids* for absenteeism, industrial accidents, quality defects, and the *standard grids* integrated into the section budgets, such as the level of cost of absenteeism, of turnover, of industrial accidents, of variation in the product quality, of variation in the direct physical productivity.

	Tools	Cost accounting	Variance	Control system	
Matrices of frequency dysfunctions	Provision	Realization		Social	Socio-economic
	(x)	x	Quantitative indicator	Yes but aggregated	Yes
Parametric matrices for unit cost	(x)				Yes
Matrix of total costs (multiplying two preceding ones)	☒	☒	☒ Financial indicator		Yes

Fig. 3.7. Framework for inserting socio-economic tools

iii. Elaboration of Socio-Economic Models for Choosing Investments with a View to a Socio-Economic Strategy

(a) Implicit hidden costs

The models that are actually used (financial models) for choosing investments are based, on the one hand, on a conceptual model of financial data-processing (e.g. discounted cash-flow, calculation of internal rate of return) and, on the other hand, on the hypothesis of the data. These hypotheses (estimated turnover, provisional trading account, preliminary estimate for realizing the investment) are based on prevision proceedings which are little short of a prognosis; though a prognosis is often a 'trade-off' between the finance, production, and marketing people.

It is important to stress that a prognosis should always imply some *underlying hypothesis of hidden cost*.[78] The validity of such a hypothesis of hidden costs is, however, based on '*evolution*' variables: absenteeism has doubled during the seventies in industrialized countries. Besides, practitioners and observers consider that certain types of job-design will be increasingly rejected:[79] production-line work for young workers, shift work, and so on.

This is happening whilst the firms' policies are evolving under pressure from the economic and social crisis, so that they are tending to abandon such remedies as massive recruitment of immigrant and female labour.

(b) Improving investment selection hand-book

The evolution of these socio-economic variables (absenteeism and turnover particularly, but also, and to a certain extent, product quality and direct physical productivity) should appear as quantitative hypotheses within *real scenarios*: variation of the level of absenteeism, increase in recruitment costs, investment costs, improved working conditions so as to make more tolerable some of the conditions which are regarded as more difficult or harder to bear.

Because they are explicit, the development of these scenarios presents three main advantages:

they provide information for a more elaborate and critical discussion of the basic hypotheses that appear in the investment file;

they provide realistic and strong bases for the financial calculation (provisional trading accounts which involve hidden costs) and consequently the decisions are taken on bases that are more plausible too;

they start a process of active participation of the different levels of decision and *management* in order to *encourage* planned investment during its preparation phase, then its implementation, then its management.

In a more ambitious perspective of stochastic decision models, the technique of developing *scenarios* leads logically to explicit alternative choices that can be demonstrated by trees or decision-making trees or PERT diagrams. Indeed, we could calculate from which hypothetical level (of hidden costs in particular, but not exclusively) the probability of non-profit of the investment is so high that one must rationally look for other solutions. For example, one could develop a scenario with explicit hypotheses of behaviour based on the structures that are included in the investment, as originally defined, e.g.

First sequence: (Traditional procedure prevails but with explicit hypotheses of the considered dysfunctions):

Investment $\Rightarrow$ Structure $\Rightarrow$ Behaviour
    e.g. organization shift work.

I	$\Rightarrow$	S	$\Rightarrow$			$\Rightarrow$		$\Rightarrow$	
				absenteeism,	a		projected		positive decision
				security,	s		economic		based on a
				turnover,	t		performances		dangerously op-
				quality,	q		level ρ (Syn-		timistic calcula-
				productivity,	p		thetic indicator:		tion which
							e.g. intrinsic		obliterates
							rate of profit-		hidden costs.
							ability)		

Second sequence: Critical reading of the preliminary analysis and correction of hidden costs hypothesis, after a social survey:

$$I \quad \Rightarrow \quad S \quad \Rightarrow \quad \begin{matrix} a_c \\ s_c \\ t_c \\ q_c \\ p_c \end{matrix} \quad \Rightarrow \quad \rho_c \quad \Rightarrow \quad \begin{matrix} \text{negative decision} \\ \text{(for instance).} \end{matrix}$$

Third sequence: Consideration of all possible solutions.

The conclusion of the second sequence calls for the search to alternative investments (different technology, different geographical setting, different system of working conditions):

$$I' \quad \Rightarrow \quad S' \quad \Rightarrow \quad \begin{matrix} a' \\ s' \\ r' \\ q' \\ p' \end{matrix} \quad \Rightarrow \quad \rho'$$

possible solutions according to a financial criterion

$$I'' \quad \Rightarrow \quad S'' \quad \Rightarrow \quad \begin{matrix} a'' \\ s'' \\ r'' \\ q'' \\ p'' \end{matrix} \quad \Rightarrow \quad \rho''$$

(c) Socio-economic strategy[80]

The socio-economic strategy of the firm should allow one to select $\rho'' < \rho'$ but at the same time it should provide some structures for better working conditions (better social performances $\psi' > \psi''$): as long as the social strategy of the enterprise (an industrial group, for instance) needs an outstanding achievement in order to change the mentality of its decision-makers, so as to meet the union demands on the one hand, and also to follow a certain evolution of public opinion.

Roughly speaking, the socio-economic strategy can be based on the following axiomatization:[81]

any investment, thus any financial model for selecting investments, implies implicit hidden costs (some call it '*porousness*' of work);

making hidden costs explicit is a dynamic force in the search for socio-economic solutions, because it starts a process of research into accounting to look for the relation between economic efficiency and social efficiency;

the search for economic solutions can end either in the *adjusting of* long-term strategies (adequacy of social conditions → economic conditions) or in *development strategies*: innovating actions or collective creation.

The author is currently developing a model of dynamic analysis for the economic activity of the enterprise, for a further elaboration of the experimental research in the field of socio-economic strategy that he has undertaken with several firms. The model is based on three main effects: Heredity (= the firm's memory), current events (short-term policy), and desired, and/or forecast, development (strategy). The model is very close to the perspective of Active Units, a concept which is the essential contribution of François Perroux.[82]

iv. *Applications of the Socio-Economic Analysis Method*

The numerical evaluation of hidden costs is, first of all, a method for an integrated social and economic diagnosis of the enterprise and it is independent of any occasional change of the system: [structure ⇔ behaviour.] It implies an elaborate social and organizational analysis that ends in fixing and determining a certain value of hidden costs. This value is the measure of two elements, as it is both:

an indicator of the variations of *global inefficiency* (five socio-economic variables) or of partial inefficiency (one of several variables). This appears clearly with the cost of absenteeism in a wire-drawing mill, which has been evaluated as amounting to 19% of the production budget, with the cost of the quality variation which has been evaluated in a shoe factory at 5.3% of the standard production cost, or with the cost of differential turnover of unskilled workers in an automobile plant, which has been evaluated at 8 000 000 F for one year.

an indicator of the potential plasticity of the system [structure ⇔ behaviour] which determines the approximate extent to which actors and partners can act as far as productive activity is concerned.

The evaluation of hidden cost variations is an index of social and economic performance, which can be imputed, in the main at least, to the observed variation of the system [structure ⇔ behaviour]. Thus it is a tool of control (socio-economic audit).

As for the enterprise's policies, clearly this system can work on two different fields. As we have seen above, it works for the improvement of traditional processes for choosing investments (the objective being to avoid the strategic errors that have been made before) and it works for the *planning of a social policy* (particularly for improving working conditions) that is associated to an economic strategy. In this case, the objective is to show the financial resources that will allow one to realize the social programme of the enterprise. Within the general pattern of our experimental researches, we made partial evaluations on realizations and experiments which are in the line of social development policies: participation in action for improving safety (wire-drawing mill), improvement of the process of recruiting personnel (automobile plant), several experiments into new forms of job-design (shoe factory, domestic electrical appliances factory, in particular).

The evaluation of hidden costs is very efficient when inserted into the process of social development according to Fig. 3.8.

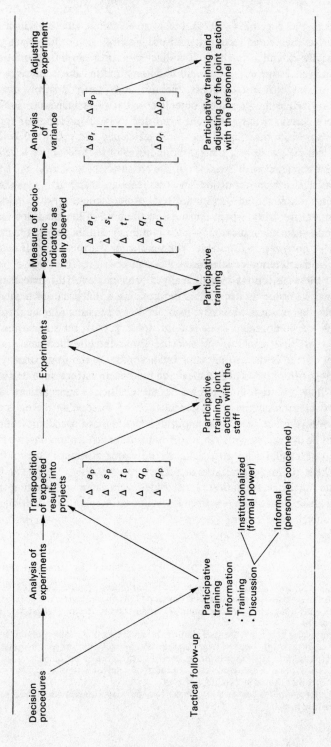

Fig. 3.8

Right from the beginning (1974), the socio-economic analysis which is presented here has used some auxiliary methods which ever since have been greatly and successfully extended to other disciplines in France: surplus accounting and the value analysis. However, one should underline that in value analysis, which is composed of two different elements, the functional analysis is very useful for our procedure, while the dominant objective of the value analysis (reduction of costs) is, to a certain extent, different from that of our approach. Our approach attempts a *joint maximization* of economic efficiency and social efficiency and this might sometimes imply a substantial increase of *unit* costs (we have seen it in the automobile plant with the costs of the recruiting procedure).

The numerical evaluation of hidden costs, though it appears to be essential, has its limits, which should be pointed out. *Numerical* costs, when calculated, have only a *relative* value, which depends on the level of the 'standard' that has been determined for the indicators of dysfunction. The principle that these costs really exist is, however, indisputable. The significance of these costs is related to the quality of the determined standard (relevance).

However these objections are not really a problem, since the determining of the costs has no value in itself. This determining is only one element in the aiding of decision-making. Similarly, in order to be consistent, and according to the principle of homogeneity, one should not expect to get a *numerical* value from these costs that would be more accurate than the other financial elements, such as the 'visible' costs, as they are fixed according to the traditional accounting methods, or the predicted technical and marketing performance. Indeed, the basic data that are traditionally used in the decision-making process are obviously very precarious, and the sophistication of forecasting methods cannot conceal this. In the last resort the important fact is that the accuracy of hidden costs should be in keeping with the accuracy of other elements.

Finally, one should take into account the major aspects of the method of diagnosis, the social and organizational analysis which is the complement and the basis of the financial evaluation. It provides a valuable contribution for the scholar and especially for the practitioner.

NOTES

(1) Quoted in A. Bienaymé, *La Croissance des entreprises*, Bordas, Paris 1971, vol. 1: *Analyse dynamique des fonctions de la firme*, p. 151.
(2) Cf. H. Savall, 'Formation et conditions de vie au travail', *Revue Française de gestion*, Mar.–Apr. 1977.
(3) In a firm near Lyon it was noticed that the introduction of a production line involving job-enrichment techniques led to an average of 15 applicants per job, as against 5 per job previously (interview with P. Beard, Institut Entreprise et Personnel).
(4) This does not, of course, exclude the possibility of delay or historical accident.
(5) 173 hrs. per month out of 720 hrs. (24 × 30).
(6) 5 working days per week or 8, 9, or 10 hrs. per day (sometimes more if travelling time is added).

(7) On the opposition between economic and social planning, cf. *Cycles d'Études européennes de Toulouse 1964*, vol. I, U.N., Geneva, 1965.

(8) Cf. P. Bois, report quoted above, ch. 2, note 94.

(9) Cf., in *Intersocial*, cancellation of experiments in progress at General Motors.

(10) Cf. the case of the Post Office Giro Centre at The Hague (H. Van Beinum).

(11) Donnadieu, 'La planification du changement social: recherches et perspectives', at the Congress of the Association Nationale des Directeurs et Chefs de Personnel (21–23 Mar. 1974).

(12) The aim-low hypothesis corresponds to the application of the experimental method, but it does, in fact, involve all the disadvantages of one-off laboratory experiments. We have already discussed the difficulties encountered when such experiments come to be extended throughout the organization.

(13) Cf. Donnadieu, op. cit.

(14) The agreements linking the Ministry of Labour to firms which benefit from FACT subsidies (Fonds d'Amélioration des Conditions de Travail) for carrying out pilot studies now include an obligation to make an economic evaluation. The method used is one worked out under the auspices of the ANACT. (Cf. ch. 1, note 155.)

(15) Cf. below, p. 121.

(16) Cf. D. Dautresme, 'Quelques réflexions sur la productivité dans la banque', *Bulletin du ministère des Finances*, Nov. 1974.

(17) Cf. *Le Monde*, 4 July 1974, p. 8, 'Parmi les accusations du rapport Chinaud . . .'

(18) Cf. also on this point the conclusions drawn in the Reynaud report (Ch. 2, note 94) about the inadequacy of the accounting systems and practice for an over-all analysis of the costs. The report only suggests elements for a 'new financial and accounting approach'; it does not suggest any precise method.

(19) Cf. pp. 130 ff.

(20) Cf. Dautresme, art. cit.

(21) Bibliography: E. Marquès, 'Gestion du capital humain', *Le Management*, Dec. 1973, p. 53; H. le Cloarec, 'La prise en compte des ressources humaines', *Direction et gestion*, May–June 1972; J. Hekimian, C. H. Jones, 'Put People on your Balance-sheet', *Harvard Business Review*, Jan.–Feb. 1967; M. Balland *et al.*, 'Données quantifiables de la gestion du personnel', internal document of Institute Enterprise et Personnel, Paris, 1973; J. Lehn, P. Reveillion in *Le Monde*, 27–8 May 1975, p. 26, 'Mesurer le social'.

(22) We shall only mention a few here, since it is not our aim to examine all the research in this area. Cf. E. Marquès, *La Comptabilité des ressources humaines*, Hommes et Techniques, Paris, 1975.

(23) B. Lev, A. Schwartz, 'On the use of the Economic Concept of Human Capital in Financial Statements', *Accounting Review*, Jan. 1971.

(24) W. J. Giles, D. F. Robinson, *Human Asset Accounting*, Institute for Personnel Management, London, Oct. 1972.

(25) In this respect E. Flamholtz's theory cannot be criticized. Cf. E. Marquès, 'Gestion du capital humain'; E. Flamholtz: 'A Model for Human Resource Valuation, a Stochastic Process with Service Rewards', *Accounting Review*, Apr. 1972; 'Towards a theory of Human Resource Value in Formal Organisation', ibid., Oct. 1972; and 'Human Resource Accounting: Its role in Management Planning and Control', *Economisch en Social Tijdschrift*, Antwerp, Feb. 1973.

(26) Cf. Flamholtz's theory cited above.

(27) Which we consider auxiliary elements, in the cost-accounting sense.

(28) A. Cibert, *Compatibilité analytique*, Dunod, Paris, 1970, p. 208.

(29) The hypothesis that the two workshop crews are different could be made without altering the validity of the method. In that case the variance in relative value $(e_i)'$, (e_2), $(e_{2/i})'$, $(e_i)''$, $(e_2)''$, and $(e_{2/i})''$ would enable us to draw a comparison in spite of the difference between the group sizes. In the same way it is not necessary for the monthly fixed costs (10 000 F in this case) to be the same for the two workshops. In the example where figures have been used so as to make it clearer, the calculations, although they are fictitious, correspond to the results observed in the experiments we have observed as far as the indicators used are concerned (absenteeism, turnover, rejects, productivity). As regards productivity, however, we could have taken one of the

numerous examples where direct productivity increases with the new organization. We have not done this, in order to avoid taking only hypotheses which favour the new organization as far as the results are concerned.

(30) On new ways of evaluating absenteeism and turnover cf. J. Noharet *et al.*, 'Le travail non qualifié. Propositions et examples d'actions', internal paper, Institut Entreprise et Personnel, Lyon, Oct. 1973.

(31) In the general and not the strictly accounting sense.

(32) In France every enterprise has an industrial accident rate per category of worker. This varies from year to year and is fixed by the Sécurité Sociale based on the accident statistics for the sector and the enterprise.

(33) Cf. pp. 130 ff.

(34) Cf. pp. 137 ff.

(35) Cf. p. 28.

(36) Incompressible absenteeism is the rate of absenteeism which cannot be reduced by improvement to the job-design or working conditions. It corresponds to reasons for absence which cannot be eliminated (sickness, accident, 'justified' personal reasons).

(37) In the classical sense of cost-advantage analysis.

(38) L. E. Davis, 'Job design and productivity', *Personnel*, Mar. 1957.

(39) In France H. Dunajewski has made a study of the improvement of extrinsic working conditions with no effect on productivity and where the decision did not arise from any economic calculation. 'Décisions d'amélioration des conditions de travail sans influence sur la productivité: étude d'un cas particulier aux garages en France', LEST–CNRS, Aix-en-Provence, Sept. 1973.

(40) In France at the moment = 0.5% Taxe d'Apprentissage and 1% Taxe de Formation, i.e. 1.5% of the total wage bill.

(41) In the marketing sense.

(42) In France Peugeot has based publicity on this.

(43) A.-J. Rigny, *Structure de l'entreprise et capacité d'innovation*, 1973, p. 46.

(44) Ibid.

(45) Cf. A. Wolfelsperger, 'La détermination des conditions de travail dans l'entreprise', *Revue d'Économie Politique*, Mar.–Apr. 1973, p. 357; G. Becker, 'Economics of Discrimination. A theory of the allocation of time', *Economic Journal*, no. 5, 1965, p. 493; G. Becker, *Economic Theory*, Knopf, New York, 1971; K. Lancaster, 'A new approach to consumer theory', *Journal of Political Economy*, Apr. 1966, p. 132; J.-D. Owen, *The price of leisure (an economic analysis of the demand for leisure time)*, Rotterdam University Press, 1969; J. S. Dyer, M. Hoffenberger, 'On the evaluation of the quality of working life: some reflexions on production and cost, and a method for system definitions', 1972, unpublished document.

(46) R. Tchobanian, 'Projet de recherche. L'Économie des conditions du travail: étude des coûts et analyse dynamique', LEST–CNRS, Aix-en-Provence, 1974, unpublished report; idem, 'Réflexions sur l'analyse économique des conditions de travail', ibid. 1972.

(47) D. Gélinier, 'Peut-on mesurer la rentabilité des investissements sociaux?', *Le Monde*, 30 Oct. 1973.

(48) We would have preferred 'productivity'.

(49) Cf. 'Committee for the quality of working life', meeting at Canterbury, 17–20 Aug. 1973; 'International Summer School: Quality of working life', Netherlands 11–31 Aug. 1974.

(50) The Renault dispute at Le Mans in 1971 made a considerable impact on public opinion. Since then the French press has regularly featured information about industrial working conditions and has made an important contribution to generating public awareness.

(51) J.-Y. Eichenberger, preface to A. J. Rigny, op. cit.

(52) FNEGE and CESI have set up working parties along with industrialists. Cf. 'Formation et amélioration des conditions de travail', Secretary of State for Manual Workers, INFFO, Paris, 1977. Since the appointment of a Secretary of State several legislative or statutory measures have been taken with a view to urging firms to diagnose (social balance sheet) and to improve the conditions and training of manual workers [footnote, 2nd edition].

(53) It is very much to be feared that, by adding a further body at the level of the works committee, the 1973 law has made the task of managing even more difficult. The law has not really done anything to bring about projects for improving working conditions. Works' Committees do not have very much power to encourage experiments.

(54) 'Rapport du Comité d'étude pour la réforme de l'entreprise présidé par Pierre Sudreau', *La Documentation française*, Feb. 1975.

(55) The budget originally allocated was only sufficient to cover documentation, diffusion of information, methodological preparation. Cf. ANACT's first 'information letter', 'Présentation de l'Agence Nationale pour l'amélioration des conditions de travail', May 1975.

In 1976 and 1977 the budget was increased and ANACT was able to carry out pilot studies, to extend its operations throughout France, to develop training projects (cf. ANACT information letter, no. 11, June 1977).

In 1976 the Minister of Employment set up FACT (Fonds d'Amélioration des Conditions de Travail) so as to allocate funds to various projects and experiments. ANACT makes a technical study of applications, and subsidies can be as high as 30% for investments and 50% for prior study work [footnote, 2nd edition].

(56) For the English edition this work has been enlarged by the addition of H. Savall's report given at the annual CERME conference, 'Le Diagnostic d'Entreprise', Nice, 21–2 Sept. 1978. Large extracts have also been published in *Revue Française de gestion*, Nov.–Dec. 1978. The report, originally translated by Mme F. Guiramand, has been adapted to conform to the present edition by M. A. Woodhall.

(57) The working group 'Conditions de Travail' was founded by H. Savall and became the Institut de Socio-Économie des Entreprises et des Organisations, in 1976. It is associated with the University of Lyon II and the École Supérieure de Commerce de Lyon.

(58) Cf. H. Savall, 'Analyse socio-économique, diagnostic et décision d'amélioration des conditions de travail', *Revue de l'Entreprise*, Jan. 1978.

(59) Cf. H. Savall, 'Formation et Conditions de vie au Travail', *Revue Française de gestion*, Mar.–Apr. 1977, reproduced in *Personnel*, Nov.–Dec. 1977. Cf. also 'Contribution de la formation initiale à l'amélioration des conditions de vie au travail', report to Secretary of State for Manual Workers, a FNEGE committee under J. Morin (PUK), secretary H. Savall, Feb. 1977, published in *Formation et conditions de travail*, Centre INFFO, Paris, 1977.

(60) An idea currently being investigated by the author, which is based on recent contributions made in sociology and political science. Cf. e.g. L. Sfez, *Critique de la décision*, Colin, Paris, 1973.

(61) Cf. F. Perroux, *Pouvoir et économie*, Dunod, Paris, 1975, and *Unités actives et mathématiques nouvelles*, Dunod, Paris, 1975; M. Crozier and E. Friedberg, *L'Acteur et le système*, Seuil, Paris, 1977.

(62) Cf. A. Reinberg, *Des rhythmes biologiques à la chronobiologie*, Gauthier-Villars, Paris, 1974.

(63) Cf. H. Savall, 'Propos d'étape de régulation socio-économique de l'entreprise par la recherche de la compatibilité de l'efficience économique et du développement humain', Report given to VIIth international colloquium of the Collège de France on the idea of regulation in the movement of the sciences, Dec. 1977.

(64) Cf. note 68 below.

(65) P. de Backer, 'Négociation et conflits dans l'entreprise: quelques indications d'application de la psychologie des conflits', *Metra*, vol. II, no. 1, Mar. 1972.

(66) Ibid.

(67) H. Savall, 'Rapport scientifique annuel à la D.G.R.S.T.', 1977, into the economic analysis of working conditions. Work carried out within the RESACT programme 1976–8, Dec. 1977, reproduced in *Cahiers Lyonnais de Recherche en Gestion*, Feb. 1978.

(68) In socio-economic terms the concept of hidden 'cost-performance' should always be used because economic cost can be linked with social performance. Cf. H. Savall, Report to the Collège de France, and A. Martinet and H. Savall, 'Dysfonctionnements, coûts et performances cachés dans l'entreprise', ISEOR, July 1978, published in

Revue d'Économie industrielle, Oct. 1978.

(69) Cf. E. Collignon, 'Évaluation financière de l'absentéisme dans une tréfilérie', ISEOR report under H. Savall, Mar. 1978.

(70) The miscalculation caused by neglecting the compensatory micro-regulations is corrected by our fifth indicator – direct physical productivity.

(71) The DGRST research programme, within the complementary RESACT programme, 1976–8, which has been renewed until 1980. The programme has the support of the ANACT, the FNEGE, and companies.

(72) Cf. E. Collignon, op. cit.

(73) Ibid.

(74) O. Uzan and M. Lopez, 'Évaluation socio-économique comparée de trois modes d'organisation: Chaînes, tâches élargies, groupes semi-autonomes. Résultats de l'évaluation quantitative (non financière) de l'absentéisme', ISEOR report under H. Savall, May 1978. The financial evaluation of all five indicators is in progress within the framework of an ANACT research contract.

(75) H. Savall, M. C. Marion, M. Lopez, E. Collignon, 'Étude du recrutement dans une entreprise automobile, 1974–77', ISEOR, May 1977. M. Lopez, 'Procédure et coût de recrutement des agents de fabrication 1977', ISEOR, May 1977; idem, 'Un indicateur de dysfonctionnement: la rotation du personnel sur embauche nouvelle', *Cahiers Lyonnais de Recherche en Gestion*, no. 1, 1978, Ph.D. programme of University of Lyon II, Lyon III, École Supérieure de Commerce de Lyon.

(76) Cf. H. Savall, 'Rapport annuel à la D.G.R.S.T. 1977, sur l'analyse économique des conditions de travail. Action sur programme RESACT 1976–1978', *Cahiers lyonnais de recherche en gestion*, no. I 1978.

(77) Cf. E. Collignon, 'Recherche sur les problèmes de qualité de produits. Mesure des coûts et recherche des causes des défauts de qualité des produits dans une entreprise de chaussures', ISEOR, June 1977.

(78) The following analysis has been tested and developed over about 15 sessions of experimental training which the author has been running for several years in large industrial groups.

(79) Cf. H. Savall, 'Formation et conditions de vie au travail', art. cit., cf. also the Report made to the Secretary of State for Manual Workers, op. cit.; cf. J. Morin, 'L'homme civil et l'homme au travail', *Le Monde*, 22 Apr. 1978.

(80) This concept has been worked on since 1974 (cf. thesis quoted 'Enrichir le travail humain . . .') It forms the basis of one of the research axes of the ISEOR research programme (H. Savall and A. Martinet, with the collaboration of some of the large French industrial companies). Cf. also A. Martinet, 'Stratégie économique et stratégie sociale de la grande entreprise', *Cahiers lyonnais de recherche en gestion*.

(81) This axiomatization is in keeping with the one developed by the author within an advisory group set up by Y. Chaigneau, director of ANACT. The group is directed by G. Lajoinie and H. Bussery (cf. minutes of meeting 22.6.67, working document).

(82) F. Perroux, *Unités actives et mathématiques nouvelles*, Dunod, Paris, 1975.

CONCLUSION

There is a normative aspect to our analysis which should not be allowed to discourage the reader. In effect, new forms of job-design are still in an embryonic state and it would therefore be unwise to seek to prove their effects conclusively. There is, however, a convergence of ideas which goes a long way towards validating our thesis. Firstly there has been an increase in the number of analyses questioning quantitative growth models and aiming at putting qualitative models in their place. Secondly there has been an increase in the number of ideas, projects, and corrective measures launched at the political level which confirm the emergence of a *new concept* of human activity. These have all flourished under the 'quality-of-life' banner.

1. THE CONDITIONS FOR THE VALIDATION OF OUR THESIS

Our study is based on two implicit premises. Now is the moment to explain them so as to recognise the relativity of our thesis.

A. First Postulate: the Dichotomy between Life at Work and Life outside Work is Pure Deception[1]

We have been implictly arguing from the idea that human life demands a large amount of human labour and that man's cultural development creates new needs which themselves imply an increase in production and work.

It is possible, however, to picture other scenarios for the future of work. Zero growth is one of them. Would it in this case be necessary to devote so much energy to job-design if the really important, progressive, side of life were to be taking place outside work, or if the condition for man's development were to lie in a reduction of work? We believe that these paths are unrealistic for a future which purports to be in any way human. Seen from a strictly positive point of view, no present political, social, or economic regime has ever made such a choice voluntarily or consciously.

We believe that there is a second factor which validates our thesis, namely the influence which working conditions have on our way of life. It will not be possible to improve the latter without improving the former. We are, however, willing to admit that in absolute terms our postulate is a fragile one.

B. Second Postulate: Social and Economic Organization is a Rather Barren Idea

The theme of specialization is a subject of universal debate. The success of the Taylor system can be explained by the convergence of a large number of evolutionary factors: ever greater scientific specialization, the subsequent educational specialization, the security provided by increasing specialized research, increasingly hair-splitting research subjects. This evolution led to absurd situations: the relative incompetence of specialists outside their own field, inability to communicate with others and, thereby, solve the problems posed in practice. The most important recent advances have often been the result of the *successful organization* involved in one particular project, the synthesis made by specialists who were able to communicate with one another. Perhaps this argues for a reversal of the specialist tendency evident in our methods?

The belief that productivity is synonymous with specialization and that the basis for an increase in productivity is to be found in mechanization and capital betrays a pessimistic concept of human ability.

It has been proved that as long as it is possible to overcome certain enormous difficulties (and these are the reasons why we are so behind) it is possible to organize work along lines which make for much greater human involvement.

We wish to assert vigorously that we can see no limits to what it will be possible for human work to accomplish. *Imagination* is also a *scientific instrument*.

2. A SCIENTIFIC QUESTIONING

It is our belief that the economist will find food for thought in the traditional paths which he clings to. He will, in addition, have to accept the fact that these paths will be questioned as new contributions emerge from other areas of scientific investigation. Our study is a contribution to the *epistemology* of economic thought.[2] This is something which is less and less the exclusive prerogative of Marxists and which is tending to increase vigorously. We do not have to speak of an ecumenical movement but it is nevertheless possible today to see that the enlargement of the concept of *homo economicus* is leading to more and more contributions of a scientific nature. It is a sign of hope.

B. The Probable Obsolescence of Certain Theories

In absolute terms our concept of isoproductive time destroys the validity of productivity measures (cf. p. 28) since it is necessary to link the productivity index to strictly defined working hours. The index is not transferable beyond these working hours. Large productivity variations which are due solely to an organizational factor will slightly lessen the value of the production functions.

Under the influence of organizational innovation, cost curves, viz. the cost of the labour factor, are out of place.

The decentralization of semi-autonomous groups and their total quantitative and qualitative production calls into question the whole principle of economy of scale and industrial concentration benefits (something which spatial analysis has already questioned).

B. The Hesitant Nature of the Return to Man, a Return so often Proclaimed by the Economists

No matter how important Keynes's contribution to economic thinking has been, the return to man which he proclaimed[3] appears to have been rather hesitant and not to have lived up to our expectations. In our attempts at economic theory we are still a long way from incorporating man's real or potential behaviour. Once new forms of job-design have been fully developed, the knowledge gained will force us to rewrite whole portions of economic theory.

As for growth,[4] far from questioning its very existence or its basis, we shall merely have to make sure that it is compatible with a *generalized* improvement of working conditions.

It is imperative to overcome the dichotomy between economic and social affairs[5] which has been institutionalized at government level. It would seem that in France at company level people are beginning to admit to a new form of power-sharing. This is true for both employers[6] and government,[7] who, eleven years after F. Bloch-Laine's book,[8] decided to study company reform.[9] This study makes change easier but it is *not* a *prior requisite* for the strategy of change which we are advocating.

NOTES

(1) Cf. G. Friedmann, *Le Monde*, 20 Sept. 1977, emphasizes and states that this dichotomy is pure deception.

(2) Cf. H. Bartoli, *Science économique et travail*, Dalloz, Paris, 1957; F. Perroux, 'Travail et civilisation', *Esprit*, Oct. 1956, p. 482; F. Sellier and A. Tiano, *Économie du travail*, PUF, Paris, 1962.

(3) Cf. A. Piettre, *Histoire de la pensée économique*, Dalloz, Paris, 1965.

(4) Cf. J. Denizet, 'A la croissance il faut un but', *L'Expansion*, May 1973; J. Attali, 'Vers quelle théorie économique de la croissance?', *Nef*, Sept.–Nov. 1973; A. Cotta, 'Empoi et Croissance. Une politique de l'emploi pour une meilleure croissance', government report, Jan. 1973; 'INSEE: Les Français doivent accepter une moindre croissance de leur pouvoir d'achat', *Le Monde*, 28 June 1974, p. 35.

(5) P. Pascallon, 'Pour un ministère des affaires économiques et sociales', *Le Monde*, 20 Mar. 1973, p. 19.

(6) F. Dalle, 'Vers un nouveau pouvoir dans l'entreprise: 1. Changer mais survivre. 2. Instaurer une démocratie industrielle', *Le Monde*, 25–6 June, 1974. Centre des Jeunes Dirigeants d'Entreprise, *L'Autorité de l'entreprise*, Flammarion, Paris, 1974; 3 articles in *Le Monde*, 21–5 June 1974 on the CJD congress.

(7) P. Drouin, 'La préparation de la réforme de l'entreprise. Du dedans ou du dehors?', *Le Monde*, 18 July 1974, p. 1: P. Sudreau, *Le Monde*, June 1974: 'I find it unacceptable that human capital should sometimes have rights over financial capital. . . .'

(8) F. Bloch-Lainé, *Pour une réforme de l'entreprise*, Seuil, Paris, 1963.

(9) The Sudreau report (cf. above, ch. 3, note 54) submitted to the Government 7 Feb. 1975.

INDEX OF NAMES QUOTED AND BIBLIOGRAPHY

Ackoff, R. – *A Concept of Corporate Planning*. Wiley, New York, 1970.

Aguren, S. (109)*. – *See* **Norstedt**.

Albou, P. – *Problèmes humains de l'entreprise, t. 1: les Relations humaines*, 112 pages. – *t. 2: La Vie de travail*, 116 pages. Dunod-Économie, coll. la vie de l'entreprise, 1971.

Ansoff, I. (35). – *Corporate Strategy*, McGraw-Hill, New York, 1965.

Argyris, C. (32, 33, 41). – *Integrating the Individual and the Organisation*, Wiley, New York, 1964.

Arquie, D., Nebenhaus, D., Noreck, J.-P. (109). – 'Pour une organisation des tâches', *Enseignement et Gestion*, novembre 1973.

— *Quelques expériences de nouvelle organisation des tâches en milieu industriel*, CESA-HEC, Jouy-en-Josas, ronéoté, 133 pages.

Association Française des Conseillers de Direction – *Les Ratios sociaux – essai de mesure du climat social de l'entreprise*, Les éditions d'organisation Paris, 1966, 163 pages.

Attall, J. (189). – 'Vers quelle théorie économique de la croissance?', *La Nef*, septembre–novembre 1973.

— 'Pour une nouvelle doctrine économique', *Le Monde*, 21 juin 1974.

— *La parole et l'outil*, PUF, 1975, 243 pages.

—, **Guillaume, M.** – *L'anti-économique*, PUF, 1974, 248 pages (3e éd., 1975).

Aubert-Krier, J. – *Compatibilité privée*, PUF, 2e éd., 1968, 231 pages.

— *Gestion de l'entreprise*, PUF, t. 1: 1969, 564 pages – t. 2: 1971, 576 pages.

Auerbach, L. B. – *See* **Sadan**.

Baker, G. M. N. – 'The feasibility and utility of human resource accounting', *California Management Review*, Summer 1974, vol. XVI, no. 4.

Balandier, G. (12)

Balland, M. (183). – *See* **Jacquet**.

Barnard, C. I. (35).

Barraux, J. (56, 108). – 'Vers la semaine de quatre jours?', *Problèmes politiques et sociaux*, 15–22 février 1974 (reproduction d'un article de *Entreprise*, 24 septembre 1971, 'Horaires de travail à la carte?').

— 'Pour une usine plus humaine', *Entreprise*, 8 juin 1973.

Bartoli, H. (189). – *Science économique et travail*, Dalloz, 1957, 308 pages.

Batten, J. D. – *Beyond Management by Objectives*, American Management Assoc., 1965.

Baudraz, J.-F. (108, 109). *L'Horaire variable de travail*, Les éditions d'organisation, 1973, 135 pages (1re éd.: Imprimerie Vaudoise, Lausanne, 1971).

— Trois articles, in *Problèmes politiques et sociaux*, 15–22 février 1974: 'L'horaire variable. Oppositions patronale et syndicale?', 'Les coûts d'introduction de l'horaire variable', 'L'horaire variable. Premiers essais.'

Béard, Paul. – *Vers la paix sociale. Le travail en équipes 'autonomes'*. Conférence faite sous le patronage du CNOF à la Société Industrielle de Lille,

*The numbers in parentheses refer to the pages in the book.

7 décembre 1944, 54 pages, brochure disponible au CNOF, Paris.

Béard, Pierre (182). – *See* **Noharet.**

Beauchesne, M. N. (10). – *See* **Roustang.**

Becker, G. (184). – 'Economies of discrimination. A theory of allocation of time', *Economic Journal*, no. 5, 1965.

— *Economic theory*, Knopf, New York, 1971.

Bedel, J. et Sylvestre, J.-M. (109). – 'Huit schémas d'organisation du travail', *Formation continue*, 1973, 3ᵉ trimestre.

Belleville, P. – 'Le prolétariat moderne des ouvriers spécialisés', *Économie et Humanisme*, novembre–décembre 1971.

Belorgey, J.-M. – 'La loi du 16 juillet 1971, ses objectifs, sa portée', *Chronique sociale de France*, janvier–février 1974.

— 'Formation continue. Un premier bilan', *Projet*, février 1974.

— *La Formation professionnelle continue et la promotion sociale en France*, Notes et études documentaires, nos. 3864–3865, La documentation française.

Benne. – *See* **Bennis.**

Bennis, W. G., Benne, K. D., Chin, R. – *The planning of change*, Holt Rinehart and Winston, 627 pages.

Bernácer, G. (53, 54).

Bernard, J.-P. (111). – 'Quel pouvoir pour les cadres?', *Responsables*, mai 1974.

Bernasse, J. (111). – 'Les obstacles à la formation', *Personnel*, novembre–décembre 1971.

Bernoux, Ph., Ruffier, J. – 'Les groupes semi-autonomes de production', *Revue Sociologie du travail*, octobre–décembre 1974.

— *Les Groupes semi-autonomes de production*, Édition Économie et Humanisme, novembre 1974, 269 pages.

—, **Motte, D., Saglio, J.** (10). – *Trois ateliers d'OS*, Éditions ouvrières, Paris, 1973, 215 pages.

Berry, M. – 'Le travail ouvrier. Principales approches effectuées. Problèmes à résoudre', Dossier, Groupe de Recherches en Gestion des Organisations, École Polytechnique, juin 1974.

— 'Synthèse des travaux de Royaumont', *Enseignement et Gestion*, janvier 1975.

Beullac, M. (111).

Bienaymé, A. (54, 182). – 'La politique industrielle de la France est-elle efficace?', *Le Monde*, 28 mai 1974.

— *La Croissance des entreprises*, Bordas, Tome 1: *Analyse dynamique des fonctions de la firme*, 1971, 288 pages. Tome 2: *Analyse dynamique de la concurrence industrielle*, 1973, 402 pages.

— *Entreprise et pouvoir économique*, Dunod, Paris, 1969, 180 pages.

Biggane, J. F., Stewart, P. A. (109). – 'Job enlargement: a case study', in L. E. Davis and J. C. Taylor, *Design of Jobs*, q.v.

Bineau, R. – *Pratique de l'enrichissement des tâches à l'atelier*, Entreprise moderne d'édition, 1975, 106 pages.

Björk, L. – *Les Conditions du travail en URSS*, Éd. Entreprise Moderne, 1955.

Blanchard, F. (11).

Bloch-Lainé, F. (189). – *Pour une réforme de l'entreprise*, Éd. Seuil, 1963.

— 'Le rôle public de l'entreprise', *Le Management*, octobre 1972, pp. 1–38.

Bodiguel – *La réduction du temps de travail*, Éd. ouvrières, 1969.

Bois, P. (111, 183). – 'L'Aménagement des conditions de travail au stade de la conception des bâtiments industriels', Rapport au Ministre du Travail, 1974.

Bonhomme, D. – *See* **Vernet**.

Boudon. – *L'Inégalité des chances*, A. Colin.

Bourguinat, H. – 'Environement et choix énergétiques', Congrès des économistes de langue française, Bordeaux-Pau, mai 1974, ronéoté.

Bouvier-Ajam, M. – *Histoire du travail en France des origines à la Révolution*, LGDJ, Paris, 1957, 765 pages.

— *Histoire du travail en France depuis la Révolution*, LGDJ, Paris, 1969, 604 pages.

Branciard, M. – 'Histoire d'une conversion, entreprise et formation', *Chronique sociale de France*, janvier–février 1974.

Brizay, B. – 'La participation, une nécessité économique', *Entreprise*, 31 janvier 1975.

Brossard, M., Maurice, M. – 'Existe-t-il un modèle universel des structures d'organisation?', *Sociologie du travail*, octobre–décembre 1974.

Brummet, L. (125).

Brunet-Jailly, J., Liess, M. – 'Facteurs et typologie de l'absentéisme pour raisons de santé', LEST, Aix-en-Provence, Action thématique programmée du CNRS en cours.

Bussard, A. – 'Capacité créatrice, âge et médiocrité', *Le Monde*, 22 mai 1974.

Caburol, G. – 'Appréciation de la CGT sur la mise en œuvre de la formation professionnelle et continue', *Chronique sociale de France*, janvier–février 1974.

Caire, G. – 'Participation des travailleurs dans l'entreprise: idéologies, attitudes et motivations syndicales', *Économies et sociétés*, ISEA, décembre 1971.

— *Les Syndicats ouvriers*, PUF, Paris, 1971, 608 pages.

Canapa, M.-P. – 'L'expérience yougoslave', *Projet*, mars 1971.

Carré, J. J. (54).

—, **Dubois, P., Malinvaud, E.** – *La Croissance française. Un essai d'analyse économique causale de l'après-guerre*. Éd. du Seuil, Paris, 1972, 624 pages.

Casella, A. – 'Écrous et boulons sortent des mains du peuple', *Problèmes politiques et sociaux*, 6 avril 1973 (traduction d'un article de *The Guardian*, London, 5 avril 1972).

Cavalié, J.-L. (60). – 'Le Bilan social', Centre Interuniversitaire d'Éducation Permanente, Toulouse, 1974, ronéoté.

Cazamian, P. – 'L'Évolution du travail mécanisé dans la production de masse et ses conséquences pour le travailleur', 30 novembre 1971, 11 pages, ronéoté.

— *La Crise actuelle de l'organisation du travail*, 18 pages, ronéoté.

— *Leçons d'ergonomie industrielle. Une approche globale*, Cujas, coll. Éducation Permanente, 1974, 155 pages.

Cecconi, O. – *La Société industrielle*, PUF, dossiers Logos, 1972, 96 pages.

Cekota, A. – *Bata, créateur génial*, trad. française publiée par la S.A. des Chaussures Bata, Paris, 1968, 341 pages.

Ceyrac, F. (111).

Chaban-Delmas, J. (1).

Chaigneau, Y. (186).

Charmeil, C. – 'Forces et faiblesses du calcul économique', *Économie appliquée*, no. 3, 1971.

Charnes, Cooper, Koznetsky – 'Measuring, monitoring and modeling quality of life', *Management Science*, vol. 19 no. 10, juin 1973 (The Institute of Management Sciences).

Charraud, A., Saada, K. – 'Les écarts de salaries entre hommes et femmes', *Économie et statistiques*, juillet-août 1970.

Chaumette, P. – 'A quelles conditions et sous quelles formes se développe la restructuration des tâches?', rapport de synthèse, Institut Entreprise et Personnel, Paris, février 1975.

Chedaux, I. – 'L'entreprise américaine redécouvre l'homme', *Entreprise*, 21–28 décembre 1970, pp. 25–33.

Cherns, A. (7, 12, 44, 111). – 'Negotiating the contract', roneoed.

— 'Modern organization theory', janvier 1973, 12 pages, roneoed.

— 'Research. Can behavioral scientists help managers improve their organizations?', *Organizational Dynamics*, Winter 1973.

— 'Personnel management and the social sciences', unpublished report, Royaumont, 1974.

— 'Better work lives. A social scientist's view', 14 pages, roneoed.

— 'Better working lives', unpublished report, Royaumont, 1974.

— 'Work or life', Conference of the British Association for the Advancement of Science, London, August 1973.

— 'Organization change through experiment', 9 pages, roneoed.

— 'Sociotechnical analysis', 8 pages, roneoed.

—, **Clark, P., Jenkins, W.** – 'Action research and the development of the social sciences', Tavistock Institute, London, August 1973, 12 pages, roneoed.

Chin. – *See* **Bennis.**

Chinaud. (183).

Chombart de Lauwe, P. H. – 'Une critique de la notion de besoin et l'introduction à une problématique de la demande', document présenté au Séminaire organisé par l'IRIS, Université de Paris IX Dauphine, 11–12 avril 1975, 6 pages, ronéoté.

Chotard, Y. (10).

Cibert, A. (183). – *Comptabilité analytique*, Dunod-économie, Paris, 1970, 282 pages.

Clark, A. W. – 'The client–practitioner relationship as an inter-system engagement', Tavistock Institute, August 1973, 20 pages, roneoed.

— 'Sanction: a critical element in action-research', Tavistock Institute, November 1971, 35 pages, roneoed.

Clark, P. A. (12). – *See also* **Cherns.**

— *Action research and organization change*, Ed. Harper and Row, London, 1972.

Clerc, J.-M. (108, 109). – 'Expériences en vue d'une organisation plus humaine du travail industriel: quelques aperçus sur un colloque', *Bulletin IIES*, no. 11, Genève, janvier 1974.

Cooper. – *See* **Charnes.**

Coriat (13).

Cotta, A. (189). – 'Emploi et croissance. Une politique de l'emploi pur une meillure croissance', Rapport remis à M. Edgar Faure, Ministre d'État chargé des affaires sociales, janvier, 1973, 40 pages.

— 'Les fonctions de production', cours de doctorat, Slud, 201 pages.

— *Les Choix économiques de la grande entreprise*, Dunod, Paris, 266 pages.

Courtheoux, J.-P. — 'La participation au progrès. Erreurs en économie et économie en erreur', *Économies et sociétés*, ISEA, décembre 1971.

Crozier, M. (57, 185). — *Le Monde des employés de bureau*. Résultats d'une enquête menée dans sept compagnies d'assurances parisiennes, Éd. Seuil, Paris, 1965, 238 pages.

— *Petits fonctionnaires au travail*. Compte rendu d'une enquête sociologique effectuée dans une grande administration publique parisienne, CNRS, 1955, 127 pages.

— *Le Phénomène bureaucratique*. Essai sur les tendances bureaucratiques des systèmes d'organisations modernes et sur leurs relations en France avec le système social et culturel, Éd. Seuil, Paris, 1963, 414 pages.

Cyert, R. M. (35).

—, **March, J. G.** — *A Behavioral Theory of the Firm*, Prentice Hall, 1963.

Dalle, F. (109). — 'Vers un nouveau pouvoir dans l'entreprise: 1. Changer mais survivre. 2. Instaurer une démocratie industrielle', *Le Monde*, 25 et 26 juin 1974.

Daubigney, J. P. — 'Actualité du système "Parodi" dans les comportements salariaux des entreprises', *Revue économique*, 1969, no. 3, pp. 497–514.

Dautresme, D. (10, 110, 183). — 'Rapport du sous-groupe D du groupe "Prospective du travail" intulé: "Organisation du travail" ', Commissariat général du Plan, Paris, février 1974, 35 pages, ronéoté (en collaboration).

— 'Quelques réflexions sur la productivité dans la banque', *Bulletin du ministère des Finances*, novembre 1974.

Davis, L. E. (7, 12, 43, 44, 46, 53, 58, 67, 87, 109, 146, 147, 150). — 'Job design and productivity, a new approach', *Personnel*, USA, March 1957).

—, **Taylor, J. C.** — *Design of Jobs*, Penguin Modern Management Readings, Penguin Education, 1972, 479 pages.

Davis, R. C. (16).

De Backer, P. (111, 185). — 'Négociation et conflits dans l'entreprise: quelques indications d'application de la psychologie des conflits', *Metra*, vol. 11, no. 1, mars 1972.

Decaillot, M. — 'Aspects de l'économie hongroise', *Économie et Politique*, janvier 1972.

De Chalendar, J. (108). — *Vers un nouvel aménagement de l'année*. La documentation française, Paris, 1970, 126 pages.

— 'L'horaire variable au libre', rapport au Premier ministre, *La Documentation française*, avril 1972.

Degot, V., Fixari, D. — 'L'approche quantifée des problèmes d'organisation du travail', Centre de gestion scientifique, École Nationale Supérieure des Mines de Paris, mars 1974, 11 pages, ronéoté.

Dehove, G., Édouard-Dolléans — *Histoire du travail en France. Mouvement ouvrier et législation sociale*, Domat-Monchrestien, Paris, tome 1: 1953, 419 pages, tome 2: 1955, 511 pages.

Delamotte, Y. (98/110). — *See also* **Touraine.**

Delamotte, Y. — 'Recherches en vue d'une organisation, plus humaine du travail industriel', rapport établi à la demande de J. Fontanet, Ministre du travail, de l'emploi et de la population, in *La Documentation française*, Paris, mars 1972, 96 pages.

— 'L'enrichissement des tâches, les groupes semi-autonomes', *Personnel*, mars–avril 1973.

— 'Eléments d'une action nationale en vue de la valorisation des tâches industrielles', *Ensiegnement et Gestion*, novembre 1973.

— 'Conflit industriel et participation ouvrière', *Sociologie du travail*, no. 1, 1959.

—, **Walker, K. F.** — 'L'humanisation du travail et la qualité de la vie de travail. Tendances et problèmes', *Bulletin de l'ILES*, Genève, janvier 1974.

Delors, J. (12, 48, 59). — *Changer*, Éd. Stock, Paris, 1975. 343 pages.

— *Les Indicateurs sociaux*, Éd. Sedeis, coll. Futuribles, 1971, 392 pages. Préface de Bertrand de Jouvenel, Introduction de Jacques Delors.

— *Les Transformations du mode de vie Mobilité et coûts de l'adaptation. Temps et espaces de loisirs. Problèmes du troisième âge*, A. Colin, Paris, 1970, 232 pages. Préface de J. Delors.

— *La Seconde Société industrielle* (J. M. Albertini, J. Delors, J. Y. Jolif, B. de Jouvenel . . .), études coordonnées par Guy Roustang, Éd. Économie et Humanisme et Éd. Ouvrières, Paris, 1967, 200 pages.

— 'Changer le travail pour changer la vie', *Réalités*, 1973.

— 'Une stratégie pour le progrès', *Projet*, février 1974.

— 'Pour une politique du travail. 1. Gagner sa vie ou réussir sa vie. 2. Organiser l'aventure collective', *Le Figaro*, 11 et 13 juillet 1974.

De Monès, J. (41, 45). — *See* **Plaquevent.**

Demonque, M. — *See* **Eichenberger.**

Denizet, J. (189). — 'A la croissance il faut un but', *L'Expansion*, mai 1973.

De Woot, Ph. (111). — *Pour une doctrine de l'entreprise*, Éd. Seuil, 1968, 284 pages.

— 'La participation dans l'entreprise', *Économies et sociétés*, ISEA, décembre 1971.

Dichter, E. — *Motivating Human Behavior* (McGraw-Hill, New York, 1971).

Dischamps, J.-C. — *Compatabilité générale de l'entreprise*, Cujas, Paris, 1972, 316 pages.

Dockès, P. — *L'Internationale du capital*, PUF, 1975, 287 pages.

— 'Division du travail et développement des forces productives', mars 1974, 18 pages, ronéoté.

Dofny, J. — *See* **Touraine.**

Donnadieu, J.-L. (10, 53, 57, 59, 91, 110, 118, 183). — 'La révolte contre l'efficacité', *Le Monde*, 5 septembre 1972.

— 'BSN: une prise de conscience d'aspirations nouvelles', *Professions et Entreprises*, mai–juin 1973.

— 'La planification du changement social: recherches et perspectives', exposé au Congrès de l'Association Nationale des Directeurs et Chefs de Personnel, 21–23 mars 1974, 15 pages, ronéoté.

— 'Les entreprises parlent d'expérience', *Projet*, février 1974.

— 'Carrefour sur les conditions de travail', Rapport final aux Assises nationales de Caen, 10 pages, ronéoté, reproduit dans *Professions et Entreprises*.

Douard, H. (53, 57, 58, 110). — *See also* **Reynaud, J. D.**

— 'Nouvelles approches de l'organisation du travail', *Formation continue*, 1973, 3e trimestre.

Drouin, P. (189). — 'La préparation de la réforme de l'entreprise: du dedans ou du dehors?', *Le Monde*, 18 juillet 1974.

Drucker, P. (32, 35).

Dubois, M. — 'La fin des OS?', *Formation continue*, 1973, 3e trimestre.

— 'Organisation du travail et gestion du personnel, leur évolution: entretien avec Renaud Sainsaulieu', *Formation continue*, 1973, 3e trimestre.

Dubois, P. — *See also* **Carré**.

Dubreuil, H. (36, 37, 38, 49, 58, 94). — *See also* **Rimailho**.

— *Les Standards*, Grasset, 1946, 434 pages.

— *A chacun sa chance. L'organisation du travail fondée sur la liberté*, Grasset, 1935, 524 pages, 2e éd. en 1939, 324 pages.

— *J'ai fini ma journée*, Librairie du compagnonnage, 1971.

— *Promotion*, Éd. de l'entreprise moderne, Paris, 1963, 237 pages (préface de L. Armand).

— *L'Exemple de Bat'a. La libération des initiatives individuelles dans une entreprise géante*, Grasset, 350 pages.

— *Nouveaux standards. Les sources de la productivité et de la joie*, Grasset, 341 pages.

— *Les Codes de Roosevelt et les perspectives de la vie sociale*, Grasset, 231 pages.

— *Employeurs et salariés en France*, Alcan, Paris, 460 pages.

— *La République industrielle*, Bibliothèque d'éducation, Paris, 1921 (préface de Ch. Gide).

— *La Fin des monstres. Idée d'une organisation contraire à la centralisation et à l'étatisme*, Grasset, 310 pages.

— *Le Travail et la civilisation. Esquisse de l'histoire et de la philosophie du travail*, Plon, Paris.

— *Si tu aimes la liberté*, Sorlot, Paris.

— *Le Véritable Intéressement des travailleurs à la vie de l'entreprise*, Éd. de l'Entreprise moderne, Paris.

— 'L'Organisation du travail et le système des équipes autonomes', *Revue internationale du travail*, 1951, pp. 308 et suivantes.

Dumont, J.-P. (10, 109). — *La Fin des OS?*, Éd. Mercure de France, 1973, 246 pages.

— 'Amélioration des conditions de travail: dans le domaine de l'élargissement des tâches, Renault va plus loin que FIAT', *Le Monde*, 10 juillet 1973.

Dunajewski, H. (184). — 'Décisions d'amelioration des conditions de travail sans influence sur la productivité: étude d'un cas particulier aux garages en France', LEST-CNRS, Aix-en-Provence, september 1973, 157 pages, ronéoté.

Durand, C. — *Conscience ouvrière et action syndicale*, Mouton, Paris, 1971, 260 pages.

— 'Les politiques patronales d'enrichissement des tâches', *Sociologie du travail*, octobre–décembre 1974.

Durand, C. — *See also* **Willener** and **Touraine**.

Dyer, J. S., Hoffenberger, M. (184). — 'On the evaluation of the quality of working life: some reflexions on production and cost, and a method for system definitions', 1972, 35 pages, roneoed.

Édouard-Dolléans – *See* **Dehove.**

Eggens, J.-B. – 'Introduction critique au "Job Enrichment". Peut-on enrichir le travail à la chaîne?', *Le Management*, octobre 1971.

— 'Une nouvelle carte à jouer: l'entreprise fédérale', *Le Management*, mai 1973.

— 'Peut-on parler d'une théorie générale de la firme?', *Revue Direction*, no. 1, FNEGE, Paris, mai 1975.

Eichenberger, J.-Y. (152). – 'Formation continue et entreprise', *Chronique sociale de France*, janvier–février 1974.

—, **Demonque, M.** – *La Participation*, Éd. France-Empire, Paris, 1969.

Emery, F. E. (43, 44, 45, 46, 58, 59). – *Systems Thinking*. Penguin Modern Management Readings, Penguin education, 1969, 398 pages.

—, **Thorsrud, E.** – *Form and Content in Industrial Democracy*, Tavistock Institute, London, 1964.

—, **Trist, E. L.** – 'Socio-technical systems', republished in *Systems Thinking*, ed. F. E. Emery, Penguin Modern Management Readings, 1969).

Fantoli, A. (110). – 'Étude d'un nouveau plan de l'organisation du travail, principaux aspects méthodologiques', ARPES, Milan, mars 1974, ronéoté.

Faramond, G. de (109). – 'En Suède, Volvo a inauguré sa première usine "sans chaîne" ', *Le Monde*, 11 juin 1974.

Faure, E. – 'L'aménagement du temps de travail', *Revue française des Affaires sociales*, Paris, octobre 1972.

Faverge, J.-M. – *See* **Ombredane.**

Fayol, H. (16, 17, 21). – *Administration industrielle et générale*, Dunod, Paris, 1970, 151 pages.

Fine, S. A., Wiley, W. W. – *An introduction to functional job analysis; a scaling of selected tasks from the social welfare field*, The W. E. Upjohn Institute for employment research.

Fiori, G. (11). – 'Lavorare stanca. Da necessità a virtù?', *Mondo economico*, Milan, 14 avril 1973, reproduit sous le titre: 'Le travail en question', in *Problèmes économiques*, 11 juillet 1973.

Fixari, D. – *See* **Degot.**

Flamholtz, E. (125, 183). – 'A model for Human Resource Valuation: a Stochastic Process with Service Rewards', *Accounting Review*, April 1972.

— 'Toward a theory of Human Resource Value in Formal organization', *Accounting Review*, October 1972.

— 'Human Resource Accounting: Its Role in Management Planning and Control', *Economisch en Sociaal Tijdscrift*, Antwerp, February 1973.

Flowers, V. S. – *See* **Scott Myers.**

Fontanet, J. – 'Portée et limites de la participation', *Économies et sociétés*, ISEA, décembre 1971.

Ford, H. (37, 38). – *My Life and My Work*, London, 1922.

Foster, M. – 'The theory and practice of action-research in organizations', Tavistock Institute, June 1973, 30 pages, roneoed.

Fourastié, J. (24).

Foy, N. (109). – 'Industrial democracy at Norsk Hydro', *European Business* no. 36, Winter 1973.

Franck – 'Epitaphe pour la D.P.O.', *Le Management*, novembre 1973.

Fridenson, P. (53). – *Histoire des Usines Renault. Naissance de la grande indus-*

trie (1898–1939), Seuil, Paris, 1972.

Friedmann, G. (12, 33, 38, 39, 42, 57, 58, 59, 189). – *Le Travail en miettes*, Gallimard, Paris, 1956, 347 pages.

— *Comme un brin de paille* . . . 1. 'Vers la fin des OS'. 2. 'Misères et grandeurs de l'autogestion'. 3. 'Les leçons du "socialisme à visage humain".' 4. 'Une chance pour la démocratie', in *Le Monde*, 21–22–23 et 24–25 mars 1974.

—, **Naville, P.** – *Traité de sociologie du travail*, A. Colin, Tome 1, 1961, 468 pages; Tome 2, 1962, 441 pages.

Frisch-Gauthier, J. – 'Moral et satisfaction au travail', *Traité de sociologie du travail* de G. Friedmann et P. Naville, Tome 2, pp. 133 à 157.

Froidevaux, P. (41, 42, 46, 56, 57, 58, 60, 107). – 'Rapport sur la réunion d'experts des 17–19 octobre 1973: l'absentéisme et la rotation du personnel' (Programme employeurs–travailleurs), OCDE, Paris, 15 mai 1974, 58 pages, ronéoté.

— 'Les modèles de travail et la satisfaction dans un kibboutz en Israël. Un test pour l'hypothèse de Herzberg (d'après les travaux de D. Macarov)', *Bulletin de l'IRAS*, Villeurbanne, mai 1974.

— 'Étude sur les facteurs d'absentéisme et la façon dont ils sont perçus par l'encadrement d'une entreprise', Thèse de doctorat de IIIe cycle des Sciences Sociales du Travail, Université Lyon II, 1971, 391 pages, ronéoté.

Froissart, D. – *Comment implanter la direction par les objectifs*, Entreprise moderne d'Édition, Paris, 1971, 154 pages.

— *Déléguer avec succès des responsabilités*. Un programme d'action pour la direction et ses cadres, Éd. Hommes et Techniques, Puteaux, 1970, 147 pages.

Galnier, E. (11). – 'Pourquoi s'absentent-ils?', *L'Usine nouvelle*, juin 1973 (no. spécial mensuel).

Garcin, W. – *Cogestion et participation dans les entreprises des pays du marché commun*, Éd. Jupiter, Paris, 1968.

Gautrat, J. – *See* **Roustang**.

Gazzo, M. (56). – 'L'européenne au travail', in revue *30 jours d'Europe*, novembre 1973, reproduit in *Problèmes économiques*, 28 novembre 1973.

Gélinier, O. (35, 150). – 'Peut-on mesurer la rentabilité des investissements sociaux?', *Le Monde*, 30 octobre 1973.

— *Le Secret des structures compétitives. Management ou bureaucratie?*, Hommes et Techniques, 1968, 262 pages.

— *Direction participative par objectifs*, Hommes et Techniques, 1968, 60 pages.

Gellerman, S. W. (110). – *Management by Motivation*, American Management Assoc., 1968.

— 'L'onde de choc du job enrichment', *Le Management*, avril 1972.

Gentil, B. – *L'Amélioration du travail des cadres*, Éd. Hachette, coll. Formation continue, 1973, 138 pages.

Géris (Groupe d'études et de recherches sur les indicateurs sociaux des entreprises) (Paris).

Gibson, Ch. – 'Volvo increases productivity through job enrichment', *California Management Review*, vol. 14, no. 4, Summer 1973.

Gilbreth, M. (16).

Giles, W.-J., Robinson, D. F. (126) – *Human Asset Accounting*. Institute for Personnel Management, London, October 1972.

Gillet, B. – *Améliorer la formation professionnelle par l'étude du travail*, Les éditions d'organisation, Paris, 1973, 256 pages.

Glautier, M. W. E. – 'Human resource accounting: a critique of research objectives for the development of human resource accounting models', Document présenté au Séminaire sur la comptabilité des ressources humaines. The European Institute for Advanced Studies in Management, Bruxelles, 28–29 novembre 1974, 23 pages, ronéoté.

—, **Underdown, B.** – 'Problems and Prospects of Accounting for Human Assets', *Management Accounting*, March 1973, pp. 98–102.

Gold, B. – *Explorations in Managerial Economics*, Macmillan, 1971.

Gorse, G. (10) – 'Humaniser le travail, c'est possible', *L'Expansion*, décembre 1973.

Gorz, A. – 'Le despotisme d'usine et ses lendemains', *Les Temps modernes*, nos. 314–15, septembre–octobre 1972.

— *Critique de la division du travail*, Seuil, 1973.

Gouault, J.-M. – 'L'éducation permanente selon la CGT-FO', *Projet*, février 1974.

Grandjean, E. (25, 26). – *Précis d'ergonomie. Organisation physiologique du travail*, Dunod, 1969, 276 pages.

Grossin, W. (56). – *Le Travail et le temps*, Paris, 1969.

Grote, R. C. – 'Implementing job enrichment', *California Management Review*, vol. XV, no. 1, 1972, pp. 16–21.

Gruson, C. (29, 55).

Guélaud, F. (10). – *See* **Roustang**.

Guest, P. (56).

Guillaume, M. – *See* **Attali**.

Guitton, H. – Compte rendu de l'ouvrage de P.-L. Reynaud, *Précis de psychologie économique*, in *Revue d'Économie politique*, janvier–février 1975, p. 143.

Gunter, H. – 'Une humanisation du travail orientée vers les travailleurs: quelques approches', *Bulletin de l'IIES*, Genève, janvier 1974.

Gutenberg, Richman. – *Dynamics of Management*, International Textbook Company, Scranton, Pennsylvania, 1968.

Hannoun, M. (57). – 'Jeunesse, maturité et disparition des grands établissements industriels', *Économie et Statistique*, janvier 1974.

Harbison, F., Myers, Ch. A. – *La Formation, clé du développement. Les Stratégies du développement des ressources humaines*, Éd. Ouvrières, Économie et Humanisme, Paris, 1967, 287 pages.

Hekimian, J., Jones, C. H. (125, 183). – 'Put People on your Balance-Sheet', *Harvard Business Review*, Jan.-Feb., 1967.

Herzberg, F. (39, 40, 43, 45, 58, 59, 62, 71, 75, 87, 110). – *Work and the Nature of Man*, Ed. The World Publishing Company, Cleveland, Ohio, 1966.

— *Job Attitudes. Motivation to Work*, Wiley, New York, 1959.

Higgin. – *See* **Trist**.

Hoffenberger, M. (184). – *See* **Dyer**.

Hoffman, E. B. (108). – 'La semaine de quatre jours soulève de nouveaux problèmes', *Problèmes politiques et sociaux*, 15–22 février 1974 (traduction d'un article de The Conference Board Record, New York, vol. IX, no. 2, February

1972, pp. 21–6, 'The four-day week raises new problems').

Huxley, A. (57). – *La Fin et les moyens*, Plon, Paris, 1939.

Ivaldi, J.-P. – 'Les trois étapes de construction d'un système de rémunération', *Le Management*, février 1971.

Jacob, J. – 'L'action syndicale après la loi du 16 juillet 1971', *Chronique sociale de France*, janvier–février 1974.

Jacques, E. (41, 43). – *Rémunération objective*, Éd. Hommes et Techniques.

— *Intervention et changement dans l'entreprise*, Dunod, 1972, 301 pages.

Jacquet,·J. L. (58). – 'Experiments in Human Resource Accounting in France', Document présenté au Séminaire sur la comptabilité des ressources humaines. The European Institute for Advanced Studies in Management, Brussels, 28–9 November 1974, 16 pages, roneoed.

—, **Balland, M., Vermay, A.** – 'Éléments quantifiables d'une politique de personnel', Rapport de recherches, Institut Entreprise et Personnel, Paris, décembre 1974.

—, —, **Le Cloarec, H., Perrin, D., Rheims, B. W.** – 'Données quantifiables de la gestion du personnel', Institut Entreprise et Personnel, Paris, janvier 1973, 91 pages, ronéoté.

Jardillier, P. – *L'Organisation humaine du travail*, PUF, Que sais-je?, Paris, 1973.

Jeannet, M. – *Structures et processus du changement au sein des entreprises*, Éd. Droz.

Jeannière, A. – 'Travail et non-travail au fil des heures', *Projet*, février 1974.

Jenkins, W. (12). – *See* **Cherns**.

Johnson, W. B. – *See* **Levitan**.

Johnston, D.-F. (55). – 'The future of work: three possible alternatives', *Monthly Labor Review*, May 1972.

Jones, C. H. (185). – *See* **Hekimian**.

Kahn (149).

Kahn, H. (24).

Kapp, B., Proust, O. – *Les Horaires libres. Humanisation dans l'entreprise*, Éd. Chotard et associés, 1973.

Kassam, A. – 'Données quantifiables de la gestion du personnel', rapport de stage, HEC, Jouy-en-Josas, 1974, 135 pages, ronéoté.

Katz (149).

Kaufmann, A. – 'L'informatique et la promotion sociale', *Économies et sociétés*, ISEA, décembre 1971.

Keynes (15, 33, 147, 189).

Knapp, Ch. B. – 'A human capital approach to the burden of the military draft', *Journal of Human Resources*, vol. VIII, no. 4, Fall 1973.

Kohler (35).

Kolm, S.-C. – 'Structuration informationnelle centralisée et hiérarchisée. Une contribution à la théorie des organisations', *Revue économique*, no. 3, 1969.

Koontz, H. (34, 35). – 'The Management Theory Jungle', in H. Koontz and C. O'Donnell, *Management: A Book of Readings*, McGraw-Hill, New York, 1964.

Koznetsky – *See* **Charnes**.

Krasucki, H. (110).

Krumnov, F. – 'Que faire dans les trois ans qui viennent?', *Formation continue*,

1973, 3ᵉ trimestre (extraits d'un article du *Nouvel observateur*, 19 mars 1973).

Laber, G. – 'Human capital in Southern migration', *Human Resources*, vol. VIII, no. 2, Spring 1973.

Lancaster, K. (184). – 'A new approach to consumer theory', *Journal of Political Economy*, April 1966.

Lantier, F. (112). – 'L'analyse des systèmes socio-techniques, moyen de connaissance et d'action pour les formateurs', document CEREQ, présenté au séminaire de Royaumont, mars 1974, ronéoté.

Lapassade, G. – *Groupes, organisations, institutions (Recherches institutionnelles, 1)*, Gauthiers-Villars, 1974, 228 pages.

Lassègue, P. – *Problèmes généraux de la gestion des entreprises*, Les course de droit, Paris, 1974–1975.

— *Gestion de l'entreprise et comptabilité*, Dalloz, Paris, 1972, 676 pages.

Lasserre, G. – 'Fonctions du profit et participation des travailleurs', *Économies et sociétés*, ISEA, décembre 1971.

Laville, A. (54, 110).

—, **Teiger, C., Wisner, A.** – *Âge et contraintes de travail. Aspects physiques, psychologiques et sociaux*, NEB, éditions scientifiques, BP 3, 78350 Jouy-en-Josas, mars 1975, 350 pages.

Lavoisier (21).

Lawrence, P. R., Lorsch, J. W. – *Adapter les structures de l'entreprise. Intégration ou différenciation*, Les éditions d'organisation, 1973, 223 pages.

Lebel, B. (107, 108). – 'Deux exemples de situations présentés au Séminaire de Royaumont', Institut Entreprise et Personnel, mars 1974, ronéoté.

Le Cloarec, H. (183). – *See also* **Jacquet.**

— 'La prise en compte des ressources humaines', *Direction et Gestion*, mai–juin 1972.

Lehmann, G. (56).

Lehn, J., Reveillion, P. (183). – 'Mesurer le social', *Le Monde*, 27–28 mai 1975, p. 26.

Lénine (19).

Lesiré, Ogrel H. – *See* **Tiano.**

Lev, B., Schwartz, A. (125). – 'On the use of the Economic concept of Human Capital in Financial Statements', *Accounting Review*, January 1971.

Levinson, H. (55). – *Emotional Health in the World of Work*, Harper-Row, 1964. (French trans. *Les Cadres sous pression*. Les Éditions d'organisation, Collection INSEAD Management, 1973.)

— *Les Motivations de l'homme au travail*, Éd. d'Organisation.

Levitan, S. A., Johnson, W. B. – 'Les limites à la restructuration et à l'enrichissement des tâches', *Problèmes économiques*, 7 novembre 1973.

Lewin, K. (35, 57). – *Les Relations humaines*, PUF, 1959, 299 pages.

— *Resolving Social Conflicts, selected papers on group dynamics*, New York, Harper Bros., 1948, 230 pages. (Research Center for Group Dynamics.)

Lichnerowicz, A. (12).

Liess, M. – *See* **Brunet-Jailly.**

Likert, R. (33, 125, 150). – *New Patterns of Management*, McGraw-Hill, New York, 1961, 279 pages.

— *The Human Organization: Its Management and Value*, McGraw-Hill, New York, 1967, 258 pages.

Lindsay, C. A. (58). — 'An examination and test of a modification of the Herzberg theory', *Dissertation Abstracts*, 1966, no. 26 (II), p. 6873.

Liu, M. (108, 112). — 'Réorganisation des emplois dans un atelier à automatisation incomplète', document présenté au séminaire de Royaumont, mars 1974, 14 pages, ronéoté.

— 'Putting the job satisfaction debate in perspective', *Management International Review*, vol. XIII, 1973 (4–5).

— 'Elaboration d'une pédagogie nouvelle pour la formation du personnel ouvrier', document ronéoté.

Ljungberg-van Beinum, I. – *See* **Van Beinum.**

Lobstein, J. (33).

Lorsch, J. W. – *See* **Lawrence.**

Lussato, B. (17, 21, 32, 35, 46, 54, 56). – *Introduction critique aux théories des organisations (modèles cybernétiques, hommes, entreprises)*, Dunod, 1972, 192 pages.

Luthans, F. – *See* **Reif.**

McCormick, E. J. (55). – *See* **Tiffin.**

McGregor, D. – *The Human Side of Enterprise*, McGraw-Hill, 1960.

Mahaux, R. (55). – *Le Gaspillage du capital humain dans l'entreprise*. Une enquête auprès de mille deux cents cadres et trois cents dirigeants, Éd. Marabout, Monde contemporain, Verviers, 1974, 201 pages.

Maier, N. R. (55, 56). – *Psychology in Industrial Organizations*, 4th ed., Houghton Mifflin, 1973.

Maire, E. (110).

Malinvaud, E. (21, 54). – *See also* **Carré.**

— 'Programme d'expansion et taux d'intérêt', *Econometrica*, vol. 27, 1959.

— 'The Analogy Between Atemporal and Intertemporal Theories of Resource Allocation', *Review of Economic Studies*, 1961.

— 'Interest Rates in the Allocation of Resources', in *The Theory of Interest Rates*, Hatin and Brechling, editors, Macmillan, 1966.

Malm. – *See* **Pigors.**

March, J.-G. – *See also* **Cyert.**

—, **Simon, H. A.** (32, 35). – *Organizations*, Wiley, New York, 1958.

Marczewski, J. (11). – *Crise de planification socialiste?*, PUF, Paris, 1973, 298 pages.

Marquès, E. (183). – 'Gestion du capital humain', *Le Management*, décembre 1973.

— *La Comptabilité des ressources humaines*, Éditions Hommes et Techniques, 1975, 136 pages.

Marx, K. (19, 54). – *Le Capital*, Éd. Molitor, Paris.

Mary, J.-A. – 'Direction participative par objectifs et enrichissement des tâches. Une expérience vécue de Guilliet à Auxerre', *Travail et Méthodes*, juin-juillet 1974.

Mathé, C. – 'L'investissement d'équipment et le personnel', Mémoire du CESI, Gif-sur-Yvette, 1973, 57 pages, ronéoté.

Maurice, M. – *See* **Brossard.**

Mayer, A. (51). – 'L'évolution de l'homme', *Personnel*, Paris, octobre 1969.

Mayers – *See* **Pigors**.

Mayo, E. (33). – *The Human problems of an Industrial Civilization*, Boston, 1933, Harvard University division of research, graduate school of business administration, 1946, 187 pages.

Meister, A. (11). – *Où va l'autogestion yougoslave?*, Éd. Anthropos, Paris, 1971.

— 'L'autogestion: espoir ou illusion?', *Hommes et Commerce*, septembre–octobre 1973.

— *Autogestion: les équivoques du cas yougoslave*. 1. 'De la bureaucratie au réformisme.' 2. 'Les charges de la démocratie.' 3. 'La leçon des micro-expériences', in *Le Monde*, 1, 2, 35 3 juillet 1974.

Mendès-France, P. – *Dialogues avec l'Asie d'aujourd'hui*, Gallimard, coll. Idées, Paris, 1972.

Migué, J.L. – 'La participation, l'efficacité et la théorie économique de la coopérative', *Économie et sociétés*, ISEA, décembre 1971.

Mital, G. (110).

Mitchell, T. R. – *See* **Scott**.

Monnin, P. – *Comment revaloriser le travail administratif*, Dunod-Entreprise, 1975, 106 pages.

Montbrial, T. de (54). – 'Intertemporal general equilibrium and interest rates theory', *Économie appliquée*. 1973, p. 877.

— 'Reformulation et généralisation de la théorie néoclassique de l'intérêt', *Économie appliquée*, 1973, p. 919.

Montel, J. (59). – 'L'emploi industriel et les jeunes', in revue *DIS*. Ministère du développement industriel et scientifique, Paris, janvier–février 1972.

Montmollin, M. de (54). – 'En Chine, une nouvelle morale industrielle?', *Le Monde*, 11 mars 1975.

— 'Taylorisme et anti-taylorisme', *Sociologie du travail*, octobre–décembre 1974.

— *Les Systèmes hommes-machines*. PUF, 1967.

— *L'Analyse du travail, un préalable à la formation*, Éd. A. Colin.

Morin, E. (54, 185, 186).

Morin, P. – *Le Travail dans l'entreprise et la société modernes*, Hachette.

Motte, D. (10). – *See* **Bernoux**.

Muller, E. (33).

Murray, H. (43, 45, 46, 59, 109). – *See also* **Trist**.

— 'An introduction to socio-technical systems at labour group level', Tavistock Institute, London, October 1970, roneoed.

Myers, Ch. A. – *See* **Harbison**.

Naville, P. (87, 59). – *See* **Friedmann**.

Nebenhaus, D. (109). – *See* **Arquie**.

Noharet, J., Béard, P. Poirson, P., Tarrière, E. (184). – 'Le travail non qualifié. Propositions et exemples d'actions', document interne, Institut Entreprise et Personnel, Lyon, octobre 1973, ronéoté.

Noreck, J.-P. (109). – *See* **Arquie**.

Normann, R. – *See* **Maier**.

Norstedt, J.-P., Agurens, S. (109). – 'Le rapport Saab-Scania. Une expérience de modification de l'organisation du travail et de ses méthodes', SAF, Confédération patronale suédoise, Départment technique, Stockholm, février 1973, 52 pages, ronéoté.

Novara, F. (109). – 'L'élargissement des tâches à la compagnie Olivetti', *Revue internationale du Travail*, octobre 1973.

Olson (Comité) (12). – *Toward a Social Report*, US Minister of Health, Washington, DC, 1969.

Ombredane, A., Faverge, J.-M. – *L'Analyse du travail, facteur d'économie humaine et de productivité*, PUF, 1955, Bibliothèque de psychologie appliquée, 236 pages.

Ortsman, O. (12, 58, 59, 112). – 'Une expérience très ponctuelle de formation d'ingénieurs à la démarche socio-technique', FNEGE, 12 mars 1974, 20 pages, ronéoté.

— 'Le cas de la Shell anglaise', *Enseignement et Gestion*, novembre 1973.

— 'Le Tavistock Institute. Son rôle dans la conception et la diffusion de nouvelles méthodes d'organisation du travail', *Enseignement et Gestion*, novembre 1973.

Owen, J.-D. (150, 184). – *The Price of Leisure (an economic analysis of the demand for leisure time)*, Rotterdam University Press, 1969, 169 pages.

Page, A. – *L'Économie de l'éducation*, PUF, SUP, L'économiste.

Paillet, P. – *Faut-il planifier l'éducation?*, Les Éditions ESF/Entreprise Moderne d'Édition.

Parias, H. – *See* **Touraine.**

Pascallon, P. (189). – 'Pour un ministère des affaires économiques et sociales', *Le Monde*, 20 mars 1973.

Paul, W. J. (62). – 'Des expériences vécues d'enrichissement des fonctions', *Direction et Gestion*, septembre–octobre 1972.

—, **Robertson, K.B.** – *Job Enrichment and Employee Motivation*, Gower Press, Epping, 1970.

Perrin, D. – *See* **Jacquet.**

Perroux, F. (11, 12, 54, 113, 159, 185, 186, 189). – 'La participation', *Économies et Sociétés* (cahiers de l'ISEA), tome VI, nos. 9–10, septembre–octobre 1972 (sous la direction de): numéro consacré à 'La participation (II)' de la revue *Économies et sociétés*, cahiers de l'ISEA, décembre 1971.

Perroux, F. – 'Travail et civilisation', *Esprit*, octobre 1956.

— *Pouvoir et économie*, Dunod, coll. Études économiques, 1973, 140 pages.

— Cours, in *Annuaire du Collège de France*, 1965–1966.

— *La Coexistence pacifique*, PUF, 1958.

— article in *Mondes en Développement*, no. 2, 1973.

— 'La liaison de l'économique et du social', in revue *Droit social*, mars 1943.

— 'Développer la ressource humaine', *Le Nouvel Observateur*, 2 octobre 1972.

Philip, A. – 'Participation ouvrière aux responsabilités de l'entreprise', *Économies et sociétés*, ISEA, décembre 1971.

Piettre, A. (189). – *Histoire de la pensée économique*, Dalloz, 1965.

Pignon, D., Querzola, J. – 'Dictature et démocratie dans la production', in *Critique de la division du travail*, éd. A. Gorz, Seuil, Paris, 1973.

Pigors, P. Myers, C. A., Malm, F. T. – *The Management of Human Resources*, McGraw-Hill, New York, 1964.

Planche, J. – 'La spécification des tâches', *Bulletin de l'IRAS*, Villeurbanne, juin 1973.

Plaquevent, J., De Monès, J. (41, 45). – 'Problématique des besoins', *Économie et Humanisme*, mars–avril 1954.

Poirson, P. – *See* **Noharet.**

Pollock – *See* **Trist.**

Poncelet, Ch. (10).

Ponsard, C. – 'L'imprécision et son traitement en analyse économique', *Revue d'économie politique*, janvier–février 1975, pp. 17–37.

Postel-Vinay, O. (12). – 'Colloque: Science et jugement de valeur', *Le Monde*, 14–15 juillet 1974.

Pousset, A. – *Fondements méthodologiques d'une approache cybernétique de la description et de la définition des fonctions dans l'entreprise.* Études et documents du Comité National Belge de l'Organisation Scientifique. Bruxelles, 1969, 29 pages.

Prestat, C. (108). – *See also* **Willener.**

— 'Projet de communciation sur une expérience de groupes semi-autonomes. Atelier Fil Textile', document présenté au Séminaire de Royaumont, mars 1974, 23 pages, ronéoté.

Proust, O. – *See* **Kapp.**

Pugh, D. S. – *Organization Theory*, Ed. Penguin, Modern Management Readings, 1971, 382 pages.

Pyle, W. C. (125). – *Director, Human Resource Accounting Program*, Institute for social research graduate School of Business Administration, The University of Michigan.

Querzola, J. – *See* **Pignon.**

Raimond, J.-M. (111). – 'Stratégie de la formation des adultes', *Personnel*, Paris, novembre–décembre 1971.

Rajkovic, S. – 'Une analyse du phénomène de la grève en Yougoslavie', *Borba*, 8 avril 1973, reproduit in *Problèmes économiques*, 25 juillet 1973.

Régnier, J. (111). – 'Introduction des facteurs humains dans la conception des installations automatisées et de leur exploitation', *Metra*, vol. 11, no. 1, mars 1972.

Rehn, G. (72). – 'Pour une plus grande flexibilité de la vie de travail', *L'Observateur de l'OCDE*, Paris, février 1973.

Reichenbach, R. (111). – 'Le coût humain de la formation permanente', *Projet*, mars 1972.

—, **Urfer, S.** – *La Croissance zéro*, PUF, 1974, 125 pages.

Reif, W. E., Luthans, F. – 'Is job enrichment truly feasible?', *California Management Review*, vol. XV, no. 1, 1972, pp. 30–7.

Reljic, B. – 'Le mouvement ouvrier international et l'autogestion', *Borba*, Belgrade, 17 août 1970, reproduit in *Problèmes politiques et sociaux*, 16 avril 1971.

Rémy, P.-L. (111) – *See also* **Reynaud, J.-D.**

Renault, L. (53).

Reveillion, P. (183). – *See* **Lehn.**

Reynaud, J.-D. (29, 46, 57, 59, 110, 111). – *Rapport remis à M. G. Gorse, Ministre du travail de l'emploi et de la population: Les aspects techniques,*

économiques et financiers de la valorisation des tâches d'exécution, Paris, mai 1974, 55 pages.
— Cf. in Friedman et Naville, *Traité de sociologie du travail*.
— 'Sociologie industrielle' (en collaboration avec G. Friedmann), un ouvrage collectif sous la direction de G. Gurvitch: *Traité de sociologie*, PUF, 1958.
— 'La négociation du changement' (2e congrès mondial de l'Association Internationale des Relations professionnelles), Genève, in *Bulletin de l'IIES*, no. 9, 1973.
— *Les Syndicats en France*, tome I: 320 pages, tome 2: 352 pages, Seuil, 1975. *See also* **Touraine**.
—, **Douard, H.** — 'The quality of working life. A central issue in industrial relations', in *Proceedings of the Conference on the Quality of Working Life*, Harriman, New York, 1972.
Reynaud, P.-L. (11, 12). – *Économie généralisée et seuils de croissance*, Génin, 1962.
— 'Économie politique et psychologie', Contre-rapport au Congrès des économistes de langue française, *Revue d'économie politique*, mai 1968.
— *Précis de psychologie économique*, PUF, coll. SUP. L'économiste, 1974, 268 pages.
— *La Psychologie économique*, PUF, Que sais-je?, 1964, 126 pages.
— *La Psychologie économique*, Rivière, Paris, 1954, 260 pages.
Ribet, M. – 'Les vertus de l'enrichissement des fonctions', *Entreprise*, no. 870, 12 mai 1972.
Riboud, A. (86). – 'Discours aux Assises du CNPF', 22 octobre 1972, 'Croissance et qualité de la vie'.
Rice (43).
Richman – *See* **Gutenberg**.
Richta – *La Civilisation au carrefour*, Éd. Anthropos.
Rigny, A.-J. (111, 149, 184). – *Structure de l'entreprise et capacité d'innovation*, Éd. Hommes et Techniques, Puteaux, 1973, 157 pages, préface de J.-Y. Eichenberger.
Rigoir, O. (56). – 'Revenus et salaires', *CEE*, in *Les cahiers français*, no. 151, novembre–décembre 1971, notice no. 1.
Rimailho, E. (16, 36). – *L'Organisation à la Française*, Delmas.
Rimailho, E., Dubreuil, H. – *Deux hommes parlent du travail*, Grasset, Paris, 1939, 236 pages.
Robertson, K. B. – *See* **Paul**.
Robin, R. (108). – 'Bureaux traditionnels et bureaux paysages', Étude psychosociale des réactions individuelles à l'égard d'un changement du cadre de vie professionnelle, document interne, janvier 1974, 126 pages, ronéoté.
— 'Deux approches pour de nouveaux modes de réorganisation', Expériences de réorganisation des tâches à l'Usine Kodak-Pathé de Châlon-sur-Saône, document présenté au Séminaire de Royaumont, mars 1974, 17 pages, ronéoté.
Robinson, D. F. (108, 126). – *See* **Giles**.
Rocard, M. – *See* **Tiano**.
Rodney, C. (58). – *Personnel Administration*, 1967, 30 (2), Wage and Salary Manager, The Martin Company, Baltimore (Maryland).

Roethlisberger, F. J. (33).

Romagnan, B. (10). – *See* **Roustang.**

Rosset, G. – 'La réforme de l'entreprise et l'efficacité économique', thèse complémentaire, Lyon II, 1973, 230 pages.

Roustang, G. (54, 55, 56). – 'Conditions de travail et changement social', *Connexions*, no. 9, 1974.

—, **Beauchesne, N., Gautrat, J., Guélaud, F.** – 'Recherches d'indicateurs sociaux concernant les conditions de travail', 2e partie: 'La législation et les organismes, analyse et bilan critique', LEST–CNRS, Aix-en-Provence, février 1973, 321 pages, ronéoté.

—, **Beauchesne, M.-N., Guélaud, F., Romagnan, B.** – 'Recherches d'indicateurs sociaux concernant les conditions de travail', 1re partie, LEST–CNRS, Aix-en-Provence, février 1972, 93 pages, ronéoté.

—, **Guéland, F., Beauchesne, M.-N., Gautrat, J.** – *Pour une analyse des conditions du travail ouvrier dans l'entreprise*, Librairie A. Colin, 1975, 246 pages (préface de Y. Delamotte).

Royer, G. – 'Quel prix payer la sécurité industrielle', *Le Management*, décembre 1973.

Ruffier, J. (10). – *See* **Bernoux.**

Saada, K. – *See* **Charraud.**

Sadan, S., Auerbach, L. B. – 'A stochastic model for human resources valuation', *California Management Review*, Summer 1974, vol. XVI, no. 4.

Sage, E. – *Les Problèmes fiscaux de l'entreprise*, Éd. Économie et Humanisme et les Éditions ouvrières, Paris, 1974, 255 pages.

Saglio, J. (10). – *See* **Bernoux.**

Sainsaulieu, R. (57). – *Les Relations de travail à l'usine*, in coll. de M. Crozier.

— Article in *Formation continue*, 1973, 3e trimestre, p. 21.

Salleron, L. – *Le Fondement du pouvoir dans l'entreprise*, Entreprise moderne d'Édition, 1965, 164 pages.

Salmona, M. (112). – 'Formation économique et changement social, langage et coûts mentaux', *Éducation permanente*, Paris, novembre–décembre 1973.

Savall, H. (111, 182, 185, 186). – 'Avant Keynes et au-delà: Germán Bernácer, économiste espagnol', *Mondes en développement*, no. 5, ISEA, juin 1974.

— 'Germain Bernácer, économiste espagnol (1883–1965). Une théorie générale de l'emploi de la rente et de la thésaurisation', thèse, ronéotée, Université Paris II, 1973, 602 pages.

— *G. Bernácer. L'Hétérodoxie en science économique*, Dalloz, coll. Les grands économistes, 1975, 479 pages. Préface de H. Guitton, membre de l'Institut, avant-propos de Colette Nême, professeur à l'Université Paris II.

Schade, G. (112). – 'Les femmes et l'éducation récurrente', *Éducation permanente*, Paris, novembre–décembre 1973.

Scheips, C. D. – 'The humanization of work', *Personnel*, no. 5, septembre-octobre 1972, p. 38.

Schumpeter, J. (149).

Schwartz, A. (125). – *See* **Lev.**

Schwartz, M. M. (41).

Scott, W. G., Mitchell, T. R. – *Organisation des structures de l'entreprise. Analyse des comportements*. CLM Publi-Union, 1973, 466 pages.

Scott Myers, M., Flowers, V. S. – 'A framework for measuring human assets', *California Management Review*, Summer 1974, vol. XVI, no. 4.

Sellier, F. (189). – *Stratégie de la lutte sociale en France 1936–1960*, Éd. Ouvrières, Paris, 1961, 351 pages.

— *Dynamique des besoins sociaux*, Éd. Ouvrières, 1970, 256 pages.

—, **Tiano, A.** – *Économie du travail*, PUF, 1962, 636 pages.

Servan-Schreiber, J.-L. – *L'Entreprise à visage humain*, Éd. Robert Laffont, 1973, 267 pages.

Sfez, L. (185). – *Critique de la décision*, Cahiers de la Fondation des Sciences Politiques, Paris, A. Colin, 1973, 368 pages.

Silvestre, J. J. – *Les Salaires ouvriers dans l'industrie française*, Préface de F. Sellier, Bordas-Études, 1973, 416 pages.

Simon, H. A. (32, 35). – *See* **March.**

Smith, A. (19, 54). – *The Wealth of Nations.*

Stewart, P. A. (109). – *See* **Biggane.**

Sudreau, P. (12, 59, 107, 185, 189). – 'Rapport du Comité d'étude pour la réforme de l'entreprise présidé par Pierre Sudreau', *La documentation française*, février 1975, 192 pages.

Sullerot, E. (56). – *Les Françaises au travail*, Éd. Hachette Littérature, coll. Les grands rapports, 1973.

Sylvestre, J. M. (109). – *See* **Bedel.**

Tabatoni, P., *et al.* – 'Analyse empirique des contraintes stratégiques', *Économies et Sociétés*, ISEA, 1968, no. 3.

— *Les stratégies industrielles*, Cahiers de l'ISEA, série Économie de l'entreprise, 1968, no. 3.

Tarrière, E. – *See* **Noharet.**

Tarrière, P. – 'Une méthode d'évaluation à la Régie Renault', *Enseignement et Gestion*, janvier 1975.

— 'L'évaluation globale des conditions de travail', document présenté au Séminaire de Royaumont, mars 1974, 10 pages, ronéoté.

Taylor, F. W. (4, 9, 10, 13, 14, 15, 16, 17, 18, 19, 21, 22, 23, 24, 28, 31, 36, 54, 58, 60, 104). – *Scientific Management*, Harper Bros., New York, 1911.

Taylor, J. C. (108, 109). – *See* **Davis.**

Tchobanian, R. (150). – 'Projet de recherche. L'économie des conditions de travail: étude des coûts et analyse dynamique', LEST-CNRS, Aix-en-Provence, février 1974, 53 pages, ronéoté.

— 'Réflexions sur l'analyse économique des conditions de travail', LEST-CNRS, Aix-en-Provence, 1972, 135 pages, ronéoté.

Teiger, C. (110). – *See* **Laville.**

Tézenas du Montcel, H. (12) – *Dictionnaire des sciences de la gestion*, Éd. Mame.

— *Les performances sociales des organisations*, thèse complémentaire de sciences économiques, Paris IX-Dauphine, 1973, 106 pages, multigraphiée.

Thorsrud, E. (7, 43). – *See also* **Emery.**

Tiano, A. (189). – *See* **Sellier.**

— *La Méthode de la prospective*, Dunod, coll. Études économiques, 1974, 208 pages.

—, **Rocard, M., Lesiré Ogrel, H.** – *Expériences françaises d'action syndicale* *ouvrière*, Éd. ouvrières, 1956, 435 pages.

Tiffin, J., MacCormick, E. J. (55). – *Industrial Psychology*, Allen & Unwin, London 1952.

Touraine, A. (10, 53, 54). – *La société post-industrielle*, Éd. Donoël, Paris, 1969, 319 pages.

— *L'Évolution du travail ouvrier aux usines Renault*, CNRS, 1955, 203 pages.

— *Étude de cas: un nouveau laminoir. Les ouvriers et le progrès technique* (et J. Dofny, C. Durand, J.-D. Reynaud; avant-propos de Y. Delamotte) A. Colin, Paris, 1966, 274 pages.

— *Sociologie de l'action*, Éd. Seuil, Paris, 1965, 509 pages.

— *Histoire générale du travail* (sous la direction de Louis-Henri Parias), tome 4: *La civilisation industrielle de 1914 à nos jours*, Nouvelle Librairie de France, Paris, 1961, 367 pages.

Trepo, G. – 'Une nouvelle famille d'organisateurs', *Revue Direction*, no. 1, FNEGE, Paris, mai 1975.

Trist, E. (43, 44, 46, 58, 59). – *See also* **Emery.**

— 'Epilogue: action research and adaptive planning', Tavistock Institute, London, October 1973, 21 pages, roneoed.

— **Higgin, Murray, Pollock** – *Organizational Choice*, Tavistock publications, London, 1963.

Umetani, S. – 'L'homme et l'organisation. Sociologie de l'entreprise nippone', *Le Monde*, 22–3 décembre 1974.

Underdown, B. – *See* **Glautier.**

Urfer, S. – *See* **Reichenbach.**

Van Beinum, H. (7, 8, 43, 46, 92, 102, 183). – 'The enterprise as an open socio-technical system', Foundation for Business Administration, Rotterdam, 40 pages, roneoed.

—, **Ljungberg-van Beinum, I.** – 'Organization development. "A matter of the warp and the weft" ', mars 1974, 16 pages, roneoed.

Van Vucht Tussen, J. – 'Nouveaux aspects dus à l'évolution de l'économie et des techniques', *Personnel*, Paris, octobre 1969.

Vermay, A. – *See* **Jacquet.**

Vernet, M., et J.-L., Bonhomme, D. – 'L'autogestion yougoslave: mythe ou réalité?', *Problèmes politiques et sociaux*, no. 68, 16 avril 1971.

Viaud, P. (24, 75, 111). – 'L'évolution des modes de rénumération', Conférence à la Fédération des Chambres syndicales des fabricants de cartonnage de France (1973), document présenté au Séminaire de Royaumont, mars 1974, 20 pages, ronéoté.

— 'Nouveau mode opératoire de conditionnement dans un laboratoire pharmaceutique', document présenté au Séminaire de Royaumont, mars 1974, ronéoté.

Von Bertallanfy (149).

Voronov, O. (108). – 'Le congé-éducation en URSS', *Revue internationale du travail*, Genève.

Vroom, V. H. – *Management and Motivation*, Penguin, Modern Management Readings.

Wade, M. – 'L'homme-robot n'est pas prêt de disparaître', *Vision*, novembre 1973.

Walker, K. F. – *See also* **Delamotte.**

— 'La participation des travailleurs à la gestion des entreprises: problèmes, pratiques et perspectives', *Bulletin IIES*, no. 12, Genève, 1974.

Weber, M. (32). – *The Theory of Social and Economic Organization*, Free press, New York, 1964, 436 pages.

Wickham, S. (57). – *Concentration et dimension*, Flammarion, Paris, 1966, 252 pages.

Wiley, W. W. – *See* Fine.

Willener, A., Durand, C., Prestat, C. – *Travail, salaire, production*, tome 1: *Le contrôle des cadences*, Mouton, Paris, 1972, 276 pages.

Wisner, A. (54, 110). – *See* **Laville.**

— 'Contenu des tâches et charge de travail', revue *Sociologie du travail*, octobre-décembre 1974.

Wolfelsperger, A. (150, 184). – 'La détermination des conditions de travail dans l'entreprise', *Revue d'Économie politique*, mars–avril 1973.

Wolff, J. – *Sociologie économique*, t. 1: *Sociologie de l'organisation économique*, Cujas, 1971, 620 pages.

Woodward, J. (33).

Zaleski, M.-E. – 'Utilisation de la main-d'œuvre et productivité en Union Soviétique', *Problèmes économiques*, 23 février 1972.

Zumsteg, B.-J. (108). – *L'Horaire libre dans l'entreprise, ses causes, ses problèmes, ses conséquences*, Éd. Delachaux et Niestlé, Neuchâtel, 1971, 120 pages.

— 'L'horaire variable. Principaux résultats des expériences étrangères', *Problèmes politiques et sociaux*, 15–22 février 1974.

ARTICLES, BOOKS, AND VARIOUS ANONYMOUS OR COLLECTIVE DOCUMENTS

C.E.R.F.I., 'Formation de la force collective de travail', *Éducation permanente*, Paris, novembre–décembre 1973.

'L'amélioration des conditions de travail; pour une approche expérimentale: les horaires personnalisés', *Entreprise et Progrès*, Paris, mai 1973, ronéoté.

'Les expériences d'horaires dynamiques réalisées par les adhérents d'Entreprise et Progrès', *Entreprise et Progrès*, Paris, avril 1973, ronéoté.

'Les conditions de travail et leur amélioration, enquête auprès des chefs d'entreprise', *Entreprise et Progrès*, mai 1973.

'L'amélioration des conditions de travail, résultats de l'enquête', *Entreprise et Progrès*, juin 1973.

'Liste d'expériences d'amélioration de la qualité de vie dans le travail en cours dans un certain nombre d'entreprises', FNEGE, Paris, mars 1974 (extrait de *Work in America* avec l'autorisation de l'Institute for Educational Development).

'La structuration du travail chez Philips', rapport de l'UIMM, Paris, mars 1972, ronéoté, 38 pages.

'Centre de traitement modulaire des chèques', document interne, Crédit Lyonnais, Direction de la Comptabilité et du portefeuille, Paris, 1974, 71 pages.

'Le problème des OS, rapport du groupe d'étude patronal (CNFF)' plus annexe: 'L'amélioration du contenu du travail sur chaîne (réalisation soviétique)'; cette annexe est la reproduction d'un article paru dans la revue mensuelle du Comité d'État près le Conseil des ministres de l'URSS, *Sotsialistitcheski Troud*, no. 8, Moscow, August 1971, CNPF, Paris, 1971, ronéoté (25 + vi pages).

'Le dossier des OS', Production et gestion et l'Étude du travail, BTE-Formation Promotion, Paris, mai 1973.

'Les conditions de travail, 9 cas concrets', et: 'une interview de M. Y. Chotard', in revue *Professions et Entreprises*, mai–juin 1973.

'L'intéressement et la promotion des travailleurs, la solution de M. Dubreuil', in revue *Hommes et Techniques*, août–Septembre 1967.

'Minutes de la première réunion du Conseil Intérimaire pour la qualité de la vie de travail', Canterbury, 17–20 août 1973, document ronéoté, 11 septembre 1973, 21 pages.

Centre des Jeunes Dirigeants d'entreprise, *L'Autorité de l'entreprise*, Flammarion, Paris, 1974, 279 pages.

'Nous nous orientons vers un système d'autogestion intégrale', interview de M. Vuko Dragasevic, secrétaire fédéral yougoslave du travail, in revue *Intersocial*, 5 juin 1974.

'Statistiques d'accidents du travail en 1971', *Liaisons sociales*, 5 novembre 1973.

'L'organisation et le travail dans les usines. L'usine sidérurgique de Wuhan', rapport d'une mission effectuée en Chine, juillet 1971, Paris, Assemblée Nationale, 1972, reproduit in *Problèmes politiques et sociaux* no. 171, 6 avril 1973.

AFCOD. *Les Ratios sociaux. Essai de mesure du climat social de l'entreprise*, Les éditions d'organisations, 1946, 163 pages.

Association Nationale des Directeurs et Chefs de Personnel, *Conditions de travail en URSS*, Paris, 1961.

Expériences en vue d'une organisation plus humaine du travail industriel, Librairie A. Colin, Collection Sciences sociales du travail, Paris, décembre 1973.

'Participation et besoin ouvrier', *Direction*, octobre 1968.

Progrès dans l'organisation du travail. Séminaire patronal international, Paris, 3–6 avril 1973, publié par l'OCDE, Paris, 1974.

Adjustment of Workers to Technical Change at Plant Level, Final report, International conference, Amsterdam, 15–16 novembre 1966, publié par OCDE, 1967.

'Heures flexibles', dossier, CNOF, Paris.

Les Tendances nouvelles de l'organisation industreille et des relations du travail, Paris, septembre 1973, AVA.

'Comment va le job enrichment?' (en anglais: 'Is job enrichment working?'), *Management Review*, September 1972, pp. 51–3.

'Les conditions de travail des ouvriers spécialisés et des travailleurs postés', Supplément au bulletin du militant, no. 359, Féd. Générale de la Métallurgie CFDT.

'Conditions de travail. Six OS de Detroit jugent l'expérience Saab', *Intersocial*, no. 3, mars 1975, p. 11.

'L'information dans l'entreprise: la communication passe par la considération',

Patronat, CNPF, mai 1974.

'Pour des conditions de travail plus humaines en rapport avec notre temps', document de la Circonscription exécutive CGT, in *Le Peuple*, 17–29 février 1972.

'Politiques syndicales pour l'amélioration des conditions de travail et de l'organisation de l'entreprise', *Revue française des Affaires sociales*, 1974, 46 pages.

'Systèmes sociotechniques, ergonomie, une approche bioanthropologique', Séminaire international d'experts, IRACT, Université Paul Sabatier, Toulouse, 21–22 mars 1975, Compte-rendu in *Liaisons sociales*, 11 avril 1975.

'Une éducation pour notre temps', *Échanges et Projet*, Paris, mai 1975.

Conditions de travail en URSS, Les éditions d'organisation, Paris, 1961. Préface de G. Friedmann, 276 pages.

'Danemark. Expériences de coopération mixte et de nouvelles formes d'organisation du travail dans les entreprises des métaux', *Bulletin UIMM*, avril 1974, no. 307.

'La diminution des gains de productivité et ses conséquences pour l'économie américaine', *Problèmes économiques*, no. 1264, 22 mars 1972 (traduction d'un article de *Business Week*, 1 January 1972).

'Mise en question de la compétivité de la technologie américaine', *Problèmes économiques*, no. 1264, 22 mars 1972 (traduction d'un article de *Business Week*, 15 January 1972).

'L'éducation récurrente', *Personnel*, Paris, novembre–décembre 1971.

'Mesure de l'efficacité du personnel (en Suède)', *Personnel*, Paris, no. 128, octobre 1969, p. 44.

'Dans un rapport sur la "démocratie industrielle" les syndicats britanniques se prononcent pour la co-gestion', *Intersocial*, 1er juillet 1973.

'De Moscou, des primes à l'imagination', *Intersocial*, 15 février 1974.

'Forces et faiblesses du calcul économique', *Problèmes économiques*, no. 1277, 21 juin 1972.

Lettre d'information no. 1, Agence nationale pour l'amélioration des conditions de travail, 16 à 20, rue Barbès, 92120 Montrouge, intitulée: 'Présentation de l'Agence nationale pour l'amélioration des conditions de travail', mai 1975.

Cycle d'Études Européennes de Toulouse, 1964, sous l'égide des Nations Unies: un volume publié à Genève, 1965.

Rapport du sous-group D *'Organisation du travail*, du groupe Prospective du travail, Commissariat général du Plan, février 1974.

Divers articles de la revue *Formation continue*, cf. *supra*.

Article sur l'expérience Ciapem-Thompson-Brandt, in *l'Express-Rhône-Alpes*, novembre 1973.

Cahier d'instructions et de valeurs de références en ergonomie du point de vue sécurité et conditions de travail, SAVIEM, document interne, 140 pages.

Réception des postes de travail, Régie Nationale des Usines Renault, 1974, 80 pages, document diffusé par L'APACT, UIMM, 56 avenue de Wagram, 75017 Paris.

COMPLEMENTARY BIBLIOGRAPHY TO SECOND EDITION

ANACT. – *Analyse ergonomique du travail dans un atelier de presse en vue du transfert de certaines presses dans un nouvel atelier à construire.*
— *Les conditions de travail dans la pratique des négociations collectives.*
— *Legislation, fonctionnement et activités des commissions pour l'amélioration des conditions de travail (CACT).*
— *Textes législatifs et réglementaires en matière d'amélioration des conditions de travail.*
— *L'architecture industrielle, l'architecture de bureaux et les conditions de travail.*

Aubert-Krier, J., Rio, E. Y., Vailhem, C. A. – *Gestion de l'entreprise*, 4ᵉ édition, tome I: *Structure et organisation*, PUF, 1975, 557 pages.

Avisem. – *Techniques d'amélioration des conditions de travail. Méthodes d'analyses, évaluation de projets, normes et procédures d'application*, Hommes et Techniques, Suresnes, 1977, 224 pages.

Barbash, J. – *Enquêtes sur les attitudes concernant la satisfaction au travail*, OCDE, août 1976, 44 pages.

Baudraz, J.-F. – *L'Horaire variable de travail*, 3ᵉ édition, Les éditions d'organisation, 1974, 136 pages.

Bellone, L. – *Amélioration de la condition de l'homme au travail*, Manuel d'ergonomie, Éditions d'organisation, 1976, 192 pages.

Bertaux, M. – *Groupes et équipes autonomes d'entreprise*, Chotard, 1977, 248 pages.

Bodet, P., Gaupels, L., Royer, J. – *Comment organiser un horaire personnalisé*, Dunod, 1975, 129 pages.

Bodman, E. de, Richard, B. – *Changer les relations sociales. La politique de Jacques Delors*, Éditions d'organisation, 1976, 220 pages.

Boeri, D. – *Le Nouveau Travail manuel. Enrichissement des tâches et groupes autonomes*, Éditions d'organisation, 1976, 224 pages.

Bois, P. – *L'Aménagement des conditions de travail au stade de la conception des bâtiments industriels.* Rapport au ministère du Travail, 1974.

Bolle de Bal, M. – *Accroissment de la productivité et psychosociologie du travail*, Éd. de l'Université de Bruxelles, 1976.

Borzeix, A., Chave, D. – *Réorganisation du travail et dynamique des conflits*, CNAM, Laboratoire de sociologie du travail et des relations professionnelles, Paris, 1975, 492 pages.

Burbidge, J. L. – *Méthodes de production en groupes et humanisation du travail*, ILES, BIT, Genève, 1976.

Capet, M., Total-Jacquot, C. – *Comptabilité, diagnostic et décision*, PUF, 352 pages.

Carpentier, J., Cazamian. – *Le Travail de nuit, ses incidences physiologiques, médicales, économiques et sociales*, BIT, Genève, 1976.

CFDT – *Les Dégâts du progrès. Les travailleurs techniques face au changement*, Seuil, 1977, 320 pages.
— *Conditions de travail: le dossier des négociations*, CFDT, Paris, 1975, 48 pages.

Chaigneau, Y., Piotet, F., Bussery, H. – 'Le travail demain: deux avenirs possibles', *ANDCP-Personnel*, octobre 1976.

— 'Les nouvelles formes d'organisation du travail', *Sociologie du Travail*, no. 1/76, Éd. Seuil.

— 'le taylorisme en question', numéro spécial de la revue *Sociologie du travail*, octobre–décembre 1974.

— 'Tendances nouvelles en organisation du travail', no. *Économie et Humanisme*, janvier–février 1976, 96 pages.

— 'Formation et amélioration des conditions de travail', Secrétariat d'État à la condition des travailleurs manuels, diffusion: Centre INFFO, Paris, 1977, 203 pages.

Chevalier, A. – *Le Bilan social de l'entreprise*, Masson, 1976, 168 pages.

Commissariat général du plan – *Contribution à une prospective du travail*, Éd. Documentation française.

Coriat, B. – *Science, technqiues et capital*, Seuil, 1976, 256 pages.

Dalle, F., Thiery, N. – *Dynamique de l'auto-réforme de l'entreprise*, Masson, 1976, 160 pages.

Davis, L. E., Cherns, A. B. – *The Quality of Working Life*, vol. 1: *Problems, Prospects and the State of the Art*, vol. 2: *Cases and Commentary*, Macmillan, New York, 1975, 450 pages and 387 pages.

Delamotte, Y., Walker, K. F. – 'L'humanisation du travail et la qualité de la vie de travail. Tendances et problèmes', *Bulletin de l'IIES*, Genève, janvier 1974.

Diverrez, J. – *Améliorer les conditions de travail*. Entreprise moderne d'édition, 1976, 152 pages.

Drolovic, M. – *L'Autogestion à l'épreuve. Le modèle yougoslave*, Fayard, 1977, 321 pages.

Entreprise et Progrès. – *Pour développer l'expression des salariés à la réunion d'échange*, juin 1976.

Gélinier, O. – *Stratégie sociale dans l'entreprise*, Éd. Hommes et Techniques, 1976, 261 pages.

Grandjean, E. – *Précis d'ergonomie. Organisation physiologique du travail*, Vander-Oyez, Paris, 1976.

Guelaud, F. – *Note introductive au questionnaire sur les conditions de travail*, avec la participation de Romagnan B., Aix-en-Provence, LEST-CNRS, 1972, 62 pages.

Herbst, P. G. – *Socio-Technical Design-Strategies in Multidisciplinary Research*, Tavistock publications, London, 1974, 242 pages.

Humble, J. – *L'Audit social au service d'un management de survie*, Dalloz, 1975, 76 pages.

Käpp, K. W. – *Les coûts sociaux dans l'économie de marché*, Flammarion, 1976, 352 pages.

Landier, H., Vieux, N. – *Le Travail posté en question*, Cerf, 1976, 192 pages.

Lavernhe, R., Pierre, J. – *L'Efficacité sociale. Une nouvelle stratégie des entreprises*, Privat, Toulouse, 1977, 228 pages.

Laville, A. – *L'Ergonomie*, PUF, 1976, 128 pages.

Lebraty, J. – 'La Gestion des Ressources humaines dans l'entreprise', *Revue de l'IAE*, Nice, 1976.

Lefebvre, C., Rollov, G. – *L'Amélioration des conditions de travail dans les emplois administratifs*. Chotard, 1977, 260 pages.

Levinson, C. – *La Démocratie industrielle*, Seuil, 1974, 304 pages.

Montis, J.-B. – *Analyse et mesure du climat social de l'entreprise*. Entreprise moderne d'édition, 1976, 140 pages.

Morin, P. – *Le Développement des organisations et la gestion des ressources humaines*, Dunod, 1976, 192 pages.

Mothe, D. – *Autogestion et conditions de travail*, Cerf. 1976, 98 pages.

Neme, J. et C. – *Politiques économiques comparées*, PUF, 1977, 432 pages.

OCDE – *Le Travail dans une nouvelle société industrielle*, OCDE, 1976, 64 pages.

Perroux, F. – *Unités actives et mathématiques nouvelles. Révision de la théorie de l'equilibre économique général*, Dunod, 1975, 296 pages.

Pigors, P., Myers, C. A., Malm, F. T. – *La Gestion des ressources humaines*, Hommes et Techniques, Suresnes, 1977, 368 pages.

Prost, G. – *Les Équipes semi-autonomes. Une nouvelle organisation du travail*, Éditions d'organisation, 1976, 152 pages.

R.N.U. Renault. – *Les Profils de postes. Méthode d'analyse des conditions de travail*, Masson-Sirtes, 1976, 108 pages.

Sartin, P. – *Jeunes au travail, jeunes sans travail*, Éditions d'organisation, 1977, 160 pages.

Savall, H. – 'Formation et conditions de vie au travail', *Revue française de gestion*, mars-avril 1977.

— 'Propositions en vue de développer la contribution de la formation initiale à l'amélioration des conditions de vie au travail', *Ensignement et gestion*, no. 3, 1977.

— 'Analyse socio-économique, diagnostic et décision d'amélioration des conditions de vie au travail', *Revue de l'Entreprise*, janvier 1978.

— 'Propos d'étape sur la régulation socio-économique de l'entreprise par la recherche de la compatibilité de l'efficience économique et du développement humain', rapport au VIIe Colloque international du College de France sur le thème: l'idée de régulation dans le mouvement des sciences, Paris, décembre 1977 (à paraître dans une revue de l'ISMEA).

— *See also* 'Formation et amélioration des conditions de travail', rapport au Secrétariat d'État à la condition des travailleurs manuels, op. cit.

Syntec Management. – *Regards sur le bilan social*. Hommes et Techniques, 1976, 200 pages.

Thietart, R. A. – *La dynamique de l'homme au travail*, Éditions d'organisation, 1977, 240 pages.

Tort, B. – *Bilan de l'apport de la recherche scientifique à l'amélioration des conditions de travail* (rapport), Laboratoire de physiologie du travail et d'ergonomie du CNAM, Paris, 1976.

Weiss, D. – *Les Relations du travail: employeurs, personnel, syndicats. État*, Dunod, Paris, 3e édition 1975, 216 pages.

Wisner, A., Carpentier, J. – *L'Aménagement des conditions de travail par équipes successives* (travail posté) + annexes, ANACT, 1976.